What Others Are Saying About This Book

"We are killing our customers with good intentions! Yes, we survey our customers until it hurts both them and our companies. This book is critical to helping us stop the madness and get focused on how we can really 'ACT' on the insights we gain from our customers. If you only have one reference point for building a complete strategy to measuring the contact center's quality of interactions, it must be this book. Buy it, read it slowly and 'ACT on it' with passion."
Mike Trotter, Vice President, Customer Experience, Vonage

"As every good traveler knows, the key to a successful journey is a great road map. Monger and Perkins have provided such a map when it comes to maximizing the use of customer satisfaction surveys. Easy to read and understand, this is a must-read for all contact center managers using or contemplating the use of an EQM solution."
Chuck Udzinski, Consumer Services Manager, Black & Decker

"Monger and Perkins do a solid job of integrating the trade literature with academic knowledge of the survey process. They are clearly well equipped to dispense pain relief in this field."
David Drews, Professor Emeritus of Psychology, Juniata College

"It can't be said better than is stated in the book: Herein lies the informed decision-making capability to obtaining meaningful customer intelligence. Just as the health of your business is in jeopardy if you choose to ignore the voices and actions of your customers, so is it too if your method of harnessing customer intelligence yields useless, non-actionable information. Reading this book will open your eyes to things you didn't know that you need to know."
Fredia Barry, President, Call Center Industry Advisory Council (CIAC)

"A very well-written and useful book about how to gather sound customer information that can be used to advantage by industry. The book selects the most relevant research and delivers critical and well-balanced advice that is both thoughtful and accessible. These days, business people cannot avoid measuring customer response, and this book tells them what to do, and what not to do."
Robert East, Professor of Consumer Behavior, Kingston University, London

"In 2007, we added external quality monitoring (EQM) data to our internal quality monitoring (IQM) program. Now we can calibrate our IQM with EQM data, providing a reality check on more subjective IQM data. Moving to a continuous tracking methodology versus an annual point-in-time view provides us with better trending data and better reflects impact of seasonality on our business. Most important, the Alert feature allows us to immediately get back in touch with unhappy customers. Nine times out of 10 we can correct the situation and retain a customer. This is customer metrics in action."
Sheryl Henderson, Director, Consumer Relations, Michelin North America

Survey Pain Relief:
Transforming Customer Insights into Action

By Dr. Jodie Monger & Dr. Debra Perkins

Survey Pain Relief:
Transforming Customer Insights into Action

By Dr. Jodie Monger & Dr. Debra Perkins

Published by:
ICMI, a registered trademark of Think Services,
a division of United Business Media, LLC
102 South Tejon, Suite 1200
Colorado Springs CO 80903 USA
www.icmi.com

NOTICE OF LIABILITY

This book is designed to provide information in regard to the subject matter covered. The purpose of this book is to educate and entertain. While every precaution has been taken in the preparation of this book, neither the author nor ICMI shall have any liability or responsibility to any person or entity with respect to any loss or damage caused, or alleged to be caused, directly or indirectly by the information contained in this book. If you do not wish to be bound by this, you may return this book to the publisher for a full refund.

All rights reserved. No part of this book may be reproduced or transmitted in any form or by any means, electronic or mechanical, including photocopying, recording or by any information storage and retrieval system without written permission from the author, except for the inclusion of brief quotations in a review.

TRADEMARK NOTICE

All trademarks, product names and company names mentioned herein, whether registered or unregistered, are the property of their respective owners.

Copyright ©2008 Jodie Monger and Debra Perkins

Printed in the United States of America
ISBN 1-932558-13-6

To Mark and our daughter, Emily, each is a guiding light of my life, and to my parents, Jim and Judy, who pointed me in the right direction.
Jodie Monger

To my soul mate, Frank, his mother, Bernadette Croghan Kirlin, who successfully raised five children as a widow, and my family, who loved me through everything.
Debra Perkins

x

Table of Contents

Acknowledgements xv

Part I: Why You Need a Doctor 1

Chapter 1: Foundations 3

Introduction to Pain 3
Beyond the Basics: How to Develop a Scientifically Sound Customer Measurement Program 6
Rocket Science for Contact Centers 8
Rally Cry for the Customer 9
Unskilled and Unaware 11
External Quality Monitoring 13
Plan of the Book 15
The Past and Present Constant: Change 18
Customers also Have Changed 30
Final Thoughts before We Begin 32

Chapter 2: Human Resource Issues in the Contact Center 35

Employee Satisfaction and Performance 36
Equity Theory 41
Valuing the Human Resource 44
Expressing the Value of the Human Component 47
If You Want It, Reward It 52
Employee Evaluations: A Powder-Keg Issue 54
The Changing Face of Employee Satisfaction 55
EQM Strengthens Employee Satisfaction and Performance 57

Part II: Science and Research 59

Chapter 3: The Necessity of Science 61

Contact Centers Are the Primary Interaction Point 63
Internal Call Quality Monitoring Is Insufficient 67
Sources and Risks of Survey Malpractice 73
Closing Points 79

Chapter 4: Benchmarking: The Triumph of Efficiency over Effectiveness 81

Benchmarking Definitions, Origins and Types 82
Contact Center Benchmarking and Goal Setting: Caution Required 87
Where's the Customer? 93
Practices and Metrics: Two Parts to the Benchmarking Process 94

Chapter 5: Net Promoter and EQM 97

The Net Promoter Score 98
The Logic of Net Promoter 100
Some Adaptations of Net Promoter 103
The Empirical Evidence: Is Net Promoter the "SINGLE METRIC" Needed? 104
How Does Net Promoter Compare to Key Drivers? 108
Net Promoter and EQM Each Have Uses 109

Chapter 6: The Science of Research: Detecting and Overcoming Biases 111

Questions: The Core of the Survey 115
Instrumentation Bias and Error 117
Respondent-Created Bias and Error 117
Researcher-Created Bias 121
Seven Rules for Getting it Right 125
There Is No Standard Mold 130

Part III: The Alpha and Omega of the EQM Program 133

Chapter 7: The Logic and Benefits of a Sound EQM Program 135

"Put a Tiger in Your Tank" 137
Benefits of CATs® 140
Comparisons of Data Collection Methods 141
Use CATs® to Avoid Survey Pain 145

Chapter 8: Developing a Scientifically Sound EQM Program 147

Survey Channel Slamming 148
Getting the Sample Size Right 151
Neither Qualitative NOR Quantitative: Both Are Necessary 154
Clean Versus Dirty Data 155
Not Just Averages: Scientific Analysis 158
Benchmarking with Customer Relationship Metrics: Apples-to-Apples Comparisons 169
A Quick Review of Our Main Points 170

Chapter 9: Practical Considerations of the EQM Program 173

Select an Immediate Post-Call Survey Methodology 174
Determine the Evaluation Process Flow 175
Do NOT Make Customers Pre-Select 175
Agents Can Still Influence Participation 176
Assigning the Surveys 177
You May Need More Trunk Capacity 178
Caller Behavior 178
Technology Must NOT Drive the Research 179
Determine the Service Attributes for the EQM Form 179
Select the Scale 180
Key Attributes Versus Net Promoter Score 183
EQM and ICM Must Complement 185
Select the "Why" Questions 186
Select the Real-Time Alert Triggers 187
It's about Avoiding the Pain 188

Part IV: Sharing the Wealth of the EQM Program 189

Chapter 10: CLV and ROI in the Center 191

Customer Lifetime Value 192
CLV Extensions 197
Return on Investment 201

Chapter 11: Communicating the Results 205

Know Your Audience 206
Reports for Executive Management 206
Reports for Operations Management 213
Reports for Supervisors and Agents 225
Share the Knowledge 231

Chapter 12: Actionable Intelligence 233

Proficiency of Execution 233
EQM and IQM Alignment 236
Site Usage 240
NP Sales Versus NP Service 241
Call Resolution 243
Take a Fresh Look at Your Research Efforts 244

Appendix 247
Reference Library 251
Index 261
How to Reach ICMI Press 271
About ICMI 273
Order Form 274

Acknowledgements

The art and science of experimental design was introduced to me at Juniata College in the mid-1980s by Dr. David Drews. This foundation became the vantage point from which I view the world — what is the research question and how can it be effectively measured?

For me, the application of research science to the contact center industry began in the early 1990s, and it has been a fertile research ground for Customer Relationship Metrics. The beginning can be easily tracked to the lack of an adequate answer to the question asked of many center management teams: "How do you know that your goals are satisfying your callers?" The operational metrics were easily quantified but there was no answer from the caller perspective. What else could a researcher do but design a methodology for the quantification of the customer experience? The past decade has been very rewarding and full of excitement from spending the day doing what I love.

The contact center is unique in its combination of talented people, advanced technology and dedication to the customer experience. The organizations that Metrics has worked with over the past 15 years have provided many opportunities for research along the path of the advancement of the customer experience. We have been fortunate to work with world class contact centers and the management teams that are responsible for that status. To all of the clients who have engaged us over the years, we thank you for including our research services among your management tools.

Thank you to the clients who are mentioned directly or indirectly in this book and to specialists at Metrics who assisted with this project such as Carmit DiAndrea, Mark Gray and Jim Rembach. It has been a pleasure working on this project with a talent like Debra Perkins.

Jodie Monger

Acknowledgements

A work of this nature inherently rests on experiences built up from uncountable interactions. I have suffered and have been pampered as a consumer, have been frustrated and elated as a professor, and have been suppressed and honored as an employee. These experiences and contradictions have informed and, hopefully, enriched this book.

I want to thank the professors who trained me despite the challenges I presented. Of special note are Dr. Janet Near and Dr. Dan Dalton of Indiana University's Kelley School of Business. They are exemplars of scholarship, collegiality and great champions of students.

I would also like to acknowledge Dr. Ralph Day and Dr. H. Keith Hunt who championed, organized and founded the key conferences and journals around the topics of customer satisfaction, dissatisfaction and complaining behavior. Much of the content of this book rests upon their endeavors. Just as important, each of them has encouraged and mentored literally dozens of young academics. I was greatly privileged to be among that number.

I also want to thank the students. Every day is an opportunity to make a difference and I feel this is my calling. It is neither comfortable nor lucrative, but it does have its rewards.

I have been blessed with colleagues over the years who have inspired, advised and sometimes healed me. Dr. Robert Labadie of Florida Memorial is one such individual. Among other things, he serves as the university's Assessment Officer: a job that involves much time, expertise, diplomacy, sweat and abuse, and is largely uncompensated. He is a "rabbi" who mixes much humor with lots of encouragement. He is always, and in all things, a gentleman.

My husband, Frank, is an extraordinary man. Through everything from triumphs to defeats, I have been privileged to be encouraged, defended, supported, cheered and loved by him. After years as a well-respected and highly successful business owner and manager, he sold off those businesses and moved to Florida so I could return to teaching. To make this move, he gave up wealth, position, his woodworking, hunting and marksmanship hobbies and the interconnectedness he once felt with a wide community of like-minded friends. I cannot believe he did this for me. And his reward for this sacrifice has been the loss of much of our financial wealth (hurricanes, frozen salaries, inflation, recession, insanely high property taxes, insurance and utilities) and a return to employee/working-man status and a serious lack of community.

After all those sacrifices, he often has been neglected as I pushed to reach a deadline; instead of complaining about it, he fixes dinner for me and then sends me back to the computer to finish my work. I am not worthy.

Many thanks go the Carmit, Jim and Mark who provided support on my schedule, and Jodie who is the rudder of us all.

Debra Perkins

Part I: Why You Need a Doctor

Chapter 1: Foundations

"We constantly survey, but we never seem to learn anything!"

"I can't tell you how much we spend on surveying, but it is an enormous amount. Time, effort, money — all seems to be wasted. When we are done, we don't know what to make of it. What did we learn?"

"I am tired of this. Constantly new survey results cross my desk. As a manager, I'm charged with making the changes that will improve our numbers, but often the survey results contradict each other from month to month. What am I to make of it? What action is 'right'?"

Introduction to Pain

Despite all the joys, there is so much pain in business: the pain of wasted resources; the pain of not knowing what to do with the information available; the pain of believing the data and implementing a new action program only to find that the actions did not achieve the desired results; the pain of having the responsibility to act without having believable intelligence.

We hear about this pain all the time at conferences. We hear about the magnitude. We hear about the intensity. We hear about the sense of hopelessness.

We are doctors, and we are here to help with the pain.

Unfortunately, we cannot hope to cure all of your business pains, but we can offer some relief for the pain associated with surveying customers. There are concrete actions that can be taken — and, in the pages of this book, we will reveal what those are and why they will help. It's a big promise, but we will keep it.

Let us talk a little about the type of "pain" expressed in the title of this book. Most of the distress associated with surveys comes from a deeply rooted misconception regarding surveys versus research. Frankly, most business people feel that they are competent to conduct surveys. After all, from their perspective, surveying is little more than scribbling down some questions, asking a few people to react to them, tabulating the responses and dashing off a summary. We need to be very clear on this point: *What we just described does not constitute research in any sense of the term.* It could well be called *surveying*, but it is not *scientific research*. Scientific research is a rigorous activity that follows certain rules and procedures that need to be well understood and applied if your goal is to gain useful insights to turn into actions. "Take two aspirins and call me in the morning" is NOT our *modus operandi*. We will show what needs to be done and why.

We'll start with a quick glimpse at the health services industry to illustrate the importance of being informed. These days, a cutting-edge model for health services providers is the concept of having "informed patients." Patients are handed brochures urging them to speak up if something is wrong, to be actively involved in their care, and to help health providers avoid expensive and possibly dangerous mistakes. Maybe you've noticed this trend. We recently experienced it firsthand during a visit to the emergency room following an accident. Just before we were taken into radiology, we learned that the orders at hand called for the wrong limb to be X-rayed! Even more dramatic are stories that seem to have an effective treatment outlined, like the removal of a diseased kidney, and then the healthy kidney is erroneously removed. Just as users of medical services need to be informed patients, so must the users of research be informed. This, then, is the first goal of this work: to inform.

In a recently aired television commercial, a man with rubbing alcohol and medical implements spread out on a kitchen table holds a mirror in one hand and the phone in the other. On the other end of the phone line, a physician directs the man where to make an incision. The scene then switches back to the man who asks the doctor, "Shouldn't *you* be doing this?" The point of the commercial is that we hire professionals to help us meet needs that we are incapable of fulfilling for ourselves. No sane person would undertake self-surgery unless pressed to it by the most extraordinary circumstances. One occasionally encounters stories such as the Minnesota farmer who amputated his own arm to avoid being pulled into and subsequently killed by a piece of farm equipment, and the mountain climber who did the same when his arm became wedged between rocks and he couldn't get it out after days of trying — but these are definitely extraordinary circumstances, not everyday events. All other things being equal, rational people prefer medical work to be performed in a sterile environment by a trained surgeon and anesthesiologist, using the best medications and technology. Most of us want the least cost, but we also seek safety and the avoidance of pain when we can.

Yet normally rational business people often neglect to use a professional researcher. Instead, they undertake expensive and important research without the training and expertise required to do the job right. This is the equivalent of self-surgery without provocation, an activity that is patently dangerous, as well as painful.

Alternatively, to save money, organizations often will appoint an inside staff member to oversee the survey endeavor and report on its progress, regardless of his or her experience or level of expertise with research. This is tantamount to taking your health issues to a shaman or herb purveyor rather than a trained medical professional. Most people wouldn't dream of trying to save money by performing their own medical or dental procedures, nor would they actively seek the lowest cost provider (because, as we all know, you're likely to get what you pay for). Yet many business professionals will do these very things when it comes to customer research because the cost is perceived to be lower. (Remember, cheap can turn out to be expensive.) Unfortunately, they fail to consider the pain such actions inflict on the enterprise, the customers and the employees.

This brings us to our second goal: to encourage the hiring of expertise and to do so with a knowledge base to determine the level of competence of the proclaimed expert.

Beyond the Basics: How to Develop a Scientifically Sound Customer Measurement Program

This was the original title of our book. It's a good title in that it honestly portrays our intent. As it implies, this text is dedicated to going beyond the basics into intermediate, and even to a degree, advanced scientific research toward the creation, initiation, promulgation and interpretation of a sound customer measurement program for the contact center industry. While many of the examples we employ come from that industry, the research method is applicable to all surveying attempts. We bid contracts every year for firms that have no customer contact center but, instead, outsource this function. Some of the proposals are for businesses that neither possess their own contact center nor outsource; nevertheless, they need customer intelligence and hire us to get it.

We hope to make it possible for practitioners who are not steeped in hardcore academic research to understand the lessons involved and, to do so, we will use the method of successive approximations: that is, we will employ a technique of presenting small steps in such a way that we explain each concept as it is needed. We will provide examples that will be familiar to general business professionals, as well as examples common to the contact center industry and non-profit organizations such as universities and governmental agencies. While it may not be possible to actually run the program we outline without hiring or outsourcing part of it to a trained researcher, it is more than possible to make the necessity of doing so understandable as we make the methodologies and scientific rubrics available. Herein lies the informed decision-making capability. An experienced practitioner versed in the lessons contained herein will be highly capable of *overseeing* the necessary research and appropriately utilizing it for the betterment of the customers, the business as a whole and most contact center agents, as well as the organization as a whole through return on investment (ROI) improvements and actionable intelligence. Trust of the program is critical and a third-party impartial expert adds value when internal politicking and strife challenge unfavorable results.

So why did we change the title of the book? While the above are still among our goals, it soon became clear to us that this book is applicable well beyond the contact center. Surveys are designed, disseminated, tabulated and interpreted in many business areas, not merely the contact center. Hence, we have broadened our focus in hopes of alleviating survey pain elsewhere, as well.

We see a clear need for the content presented in this book, as there is a great deal of basic material available — from our own writings, as well as many others. Further, it is apparent from some sources that the whole truth is not always clearly shared with regard to research methodologies. As a result, practitioners often expect more and different results from their measurement programs than they can achieve given the methodology utilized. We intend to lay bare to the reader the shortcomings of various research methodologies, and reveal the established scientific means to correct for those shortcomings. As you will see, the best "short answer" to methodological shortfalls lies in using a mixture of methodologies that complement each other to ameliorate the inadequacies inherent from the use of any single one. In other words, no single technique can accomplish all research tasks since every technique has some faults. But, when using multiple techniques, the weaknesses of one will be overcome by the strengths of a companion technique.

Rocket Science for Contact Centers

This was the second title we wrestled with and ultimately discarded. It's also a good title in some respects. While it is pretty "catchy," in an attention-getting way, it's also a bit more obtuse.

We have all heard the saying, "It's not rocket science!" which is used to indicate that people with less training than a rocket scientist should be able to accomplish a task. One day, it occurred to us that each of the authors of this book possesses an education at least equal to the typical rocket scientist! We each have roughly 12 years of university education, which entitles us to the honorific "doctor." Much like a rocket scientist, we have been well trained in statistics, science and research methodology. But unlike rocket scientists, we are trained to deal with topics much more complex than trajectories, mass and propulsion. True, each of these is complex and requires higher mathematics to comprehend; however, once understood, the principles remain immutable. $E=mc^2$ is an absolute.

We social scientists, however, deal with probabilities rather than absolutes because we study human behavior. Humans are notoriously difficult to work beside, sell to, buy from or manage, much less predict. Yet we are in the business of prediction. We work with probabilities every day. As a chemist friend of mind once said, he expects one molecule of hydrogen to combine with two molecules of oxygen to produce water 100 percent of the time. It would be impossible to safely conduct chemical experiments if 90 percent of the time we produced water and the other 10 percent of the time we might get hydrochloric acid. A chemical experiment is completely repeatable if the procedures are properly followed.

No such assertion can be made when working with humans.

For example, a university president asked the faculty to support each other by attending the workshops, conferences and symposia sponsored by the other schools across campus. His urging caused some professors to actively look at events outside of their own departments and, subsequently, attend them. But other professors leaving the faculty meeting were overheard to say they would most certainly *not* do any such thing unless they were paid to do so. Each professor received the same stimulus: a request from the boss to be collegial by engaging in a particular activity. The responses, however, were probabilistic.

So, in truth, it takes *more* than a rocket scientist. It takes a social scientist trained to deal in the probabilities inherent in human behavior.

We undertook the goal to encourage readers to hire the necessary expertise because we've seen tremendous resources wasted on poorly designed surveying efforts that resulted in useless, non-actionable information — even though informed managerial action was the sole function of the survey activity.

Rally Cry for the Customer

Much in the customer surveying environment seems dry, brittle, gray. Where is the enthusiasm? Where is the "active"? Where is the passion?

We considered "Rally Cry for the Customer" as a possible title for this book. By definition, rally has lots of military connotations, such as to muster or call up forces, or to stir up; a recouping or reuniting of forces. When coupled with "cry," we get a slogan to engage in activity meant to unite forces for a purpose, and our purpose is in service to customers.

There is a lot of pretense that customers are being served and that business is in the business of doing that very thing. But consider these signs that we've seen on business premises:

1. For your convenience, please return carts to the corral.
2. To better serve you, please have your deposit slip completed before you enter the queue.
3. For faster service, please remove your picture ID from your wallet.

We won't even start on the ever-changing rituals of getting through an airport!

The point is that many of the rules in business are not set up for the convenience of the customers. Rather, these urgings are to make things easier for the institution. This is a common failing in business and non-profits; making transactions as easy as possible for the institution, while expecting the customer to provide that ease.

As one of many potential illustrations of this point, we use a specific branch of a major player in the banking industry. We are "premier" customers, but no one at the branch ever recognizes us or knows us no matter how many times we use the facility. There is always a queue regardless of when you go to the bank: at opening, lunch time, middle of the afternoon or near closing, and varying the day of the week has not been a successful means of avoiding the queue either. For the last two years, we have had to present our driver's license to conduct any activities regardless of how small. Now we are expected to present a specific, bank-issued ATM card instead, which supposedly serves as our identification. In actual fact, the ATM card does not have the holder's picture on it, so the driver's license would be a superior means of identification; but the real point of the switch was to eliminate the teller's need to input the customer's account. No big deal you say — except that we NEVER use an ATM. Literally, we have never used one, so why would we carry the card? But being a "premier" customer does not save us from the obligatory lecture that we need to swipe the ATM card every time we go to the bank, and why aren't we carrying the ATM card?

The point again, is that even our best customers do not get much customer service. Rather, we expect our customers to conform to processes engineered from the institutional point of view. This is as backward as anything can be. We need to take customer service seriously and begin to engineer the customer experience from the point of view of the customer. Hence a "Rally Cry for the Customer" would be an excellent title for this book. We want that active involvement on behalf of the customers who, after all, are responsible for every bit of financial success any organization ever achieves. We want that sense of urgency. We want to gather our forces together, involve people and begin to give "real" service instead of "lip" service.

Agents often are the most enthusiastic about this concept. Agents experience a phenomenal level of frustration when they see how to help the customer, but are not allowed the leeway and autonomy to fix the problem. We hire "people people" to service the people, but expect them to act like automatons programmed to break production quotas!

It is not only agents who see this importance in institutions. It's not uncommon for the folks in the C-level suites to talk about creating a rally cry (our term) for the customer, and the vision and the mission of the organization that they want to see as interwoven with the directive of customer centrality; but the vision will never be realized with the current research that is being conducted. Research is not a disconnected thing but a fundamental input for a dedicated and engaged workforce.

It's an input for goal setting, an outcome of goals.

It's an input for coaching, an outcome of coaching.

The Rally Cry is the spirit and culture of the company and the common goal for customer service and satisfaction that returns profit to the organization.

We have adopted the "Rally Cry for the Customer" as a central theme at Customer Relationship Metrics because it fully embodies the input and the output for and from our research, but we ultimately rejected it as the title for this work. That decision largely rested on the need to get the surveying piece and the pain caused by useless "pseudo-research" in front of the buying public. Maybe "Rally Cry for the Customer" will be the title for our next book.

Unskilled and Unaware

Lest anyone should believe that we are overstating the case, we'd like to draw your attention to a very nicely conducted piece of research titled, "Unskilled and Unaware of It: How Difficulties in Recognizing One's Own Incompetence Lead to Inflated Self-Assessments," by Justin Kruger and David Dunning. In this research, subjects were asked to rate their competence in certain domains and then take tests within those domains (humor, grammar or logic). Those scoring in the bottom quartile of the distribution on performance nevertheless had self-rated their abilities very favorably, despite their clear inabilities in the area. To quote from the authors:

> People tend to hold overly favorable views of their abilities in many social and intellectual domains… [we] suggest that this overestimation occurs, in part, because people who are unskilled in these domains suffer a dual burden: Not only do these people reach erroneous conclusions and make unfortunate choices, but their incompetence robs them of the metacognitive ability to realize it… Several analyses linked this miscalibration to deficits in metacognitive skill, or the capacity to distinguish accuracy from error. Paradoxically, improving the skills of the participants, and thus increasing their metacognitive competence, helped them recognize the limitations of their abilities.

So the inability to properly diagnose when to call in a specialist is by no means limited to any certain group of people. People, in general, believe that they possess expertise that they do not. It is only when they are trained and, therefore, more knowledgeable in the area, that they understand just how little they know and how much more there is to learn.

Interestingly enough, the research also pointed out that those who actually possess expertise *overestimate* the degree to which *others* also possess this specialized knowledge. Evidently, the possession of this specialized knowledge biases the possessors to the belief that it is widespread, when, in fact, it is possessed by a very limited subset of the population. So now it's possible for you to understand our Gestalt moment when we realized that conducting research actually *is* like "rocket science."

A primary goal of this book is to narrow the knowledge gap that exists between the unskilled and the skilled "ends" of the continuum. Being a researcher or knowing how to conduct an engagement with a researcher moves one toward the goal of harnessing customer intelligence. The first step to alleviating survey pain is to become educated to the difference between surveying and research. The second step is to recognize the limits of the expertise available in-house compared to the amount needed for a competent research program.

Relax. The doctors are here.

External Quality Monitoring

There are lots of stories and examples throughout this book, a great many of which come from our own research and personal experiences. Our thought was to select the examples that everyone will be able to understand regardless of business area. In service to that thought, we will explain the jargon and interpret for the layman.

Our primary focus will be on the customer measurement program within the contact center environment; that is, the program the contact center has put in place that is designed to hear the wants and needs of its customers. (Contact centers are typically known as the 1-800 call centers that provide technical assistance, customer service, sales and intermediary services between customers and other elements of the business, just to name a few functions.) In general, we will refer to the data that is to be collected by this program as the **external quality monitoring** program or **EQM**. By this, we're referring to a suite of methodologies and programs covering the various communication channels rather than a single, one-shot instrument that gives an "answer." An EQM program offers a strategic-level look at customers' wants and needs. We have coined this particular phrase to describe what we are doing here because it is intuitively understandable that customers evaluate/monitor their experience.

We are all more or less familiar with **internal quality monitoring (IQM)** programs in which a designated person listens to an agent's calls and assesses the quality of the call according to set criteria. (This is analogous to Quality Control in a manufacturing environment.) A very large percentage of all contact centers in the world have such a program in place. The program we propose will accomplish the same *quality* purpose as IQM with the added benefit of *listening directly to the Voice of the Customer.* Other people's suppositions about what customers want or need are often palmed off onto contact centers as the voice of the customer, but only a program such as the one we will detail can actually do the job. Only true *data collected from customers* can provide the intelligence needed to properly direct contact center activities.

As an aside, other consultants and researchers sometimes use the phrase "Voice of the Customer" to describe the EQM program that we're advocating. It's not a bad choice in that, to properly design the customer experience, you need to truly understand what customers themselves want and need. Additionally, it is intuitively obvious to the contact center industry when we say we are planning and implementing a program that completely complements the IQM program. But many vendors claim to capture the voice of the customer when they're only selling their product or service, which is a mere shadow of what is necessary. We abandoned the use of the term for the program itself primarily because it is possible to have a fantastic measurement program and then not use it to create a groundswell of enthusiasm leading to a Rally Cry for the Customer. Although we declined to use the phrase "voice of the customer" in our program's name, it is, nevertheless, not without some value, and we use it occasionally throughout the book. For example, "voice of the customer" has both literal and figurative meanings. It is possible to capture voice data literally one customer at a time. It is also possible to capture the sense of the customer's desires though alternative modalities, for example, such as mechanical responses to rating scales. Both are ways to capture the voice of the customer. But some methods are better than others. In general, a modality that captures the data with as little distortion as possible is preferable to the alternatives. There are many potential distortions in data collection — we'll discuss several of these and how best to eliminate them. As you'll see, different contact centers have tried varying means to collect and understand the needs of customers. We'll detail some of that information later in this chapter as we relate the history of the contact center industry and its understanding of customers in the recent past.

Plan of the Book

Before we move on with an overview of the contact center industry's history, let's take a brief look at how the content in this book is organized, and the topics on which we will focus.

In Part I, we will establish our goals and define some terms. Additionally, we'll provide an overview of the history of the contact center industry and a brief look at how consumers have changed over time. Next, we'll look, with some detail, at human resources. We stated earlier that we deal in the probabilistic behavior of humans, which is not limited to customers — it also extends to employees. What we say about one is likely, to some degree, to apply to the other. Since most businesses readily agree that their employees are their competitive edge, we thought it appropriate to expend some effort to bring employees into proper focus. Employees project the culture of the organization that is heard by its customers. Part I, then, sets our stage.

In Part II, we'll begin a systematic study of the science of research, which starts by indicating what it is not: surveying. In fact, we've coined the phrase "survey malpractice" to indicate just how bad surveying is compared to real science. We then take up two topics in research that have received a tremendous amount of press: benchmarking and Net Promoter. We've devoted a chapter to each of these two topics to put to rest many misconceptions about them.

Benchmarking studies, for instance, often have been hailed as key to running a top-notch organization. Specifically within the contact center environment, benchmarking operational information is of great interest. We will explain in some detail why benchmarking studies fall very short in providing the intelligence needed to hear the needs of the customer. Benchmarking has come under intense scrutiny because some researchers have touted it as the paramount research program within the contact center environment. In part, that's likely due to the fact that they have access to national benchmarking data, as we also have. Needless to say, there is a living to be made from gathering, analyzing and interpreting benchmarking data. It may also be that some simply fail to see the shortcomings inherent in decision making within the contact center environment based on benchmarking alone. While it is true that benchmarking studies have some validity in this environment, they are far from serving the central focus of the contact center. In fact, benchmarking data is completely deaf to the voice of the customer, and hence, only of peripheral interest at best. Therefore, we have chosen to devote a full chapter to benchmarking history, theoretical underpinning and positive use, as well as misuse, in the contact center world.

We next devote a chapter to Net Promoter. Far too many people have bought into the highly unscientific idea that it is possible to run a successful business based on a single survey question. This is an idea that must be debunked, and we do so here. That is not to say that there is NO value in the concept; rather, the benefits touted far exceed the realistic possibilities based on a single question.

Part II ends with a chapter devoted to scientific enquiry and its centrality to any survey research program, such as the External Quality Monitoring customer measurement program. The basic thesis of this entire endeavor rests on the authors' firm belief in the utility of scientific enquiry over all other means. We will cite research on the benefits of clearly capturing the voice of the customer. Additionally, we'll explain why Internal Quality Monitoring programs do not suffice any better than benchmarking studies as a means of hearing the needs of the customer. We'll then look at how to develop a scientifically sound research program. We've carefully outlined what to avoid and what must be present, emphasizing the importance of sufficient sample size and including both customer-volunteered *qualitative* data, as well as researcher-solicited *quantitative* data. We'll discuss how to ensure that the data inputs are devoid of "dirt," and the means for cleaning such so that the will of the customers can be clearly heard. We'll also provide numerous examples and explanations for scaling decisions, normalization and regression analysis, and discuss how to interpret regression output and the uses of such information for managerial decision-making.

Part III gets to the heart of the EQM program. We speak in detail about the logic and benefits of a sound EQM program, and how to scientifically develop a program meant to listen to the voice of the customer. Effective EQM programs generate positive energy and a commitment that supersedes other performance measures. Programs are designed to be continuous, positive reinforcements for delivering excellent service. When people are positively committed to a common cause to maximize the customer experience, collectively, they deliver breakout performance. A primary outcome is the generation of people power through trust and fair accountability. Because this is critically important and so much is learned through trial and error, we've included a chapter consisting of research hints. We think of these as practical considerations and hope they'll help you to avoid the problems that we've encountered in the past.

Part IV concretely demonstrates how to prove the value of the research through customer lifetime value (CLV) and return on investment (ROI). These techniques for establishing the value of the program take it out of the "fuzzy" area of qualitative analysis into the hardcore realm of standard business analysis. We demonstrate how to calculate return on investment, which is a powerful tool to use in-house to demonstrate that a soundly executed EQM program pays for itself through increased employee and customer satisfaction, retention and recommendations.

No matter how well you develop and execute your EQM program, the results will produce little benefit for the contact center unless your executive management also gets the message. Hence, we discuss the importance of communication and how best to accomplish it. Last, we look at numerous examples illustrating how the EQM program can be communicated to the best effect.

In addition to the executive levels, most areas of the organization can benefit from intelligence gathered within the contact center. Every organization aspires to be elite. An aspiration transfers into a commitment. A commitment supports a Rally Cry that is heard by customers. Quantifying and managing to what the customers are *hearing* in the experience with you cannot be accomplished with a basic survey program. The superlative is required to be elite. We'll outline the means for strategically leveraging the results of the EQM program across the organization.

As we mentioned earlier, the rest of this chapter will provide an overview of organizations' understanding of their customers by focusing on the recent history of the contact center industry. We'll also take a brief look into the psychology of customers. There is a plethora of consumer behavior texts, each consisting of several hundred pages. Additionally, the academic literature on customer satisfaction, dissatisfaction and complaining behavior offers a treasure trove of insight into caller behavior in the contact center environment. A complete survey of that literature is outside the scope of this endeavor; nevertheless, a brief view of what motivates customer behavior is useful.

The Past and Present Constant: Change

The Former "Cutting Edge"

In the contact center industry, surveying and customer satisfaction strategies have been a part of the way business was conducted for the past decade. When companies surveyed customers the process was not scientific and often used flawed methodologies and inconsistent instruments, so businesses were essentially learning inaccurate and ineffective things about the customers. Customer measurement was inconsistent across the industry as a concept of "customer satisfaction" developed, despite the fact that customer satisfaction was seen as the same for all customers — that is, customers were thought to be identical in needs and wants. Customers were perceived as a homogeneous cohort.

In those days, business gave lip service to the creed that "The customer is *always* right." Business goals were stated as 100 percent customer satisfaction, and measurement programs were slanted toward securing the goal of the metric. Since customers were perceived as homogenous, surveys asked simple questions on simple scales to detect simple needs and wants.

Quality and product offerings were considered to be competitive advantages. Product features were the most important aspect of marketing and advertising. Close secondary emphasis was placed on the company's name.

Generally, companies tried to do a lot of things, even if they didn't do them all well. Outsourcing was very nearly non-existent; rather, each company handled all of the services needed in house, even if only poorly.

Strategy was all about customer acquisition. The focus was on getting the customer to buy the product — even if only once. The focus was short-term and on product trial rather than on relationship-building.

Forecasts of future sales were predicated entirely on past sales performance. Facts and figures usually guided decision-making except where management weighed in on decisions because they thought that they understood customers better.

Dissatisfaction was generally not considered, but, when it was, it was viewed as an unmitigated negative — a concept to be whispered about and not spoken aloud.

Marketing was responsible for being the voice of the customer. They thought it was their job to understand customers and communicate that understanding to the rest of the company.

In the last 20 years or so, customer relationship management (CRM) was considered to be a software, technology or suite of products. This was the totality of what was meant by CRM. Customers were taken care of, by definition, via the CRM bundle. The presumption was that the universe was already known. CRM software solutions were, and often still are, implemented without the customer in mind.

> "CRM benefits don't come without cost or risk, not only in collecting the original customer data, but also in maintaining and mining it." (Kotler and Armstrong, 2006)

> "An estimated half or more of all CRM efforts fail to meet their objectives. The most common cause of CRM failures is that companies mistakenly view CRM only as technology and soft-

ware solution." (Rigby, 2002; Flinders, 2004)

"They forget to focus on the 'relationship' part." (Krauss, 2002)

The Present "Cutting Edge"

Times have changed business in important ways. Competition has created an environment that is unlike any other before. Today, business competes on a world stage; and for better or worse, globalization is here to stay. Gone, or nearly so, are the days when businesses operated on a national scale at most. In those days, a company could expect to have special obligations to the host country, and in return, the business could expect to receive special benefits such as some protection from foreign competitors, research subsidies or tax breaks. As long as lobbying remains the favorite sport in national capitals, certain governmental special treatments, such as tax breaks for some industries, can still be expected; however, the Free Trade legislation in Europe and the Americas has forever altered the complexion of competition. With the benefits of the free movement of capital and labor has also come free movement of competitors across national borders.

Additionally, deregulation in several industries has created opportunities for new competitors while seriously undercutting the slow-moving giants that were deregulated. For example, witness the telecommunications industry. Back in the days when the telephone industry consisted of Bell Telephone, *Rowan & Martin's Laugh-In*, a popular sketch comedy television program, featured a long-running series of skits showcasing the humor of Lily Tomlin as Ernestine, a wisecracking telephone operator. Paraphrased, the standard ending to the skit was, "We're Ma Bell. We don't have to care." Businesses that treat customers cavalierly today may find themselves out of business tomorrow as customers desert them for competitors.

Even governmental entities are making attempts to serve customers better. For example, the Internal Revenue Service (IRS) is promoting itself as a "kinder, gentler" IRS, and offers certain tax help options. The Commonwealth of Virginia is trying to overhaul its Department of Motor

Vehicles contact center by creating a more user-friendly system and positive service experience. Various offshoots of the Florida Medicaid program are highly focused on the customer experience through its outsource contact center provider, and continue to leverage customer intelligence to engineer the call experience and to gather valuable feedback about its agency's programs.

Keener competition over time has resulted in a shift in focus. CRM is now seen as both the processes and the tools used to implement a company's customer relationship strategy. The supposed "voice of the customer" has become the most critical element in process design, software and hardware purchase decisions. Previously, the purchased CRM bundle drove the customer relationship; now the characteristics of the desired CRM strategy drive the purchase of the appropriate bundle of consulting services, technology and software. Emphasis is now on the building of relationships.

Intuition and customer data are strong factors in decision-making. Decisions are based on asking customers what they want. Customer satisfaction is no longer considered a steady measurement across all customers; rather, it can mean different things to different customers.

Many of the industry's leaders now view the customer as king… but *not* always right. One hundred percent customer satisfaction is now seen as an unrealistic and unwise goal, and new goals are articulated to replace one that is impossible to reach. Companies realize the value in customers and many treat them differently today. Customer segmentation has taken root and is used to target the organization's truly valuable customers for the most attention and the highest level of customer service; hence, the birth and growth of "premier," "platinum" and other such customer designations with the attendant "special" services, such as free checks, lower rates on other services, etc., and expedited service to higher skilled agents.

Companies are trying harder to uncover the customers' needs. They have begun to ask more questions and different kinds of questions in order to expose the bedrock issues. Often these take the form of more qualitative and fewer quantitatively scored questions.

Customer service has become a powerful competitive advantage. It is how companies use the customer knowledge that they have gained. How far does customer information permeate into the organization? This alone can be the competitive advantage that turns so-so performance into stellar profits. Acquiring information about the will of the customer from and about frontline agents, and passing it along to the necessary department heads to take the necessary action is mission critical to business today.

Communicating the value of the services that the company provides is the most important aspect of marketing and advertising in the new millennium.

Companies focus on core competencies and try to do only a few things well. Outsourcing is common. Firms seriously consider the "hire" or "buy" decision when evaluating the need for additional expertise. Programmers, technical maintenance personnel and researchers are often under contract rather than hired. Some organizations come to rely completely on outsourcing, moving the entire customer care function to domestic, off- or nearshore facilities.

With competition in the marketplace rising, companies must ensure customer satisfaction, not just by continuing to provide good service, but also by providing a *differentiating level* of service and value to its customers. Today, strategy is all about customer retention and generation of positive word-of-mouth, and the focus is on the depth of the relationship with the customer. Long-term focus is the key. Customer lifetime value and customer loyalty come into play for company strategies and become a part of the mission statement.

Future performance projections are based on present performance. The past no longer provides much guidance because the pace of business is too fast. Businesses see that they can build on present strengths, and therefore project into the future on that basis.

Dissatisfaction and satisfaction are seen as opportunities for improvement. As such, they are openly discussed and mined for options that will appeal to customers.

Senior management is often responsible for the voice of the customer; oversight of the function reports directly to top executives. Often it is acknowledged as simply too important to delegate. Since this provides the most critical link between a company and its customer asset base, the responsibility to acquire, maintain and grow customer relationships rests almost squarely on senior management's shoulders.

Today, knowledge and responsiveness are required for the company to be successful. Hiring and training have become a priority for contact centers. It takes knowledgeable agents to provide the level of service to customers that they expect.

The Voice of the Customer: The Missing Link, Then and Now

Despite the recognition in recent years that customers are not homogeneous and, therefore, have varying needs, wants and service requirements, and despite the improvements companies have made in tailoring the business to the needs of the customer, the directives from the "voice of the customer" are conspicuously missing from most discussions. Unfortunately, the talk focuses most often on the technology; about the integration of that technology; about ways to get people within the organization to use the technology; about ways to get the customers to use the technology, even when what they often want is human interaction; and about ways that we *believe* our customers will benefit from the technology. Yet we seldom listen to the actual "voice of the customer." **Listening** to the voice of the customer through an EQM program allows the customer to design the experience. Instead of expecting marketing or some manager who rarely actually interacts with a customer to know what the customer wants, listen to what the customer says. Listening is a forgotten art.

Where is the best place to listen to the will of the customer? Clearly, the superior listening post is the contact center. Ironically, in many organizations this intelligence resource is largely untapped. Organizations try to collect customer wants and desires through advertising and marketing or other means. But today, the vast majority of all customer service interactions occur electronically — by telephone and the Web — via dynamic or two-way communications that flow through the contact center.

Contact centers are never at a loss for numbers. Managers live by their center's statistics. They continuously post numbers, report operational metrics, worry or feel elated by these numbers and even benchmark operational metrics against other contact centers. What if they were celebrating or worrying at the wrong times? This is exactly what can happen if the center is not reporting and analyzing the caller's perceptions of the service delivery.

Caller perception is the reality. Whether it's real or only perceived by the caller, the caller evaluation is the reality that managers must handle. It is more real than the service level or average length of call or any other operational metric. Despite this fact, the list of metrics managers watch on a daily basis often does not include caller feedback. Does it really matter what the operational metrics look like if the center does not know whether it is effective to the callers? Without the customers' feedback, it is impossible to know whether the operational metrics are out of line.

The point here is that the difference between efficiency and effectiveness is the difference between a lingering financial death and organizational health and wealth. Efficiency has been defined as "doing a thing right." It entails accomplishing the task at hand via the lowest cost means. Effectiveness, on the other hand, has been defined as "doing the right thing." This definition implies selecting the critical task to accomplish and then doing it. If it were necessary to choose to be efficient *or* to be effective, clearly it would be superior to be effective so that, at least, the most important task is accomplished. There is no advantage to doing a wrong thing well, while there is much advantage to doing what is necessary even when doing it poorly from an efficiency standpoint. Efficiency should be an outcome of an effective process.

Note that the metrics that centers collect generally fall into the "efficiency" category. Average length of call is just one of more than a dozen such metrics. The important point is that the customer doesn't care how long the call takes, whether it is their call, someone else's or the daily average. What the caller cares about is whether or not the issue that motivated the call is resolved quickly, pleasantly and in their favor. Only their call is important. All the metrics in the world matter not one iota to callers. Just listen to the "voice of the customer" from any contact center and this will become apparent.

Ideally, the goal to pursue is to provide effectiveness while being reasonably efficient. Effectiveness requires customer centrality to guide the center, essentially to operationalize the Rally Cry for the Customer. Making operational metrics the driver of the center's reward structure is the triumph of form over function; putting the cart before the horse; throwing the baby out with the bath water. Choose a cliché. They are all true when efficiency is the sole guide.

With that said, should operational metrics be completely ignored? What actions should be taken when X drops below a certain point or Y increases above a certain point? Presumably actions taken reflect the assumption that these movements ultimately affect caller satisfaction. In many cases, they probably do, but it cannot be proven unless the center's dashboard has a complete set of both satisfaction and operational metrics. In other words, correlate the operational metrics with the customer feedback from the EQM program to help determine when and what remedial actions can be fruitfully pursued.

Quantifying operational metrics is not an issue given the technology and software that is widely available; so the challenge becomes one of accurately measuring service delivery from the callers' perspective. The ideal method to collect callers' perceptions in a contact center is through real-time, post-call surveys.

Technology: Enabler or Paralyzer?

When the Internet stormed into our lives years ago, experts predicted the demise of phone contact by consumers. Many pundits forecasted that consumers would be using the Internet for *everything*... from grocery shopping to buying cars. Despite the successes of online services like Peapod and Autotrader.com, and all the hype associated with the Internet and email, it has become obvious that customers will never abandon the phone for doing business. The Internet has become *a* medium for communication, but not *the* medium for communication. Although today's consumers use email and other self-service technologies, self-service has not replaced the need for service by a live agent. Instead, these technologies have elevated the need for an effective contact center. More complex issues that cannot be resolved via the Internet or email find resolution via phone calls or chat sessions with agents in the contact centers. Additionally, *someone* must respond to tech traffic one way or another. Although we will return to the discussion of technology momentarily, the role of the agent is mission critical and deserves consideration here.

Even with all the new technologies in place, skilled agents are the foundation of the customer service function. This fact of life is given "lip service" by most companies and may even be believed by some, yet many agents are made to feel like nothing more than cogs in a wheel. Their needs are often ignored in favor of technology improvements. The hard, cold fact is that people are often left out of the equation. One equation to express these relationships is:

Customer Satisfaction = people + process + technology

We would argue, however, that the above equation fails to capture the concept of synergy. Synergy is the surplus over the simple summation of resources applied. A company is said to have synergy when the whole is greater than the sum of the parts. The appropriate equation then should be:

Customer Satisfaction = people x process x technology

Note that people are the foundation of synergy. If there is synergy anywhere, it is due to the personnel. They are the pivotal resource and the absolutely essential component to build a Rally Cry for the Customer.

The reality for most contact centers is that agents are expected to adjust to changes in technology and processes as readily as technology and processes can be changed. It is the technology and the processes that act as the givens or constraints and the people who are expected to wrap themselves around them. Often, each new process or technological innovation further dehumanizes the agents. With this history in place and the advent of offshoring, it is little wonder that agents look askance at additional innovations! But without well-trained, engaged and motivated agents the entire customer service function breaks down. It is the processes and technology that need to be slaved to the people, and not the reverse. With appropriate technology and processes in place, it is possible to help agents to become world-class generators of customer satisfaction.

One such technology is the Completely Automated Telephone survey (CATs®) system, which we'll discuss later in detail. Briefly, however, CATs® allows for the capture of customer evaluation data quickly, conveniently, accurately and at a reasonable cost. Because the system is so timely and accurate, feedback on agent performance is readily available for training and reward purposes. Such a system can only serve to assist agents to become better decision-makers as better-targeted training can be devised to pinpoint areas that need coaching. Additionally, research demonstrates that a timely reward for a job well done is reinforcing and tends to lead to repetition of the behavior. That is, just as timely corrections lead to improved performance, timely rewards contribute to additional performances worth rewarding. It can very nearly become a self-sustaining system. Automated survey applications are not equivalent to one another. A technology solution to collect data does not make a research program and does not produce an equivalent amount of meaningful rewards and coaching opportunities.

Agents aside (and the industry simply cannot afford to put them aside), sometimes the technology itself seems to take on a life. Data is updated so frequently in the systems that the concept of "outdated" has drastically changed. Now metrics that are only a few hours old may be thought of as outdated! In truth, frequent reporting can weigh down the process. In addition to frequency, there is the issue of just too many reports overall. Not every piece of data is worthy of reporting to everyone. There is such a thing as too much. It can become difficult for managers to focus on what is important because so many reports are being generated. Report by exception would seem to be a reasonable alternative to excessive reporting. That is, only ask for reports on variables that are above or below certain set minimums or maximums. The alternative is to spend a major portion of every day analyzing data that basically says everything is "normal."

Although information systems have come a long way, they still may not be able to integrate customer information from different organizational sources. As a result, the various sources are analyzed separately, instead of as one cohesive data set. Data analysis is scattered and fragmented. Different pictures may emerge due to these varying data sources of the same happenings at the same time, which may result in a biased view of the customer's perspective.

Sometimes technology leads organizations to tie staff responsibilities, performance evaluations and rewards either to the wrong type of data or to data from the wrong systems. It may even lead businesses to forget the customer entirely. Many managers just assume the technology is working the way it is supposed to, but never investigate it further. Unexamined assumptions can easily lead to fallacious conclusions.

In the never-ending search for means to drive down costs in the contact center, we have readily adopted technological advantages as they have become available. However, organizations often do not look at technological advances from the customer's perspective. For example, it may be more cost-effective for a company to use an interactive voice response (IVR) system than have its agents take calls, but the menu options are typically selected from the company's perspective and for its convenience. Someone who helped to set up the IVR *may* have considered to some degree what may be helpful to customers (or not), but that doesn't mean the customers' actual perspective was captured. Customers almost universally want the option early on to speak with an agent. Yet, this option often is presented very late in the menu, *if at all.* As IVR strategy, this may or may not be effective. The goal is to have options that facilitate self-service, proper call routing and a positive customer experience and not cause customers to just opt out to an agent. Recently a new client told us that their IVR was studied with a customer assessment prior to implementation... FIVE years ago. This just won't do! Customer experience measurement is not a once-and-done deal.

This brings up the topic of speech recognition used to greet callers when dialing into a customer service and support center. Ultimately, is speech recognition technology an enabler or a paralyzer in the customer interaction? For those customers who are technologically naïve, such as some elderly and those with inadequate education, the necessity of pushing buttons for each selection can be uncomfortable or even impossible. For these types of customers, speech recognition technology, at least to some degree, can be an enabler for customers faced with IVR menus.

Unfortunately, there seems to be a perception in the industry that, if the customer can speak the response instead of pressing a button, it is acceptable to keep asking questions long past reason. However, it is just as important to create efficient menus with speech recognition applications as with push-button technology. From the customer's perspective, speech recognition cannot compensate for lengthy menus. The recent ad campaign from CitiBank concretely demonstrates the case in point. In its television commercial, we see a guy answering untold numbers of idiotic questions — first in his kitchen, then in the bathroom and later on the subway, just to be disconnected as the train enters a tunnel with the issue unresolved. As the campaign slogan says, "Sometimes you just want to talk to a person. Just dial 0 to talk to an agent."

Lastly, sometimes the industry is guilty of putting technology in place just for technology's sake. This is the "keeping up with the Joneses" syndrome and a negative result of benchmarking. Little effort is made to dovetail the new technology into the existing processes or to change the processes to match the technology. For example, customers often are asked to respond to menus that ask for their account numbers, zip codes, mother's maiden name, first elementary school attended and who knows what else — only to be asked to repeat the same information to the live agent. While the technical teams may have a good reason for this, the customer perceives it to be needless repetition that is a waste of time — and make no mistake, they resent this gap that exists between your IVR and the desktop populated by CTI (computer telephony integration)!

Customers also Have Changed

More Knowledgeable... More Demanding

Customers have access to more information than ever before, and not only through books, newspapers, magazines, radio and television. The Internet has increased information access for customers in a big way. Now it takes very little time or effort to find out almost anything, from how to build a bomb to the ratio of churches to taverns in New England in the 1990s. Commercially available consumer goods are even simpler to research than obscure facts; a quick Google search will turn up vendors of the desired products and services along with ratings collected by a variety of sources.

The pace of life is ever quicker, and consumer preferences change just as quickly. This ever-quickening rate of progress has made convenience almost a moot point. Commerce and socializing continue 24/7. Some banks have returned to Saturday afternoon hours and some are open on Sunday. Others have opened smaller branches in grocery stores with extended hours. Urgent care centers make physician advice available during extended hours. People can shop catalogs by phone, buy auto insurance and research furniture purchases at 3 a.m. using the Internet.

Along with this wealth of information comes newfound consumer self-awareness. Consumers now have the power of choice — and they know how powerful they are in the marketplace. Customers want to deal with companies who treat them special and provide more than the standard care. They want companies to take a personal interest in their well-being. They want individual, one-to-one efforts made to keep their business. Customers who don't get the service they expect will stop patronizing the business, and they may engage in negative word-of-mouth by telling friends and relatives about their experience. These are the more benign actions consumers may take. Those who become angry enough tell their stories to other consumers online. (To see an example of this rather extreme consumer activism, do a Google search on "Jennifer Convertibles.")

Why They Say the Things They Do

Customer perception is the reality every business lives with. As we alluded to earlier, the actual facts are less important than the customer's perception of the facts. It's difficult to accept this concept while, at the same time, maintaining that objective reality exists; nevertheless, it's true. Let's briefly examine the reality that customers perceive and how it's built up. Consider the following points:

• In any social behavior, including buying transactions and service interactions, how consumers think about themselves will influence how they behave.

• When buying a product or service, people often see that purchase as a reflection of themselves, their personality and, at some deep level, who they actually are. They also make inferences about other people who buy the same products and services. By extension, purchasing then affects what buyers think about the people who sell the goods and services they choose.

• Customers will approach the service interaction with expectations of how the interaction will go and what role they will have to play in it. This will influence the nature of the interaction, even before it occurs.

• When dealing with customer service via the telephone, the consumer's prior experiences and the experiences related by others will form much of the caller's expectations. Those expectations will be subsequently impacted by whatever other data is available during the call. Interestingly, the caller only has the sound (tone) of the agent's voice and his or her actual words with which to make inferences. Therefore, tone and word choice figure prominently in judgments about contact center incidents.

• Consumers are motivated to categorize others (including agents) because it makes their lives simpler. Therefore, they will know (or think they know) how to deal with a situation better — especially one in which they are dealing with people they don't know — because they have previously categorized it and stored it in their memory for easy recall in the future.

- Customers expect to be treated in a manner consistent with their role as customer in the interaction. Consumers evaluate service institutions and personnel positively when the personnel treat them as individuals who have specific needs to be met by the service interaction.

- Research has shown that satisfaction and/or dissatisfaction in one's life role may be transferred into other life roles, such as the consumer role. In other words, frustration or dissatisfaction with a product or service may actually stem from the consumer's feelings of frustration in another life role. However, they will transfer this dissatisfaction to the agent and the service interaction.

- Consumers' own self-perceptions bias their judgments in such a way that consumers often see themselves more positively and their role more valuable, important or influential than is actually the case. They will see themselves as the most valuable customer to your business during the service interaction. While this self-serving bias allows people to take responsibility for their successes, it also causes them to blame others for their failures. This is an important concept in service interactions since research has shown that blaming others for product dissatisfaction permits one to direct anger outward, toward the company, rather than to oneself.

Final Thoughts before We Begin

The contact center industry and customers themselves have changed a good deal over time, and continue to do so. Many times, those changes have made positive impacts on the bottom line via benefits received from technology and process improvements.

We have taken a brief look into the minds of callers. Now we will explicitly demonstrate the ultimate usefulness of the EQM system to the agents, organization and customers. In so doing, it will be necessary to look at the science of evaluation as currently practiced in the industry, and how the application of certain rules can improve the quality of the evaluations made within the center.

Without further ado, let us begin the process of easing the pain.

Chapter 2:
Human Resource Issues in the Contact Center

In the rush to perform, we often forget that a well-considered strategy should be the driving force behind all the tactics we elect to implement in the business. What are the competitive advantages the organization already possesses and where does the organization want to go? Do we only care about this quarter's bottom line or are we focused on long-term relationships and the profits that flow from them? What kind of corporate culture do we have and what do we hope to create in the future? The answers to these questions tell us whether we should "make" or "buy" our talent; and the "make/buy" decision informs our recruitment, selection and training programs. But no training program can hope to flourish without a sound understanding of the principles surrounding the issues of motivation and rewards. If training is to succeed, then the contingencies must be properly arranged to support that success. Lastly, we look at how the EQM program supports and enhances the Human Resources function by creating engaged agents who are dedicated to the Rally Cry for the Customer.

Employee Satisfaction and Performance

At the root of every organizational goal is profit, which can be driven by the employees' performance in serving customers. Therefore, firms strive to obtain high performance from their employees. But what drives high performance? Is there a link between employee satisfaction and performance? Much of the following arguments were derived from the classic work of David Cherrington, Joseph Reitz and William Scott, titled "Effects of Reward and Contingent Reinforcement on Satisfaction and Task Performance" (*Journal of Applied Psychology*).

Over the years, management experts have proposed various hypotheses about what drives employee performance. The first theory to be widely accepted posited that satisfied employees provided higher levels of performance. This is intuitively appealing assertion was founded largely on a misinterpretation of the work of F.J. Roethlisberger and W.J. Dickson in the classical Hawthorne experiments reported in *Management and the Worker* (1939).

The original experiments were designed to uncover the optimal lighting conditions to maximize worker performance in a factory. During the experiments, the researchers stumbled onto the realization that social forces had as much or more to do with output as production equipment. (At one point, the lighting in the experimental area was reduced to the level of "moonlight," and production still *increased* due largely to the "special treatments" received by the workers participating in the studies.) The misinterpretation of these experiments gave rise to the human relations school of management and the work of its supporters, such as Elton Mayo. However derived, we now have the first hypothesis:

> H1: Satisfaction leads to performance.

The obvious prediction arising from this hypothesis is that those who are satisfied in Time 1 should produce highly in Time 2.

Somehow, over time, the reverse also came to be believed; that is, performance leads to satisfaction. This is also intuitively appealing, as it is widely known that the feeling of accomplishment that comes from a job well done could also be called satisfaction. This theory was reviewed by D.P. Schwab and L.L. Cummings in 1970 in their work, titled "Employee Performance and Satisfaction with Work Roles: A Review and Interpretation of Theory," and by others since. So we now derive the second hypothesis:

> H2: Performance leads to satisfaction.

The obvious prediction arising from this is that those who are successful, high performers in Time 1 should also report feeling satisfied in Time 1. Engineering the environment to enhance success should lead to happy workers via their successful performance. In essence, successful people are happy people.

Based on studies in both behavior reinforcement and mood theory, the next competing hypothesis that can be derived suggests that there is no inherent relationship between satisfaction and performance; rather, satisfaction is a function of rewards. This is also an intuitively appealing hypothesis as it makes sense that those who get rewards will be happy to have received them; contrariwise, those who do not receive rewards will be unhappy to have been left out. This leads to hypotheses 3 and 3a below:

> H3: There is no inherent relationship between satisfaction and performance.
> H3a: Satisfaction is a function of rewards.

In other words, if one wishes to have happy staff, simply distribute many rewards regardless of the level of performance. Such rewards are often labeled as non-contingent rewards.

As a corollary, primarily from the Operant Conditioning literature, it has been suggested that performance can best be enhanced where rewards are distributed appropriately, and, alternatively, retarded where rewards are distributed inappropriately. These suggestions lead to the following hypotheses:

> H3b: Performance is a function of the linkage between performance and rewards.
> H3b1: Appropriate linkage leads to higher performance.
> H3b2: Inappropriate linkage leads to lower performance.

These competing hypotheses were tested in a remarkably simple experiment in which students were asked to perform a test-grading task. After Session 1, the completed materials were collected to be counted later so as to determine the level of performance each person achieved in Session 1. Rewards were randomly distributed to the participants so that there was literally no relationship between rewards and performance *a priori*. All were then asked to rate their satisfaction with the task just completed and these materials were also collected for scoring. Next all subjects were asked to continue the task learned in Session 1 in Session 2 and at the end the materials were collected so that performance results for Session 2 could be tallied. As expected, the task was more familiar in the second session so all groups performed better in Session 2 due to that prior practice.

The performances achieved during Session 1 were divided into High and Low achievers to form two groups. Then, as rewards were randomly distributed, it was possible to divide each of those two groups into rewarded and unrewarded leaving a total of four groups. When the data were all collected, graded, and sorted, the following table could be constructed which would allow us to see which hypotheses hold true.

Tests of Competing Hypotheses of Satisfaction, Rewards and Performance

Group #	Session 1 Performance	Session 1 Rewarded?	Session 1 Satisfied?	Session 2 Performance
1	High	Yes	Yes	High
2	High	No	No	Low
3	Low	Yes	Yes	Low
4	Low	No	No	High

Source: Extrapolated from "Effects of Reward and Contingent Reinforcement on Satisfaction and Task Performance," *Journal of Applied Psychology*, Cherrington, Reitz and Scott (1971).

According to H1, satisfaction leads to performance. If that is true, then those who rated themselves as satisfied after Session 1 should have high performances during Session 2. Those who rated themselves as satisfied after Session 1 are Groups 1 and 3. An examination of the last column for these two groups (performance during Session 2) shows that they were not uniformly high performers in Session 2; so H1 fails. Specifically, Group 3 self-reported satisfaction after Session 1, but turned in a low performance during Session 2.

According to H2, Hypothesis 1 is actually backward and it is performance that leads to satisfaction. To test this, we would need to examine whether those whose performance was high in Session 1 also rated themselves as satisfied. Looking at Groups 1 and 2, which were the high performers, and comparing them to the satisfied column, we see that some were satisfied and others were not (Group 1, the former; Group 2, the latter). Therefore, H2 fails. From this, we can conclude that, whatever the relationship between satisfaction and performance, it is not a simple, direct one.

We will only assess the veracity of H3 after we look to the sub-hypotheses. H3a says that satisfaction is a function of rewards. For this to be true, then those who were rewarded after Session 1 (Groups 1 and 3) should have rated themselves as satisfied. We can see that this is so. We can also look at Groups 2 and 4 and see that those who did *not* receive a reward did *not* rate their feelings as satisfied, so we then have a second test of the veracity of this hypothesis. This leads to the conclusion that H3a is true: Satisfaction is indeed a function of rewards or the lack thereof. Those who received rewards will self-report as satisfied, and those who do *not* receive a reward will *not* report as satisfied.

H3b departs from the satisfaction/performance controversy to look at the relationship between rewards and performance. As we did for H3a, we will set aside judgment for H3b until we have assessed the sub-hypotheses. For H3b1 to be true, those groups who were rewarded appropriately for their work in Session 1 should perform well in Session 2. Group 1 performed well in Session 1 and received a reward. This is appropriate, and we can see that their performance during Session 2 was high. Group 4 performed poorly in Session 1 and did not receive a reward. This is also appropriate and, as we can read from the last column, they were also high performers in Session 2. Note what it means to be appropriately rewarded: If you perform highly, you get a reward, and if you perform poorly, you do not.

For H3b2 to be true, those groups that were inappropriately rewarded should score lower performances. Again, we need to think about what it means to be inappropriately rewarded. If you performed well but did not receive a reward despite that performance (Group 2), then that would be inappropriate. Also, if you do poorly and are rewarded for that poor performance (Group 3), that, too, would be inappropriate. We then have Groups 2 and 3 to assess in Session 2, and find that both groups performed poorly. This confirms H3b2 that those who are not appropriately rewarded (i.e., received an undeserved reward or failed to receive a deserved reward) perform poorly in a subsequent session.

Since both H3b1 and H3b2 are confirmed, then H3b is true, as well. Likewise, since both H3b and H3a have been found to be true, then H3, as a whole, is also true.

What, then, has been learned from this exercise?

1. There is no simple, straight-line relationship between satisfaction

and performance.

2. If you want happy, satisfied workers, then distribute many non-contingent rewards. Give freely and often to everyone, and everyone will be happy (but not necessarily productive).

3. If you want productive workers, then distribute contingent rewards. Give meaningful rewards, but only to those who *earn* them. Interestingly enough, rewarding positive performance leads to higher performances. Denying a reward during periods of poor performance tends to lead to better performance in the future.

These conclusions naturally lead to considerations of equity since it is likely that equity theory underlies many of the previously mentioned results. Rewards, appropriately distributed, will then be able to drive performance to higher levels, but only so long as they are actually appropriate.

Equity Theory

It could easily be argued that many of the previously mentioned effects were obtained without conscious thought on the part of the participants, although one could also argue that, based on the logical outcomes, cognitive activity, in fact, *drove* the results. As the subjects' cognitions were not collected during the experiment, all we have is speculation. Equity theory, however, provides one clear and widely accepted framework for explaining employee behavior in the work environment.

In the simplest terms, equity theory suggests that individuals compare their job inputs *and* outcomes with those of others, and then respond to eliminate any inequities (Robbins, 2005). Note that people look at their inputs and outcomes, rather than one or the other, so equality itself is not the issue. It is, therefore, not enough that salaries are the same (outputs) *or* that the workload is equally distributed (inputs); rather, ratio comparisons are made. The following table shows the comparisons made in equity theory.

Equity Theory

Ratio Comparisons*	Perception
O/Is<O/Ir	Inequity due to being under-rewarded
O/Is=O/Ir	Equity
O/Is>O/Ir	Inequity due to being over-rewarded

*O/Is represents the ratio of outputs to inputs of the subject
*O/Ir represents the ratio of outputs to inputs of the referent (comparison other)

The referent selected is important in making equity comparisons, and there are four referents that could be selected (Goodman, 1974):

1. Self-inside: An *employee's* experiences in a different position *inside* her current firm.
2. Self-outside: An *employee's* experiences in a situation or position *outside* her current firm.
3. Other-inside: *Another* individual or group of individuals *inside* the employee's current firm.
4. Other-outside: *Another* individual or group of individuals *outside* the employee's current firm.

A variety of variables impact which persons will be chosen as referent for comparisons. Those with little information or experience are likely to use themselves, for lack of better and more information. Both women and men tend to choose same-sex comparisons. Upper-level managers, professionals and those with better educations tend to make more outside comparisons, as they will have access to more and better information.

So what will a person who perceives an inequity do about it? There are several options, depending on the circumstances, from which a selection can be made.

1. Change their inputs (exert less effort).
2. Change their outcomes (ask for a raise).

3. Change their perceptions about themselves (I work harder or less hard than others).
4. Change their perceptions about others (the position "X" holds is a lot harder than I thought it was).
5. Change referents ("I may not make as much as my brother-in-law, but I make more than my Dad at this age").
6. Leave the field (quit).

There are four hypotheses that we could turn to research to evaluate based on being over-rewarded or under-rewarded; but, in truth, the research shows that the over-rewarded hypotheses do not stand up well to testing, and this is probably because we humans have greater tolerance for being over-rewarded than we have for being under-rewarded. So to simplify, we will only look to the under-rewarded situations.

1. When under-rewarded and paid by time, people will tend to produce fewer units or lesser quality.
2. When under-rewarded and paid by quantity of production, people will tend to produce a high number of low-quality units.

Of course, agents are paid in both forms in the contact center. There are hourly payments as well as production bonus situations for number of calls taken.

Before leaving equity theory, it is important to note that the previous discussion focuses on what has been called **distributive justice,** or fairness in the amount and allocation of rewards. More recent equity research has articulated **procedural justice,** which focuses on the perceived fairness of the process by which those distributions are made. Both are important in the workplace. That is, not only should the amounts and allocations of rewards be fair, they should be *seen* to be fair because the procedures for the allocations are constant across employees.

Evidence in the research suggests that, as may be predictable from the study of human nature, distributive justice is more important than procedural justice in employees' satisfaction evaluations; nevertheless, procedural justice judgments have effects, as well, although they tend to be more in organizational commitment, trust in the boss and intention to quit (Konovsky, 2000). This suggests that managers should share information on how decisions are made (in addition to the decisions themselves), use the same standards for everyone to ensure consistency and unbiased procedures, and actively manage the perceptions of procedural justice held by employees (Robbins, 2000).

Valuing the Human Resource

Before we move on, it's important to consider the strategy decision and to reason out where it directs our attention.

Jeffrey A. Mello has written an eminently readable book, *Strategic Human Resource Management*, which is used in the MBA program at Florida Memorial University, as well as other institutions offering graduate business education. We consider this text to be recommended reading for our audience, too, as it is targeted to executive-level or graduate student readers. It will give you a much more complete understanding of the topic than we are able to convey in this short chapter. In his book, Mello concretely demonstrates his argument that the human resource function can and should be strategically deployed in the service of the company strategy. His oft-repeated theme is that there is no "one best way"; rather, human resource tactical and strategic choices should be predicated on the organization's overall strategy. Doing so ensures that the company's people resources and expertise are available in sufficient quality, quantity and in a timely manner.

It is fairly simple to find companies that claim to place a premium value on their human resources. A well-known example is IBM, whose case history has been widely published in business literature. The following version was largely taken from *Law and Ethics in the Business Environment*, by Terry Halbert and Elaine Ingulli.

For many years, IBM never laid off a single employee. This focus on employees was an outgrowth of the IBM Principles, listed below.

IBM Principles

1. The marketplace is the driving force behind everything we do.
2. At our core, we are a technology company with an overriding commitment to quality.
3. Our primary measures of success are customer satisfaction and shareholder value.
4. We operate as an entrepreneurial organization with a minimum of bureaucracy and a never-ending focus on productivity.
5. We never lose sight of our strategic vision.
6. We think and act with a sense of urgency.
7. Outstanding, dedicated people make it all happen, particularly when they work together as a team.
8. We are sensitive to the needs of all employees and to the communities in which we operate.

But times and technologies changed, and IBM was not agile in the face of these changes, therefore violating part or all of Principles 1, 2, 4, 5 and 6. This led to the offshoring of jobs, which violated the spirit of Principle 7, and the fact of Principle 8, as facilities were closed, communities devastated, and good jobs disappeared. That is bad enough, but it gets worse.

In late 2003, the *Wall Street Journal* reported that IBM planned to move nearly 5,000 jobs overseas to save expenses… Employees at IBM facilities in Texas, North Carolina, New York, Colorado and Connecticut would be affected; IBM had already hired hundreds of engineers in India to begin taking on their work. According to the *Journal*, IBM workers slated for replacement throughout 2004 would actually be expected to train their foreign replacements. (Halbert and Ingulli, 2006)

The requirement to train your replacement "adds insult to injury," as the saying goes.

As we see in this example, some companies give "lip-service" regarding the value of their people, but they do not always live up to their proclaimed standards. (It would be easy to find a large number of examples of companies that claim to place a high value on their human resources, but fail to invest in them and then freely replace them at will.)

Mello contends that companies would be well-served to adopt a system to value human assets in much the same way that other assets, such as land, equipment and brands, are assigned values. This does not imply that people are only numbers and disposable; rather, the intent is to make it clear just *how* valuable the human component is to any company. However, compared to other assets, the human component is uniquely difficult to assess due to several factors that can be overcome, but require effort to do so.

1. Investments in the human element require a longer-term perspective, as they are less likely to mature in the near term. This longer-term perspective increases the risk that an investment in people will be made without a benefit being received by the firm.

2. Unlike other assets, human investments can decide to leave, and this, too, increases the likelihood of a low return on the investment.

3. Combine the first two points with the fact that American business is intensely focused on short-term returns: next week, month, quarter or year. While in American business, it's rare to plan five years into the future, it's a very common practice in, say, Japan. (A recent example of the longer-term perspective of some foreign companies is the investment by Toyota in the NASCAR team owned by Michael Waltrip. Although the team's performance has been very disappointing for the fans in this first year, Toyota has made it clear that they have no intention of withdrawing financial support, and that they're in the game for the long haul.)

4. Organizations that are doing well may not see the need to change an investment perspective. Things are "fine," so there is no urgency attached in a non-emergency environment.

5. Companies that are doing less well are typically in need of a quick boost and are unwilling or unable to adopt a patient investment perspective. They see the need for salvation today, not at some unspecified future time.

Interestingly, companies that invest in the human component and adopt a long-term investment perspective gain a competitive advantage that is very difficult for competitors to imitate. By contrast, new technology can be purchased and brought online, patents and licensing agreements secured, market share purchased through blanket advertising campaigns and aggressive pricing, brands bought or sold — these are all tactics that can be implemented by one firm and copied by the competition in a few months. But once an organization creates a competitive advantage through its *people*, it is rarely also achieved by a competitor in the same industry. Companies can maintain their HR-generated uniqueness — and high-performing competitive advantage — by expressing their appreciation to the people who make it all possible in both monetary and intangible terms.

Expressing the Value of the Human Component

Jeffrey Pfeffer, professor of organizational behavior at Stanford University, and a well-known and highly respected researcher and author, suggests that there are some 13 or so practices for managing people, which are key to retaining competitive advantage (Pfeffer, 1995). These suggestions seem to fly somewhat in the face of the typical ways in which we manage contact centers, and so they're worth a close examination.

1. Employment Security. Business has become almost fixated on offshoring options. While it is true that short-term costs can be reduced via offshoring due to the lower cost of labor in much of the world compared to Canada and the United States, this is clearly not sustainable in the long run as the middle class that has been the economic engine driving profitability and good times for much of business throughout the world cannot continue when good paying jobs disappear from North America. (In an aside, even Wal-Mart, one of the largest importers of goods from China in the world, has recently made news by contending that the low wages in America are leading to shopper's inability to afford even the cheaper goods offered in their stores. What Wal-Mart is seeing is a more pronounced "payroll cycle," such that many Americans are now waiting to go the store until they receive that next paycheck. The implications are numerous, but include the likelihood that many consumers no longer have emergency funds available and so must live paycheck-to-paycheck. (This *CNN* discussion titled, "New Recall Issued for Chinese Toys; America's Middle Class on Verge of Collapse?" aired on August 14, 2007. To view the transcript, go to http://transcripts.cnn.com/TRANSCRIPTS/0708/14/ldt.01.html.)

Employment security signals to the workforce that the organization is making a long-standing commitment to their well-being. It also likely changes the nature of the relationship between the firm and its people from one that is purely economic to one based on social exchange, as defined by Peter Blau in *Exchange and Power in Social Life*. The economic exchange between a company and its employees is defined in terms of dollars paid by the firm for the time spent by the employee — an exchange that is ongoing for each pay period. Firms that take a longer-term perspective demonstrate a standard of care for their people that goes beyond the contractual pay-period requirements. The social norm of reciprocity, in which as benefits received from one party are returned to the giver in some form, kicks in. That is, when the firm makes a commitment to employment security for its workers, those workers, in turn, feel an obligation to reciprocate and take a long-term view of the needs of the firm. When people are treated as interchangeable parts, they respond with the minimum that economic exchange will allow. This may mean being physically present, but also totally unengaged, such that one simply goes through the motions. When treated as valued assets, their response will be more expansive and generous, and firm survival becomes a focal concern.

2. Selectivity in Recruiting. If a firm commits to employment security, it behooves it to select wisely so as to only offer positions to those who at least meet minimum standards. Studies, undertaken in environments where production differences were possible, indicate that the best workers produce about twice as much as the worst workers (Schmidt and Hunter, 1983). Many companies screen very little for specific skills on the assumption that these can be learned by nearly everyone; however, if the expectation is for long-term employment, the employee's fit to the firm then comes very much into play. Rather than assessing the job/skills fit, many firms are now assessing the person/organization fit and doing so with great care. Southwest Airlines has long been known for this focus on the person/organization fit, and conducts interviews with this specifically in mind.

3. High Wages. In this day of offshoring to save wages, it may seem counterintuitive to suggest paying higher salaries. But doing so can yield handsome dividends, as higher wages will attract a larger pool of applicants, which can lead to higher quality applicants and greater selectivity for the organization. Most importantly, high wages signal that the people are considered important, just as low wages indicate a perceived interchangeability and, hence, the lack of importance for employees.

4. Incentive Pay. Better performers should receive more pay. Following such a policy unambiguously signifies what the firm values. As Pfeffer points out, "Consider the alternative — if all the gains from extra ingenuity and effort go just to top management or to shareholders... people will soon view the situation as unfair, become discouraged, and abandon their efforts." Many companies are known to utilize incentive pay to good effect. Retail sales clerks at Nordstrom, restaurateurs working for Au Bon Pain, and assemblers within Lincoln Electric all receive substantial incentive pay that boosts their paychecks well above industry averages while earning above-industry-average profits for the firms. Some companies, like Eureka and Montana-based Lincoln Electric, also pay bonuses based on the overall profitability of the company, in addition to individual incentive pay.

5. Employee Ownership. There are two clear effects of employee ownership interests in the firm. The tug-of-war that often exists between labor and capital is largely avoided because each has partially become the other. The "us/them" delineations simply no longer apply. Secondly, employee-owners look to the future and the long-range effects of today's decisions. While this has traditionally been a perspective only expected from managers, workers who are also owners often take it up, as well.

6. Information sharing. If people are to be the source of competitive advantage, then it follows that information needs to be shared and acted upon within the organization. *ICMI's Member Research Report on Customer Satisfaction Measurement* (2007) found that information flowing out of contact centers was not always welcomed and acted upon as valued intelligence by other parts of the company. But this perspective is likely to change as information sharing grows more common. Finding a flaw within another department or group is an unrecognized blessing, because it is impossible to improve unless issues are properly diagnosed. Only then can real, truly substantive changes occur.

7. Participation and Empowerment. Decentralization of decision-making is paramount to getting people to take ownership of the firm's processes and outcomes. Specifically, we advocate pushing decision-making power, as much as is practical, down to the agent level. Agents who see what needs to be done for a customer but have no power to give it feel frustrated over their inability to affect a positive outcome. As the retail icon Nordstrom stipulates under Nordstrom Rules:

Rule #1: Use your good judgment in all situations. There will be no additional rules.

8. Self-Managed Teams. It's one thing to form a team and quite another to allow the team to manage itself. While the team structure will not fix everything and definitely requires executive sponsorship, nevertheless, there have been many highly positive outcomes from the institution of self-directed teams. These teams set their own standards, handle their own problems, and are responsible for disciplining and rewarding the members. Such a structure can eliminate several levels of management, as well as the resources needed to sustain them and the bureaucracy that inevitably emerges to prop them up. In addition, members of self-managed teams tend to be engaged, cooperative and loyal.

9. Training and Skills Development. Managers often complain about wasted training and development dollars, when the real issue is that, once trained, the employees are given no opportunity to use the skills they've acquired. By definition, training is expected to have a short-term payback, while the payback for development is longer-term. Both require the opportunity to practice, firsthand or by assisting others, for the learning to be properly internalized. "Skills" acquired and never used are soon forgotten, and the money paid to acquire them is truly wasted.

10. Cross-utilization and Cross-training. The motivational effects of variety are not to be underestimated. Cross-utilization and cross-training help employees to "stay fresh" and engaged in their work. Performance and results are improved as fresh eyes have a chance to look at old problems and new ideas filter into the work process. From a labor management standpoint, cross-training ensures that the necessary skill sets will be available on the floor at any given time enabling properly trained staff to step in and work effectively in times of emergency with little or no warning.

11. Symbolic Egalitarianism. There are various ways to signal that we are all on the same team, all of which have in common the idea of tearing down barriers between people. Dr. Karl Wright, president of Florida Memorial University, drives a 1988 Volvo station wagon, which can be found in the communal parking lot among the cars of students, staff, and faculty. He can often be seen walking across campus, when a phone call would bring him a golf cart and a security guard escort. He eats his meals in the cafeteria, usually with a table of students. Dr. Wright consciously decided to keep the lines of communication open by keeping exclusivity, to which he is legitimately entitled, at bay. The same thinking can be found in some for-profit enterprises. The CEO of Wal-Mart has a very modest office in Bentonville, Ark., which looks more like the office of mid-level manager at a moderate-sized firm, instead of the spacious quarters one would expect of the leader of a company whose annual revenues exceed those of many countries. The lack of barriers and obvious modesty represented by these leaders send unmistakable messages to the employees of both organizations.

12. Wage Compression. According to Terry Halbert and Elaine Ingulli in *Law and Ethics in the Business Environment*, "Plato believed that the rulers of the ideal society should be paid no more than four times more than the lowliest member of that society." This would be an extreme example of wage compression. What we see in big business today is often the direct opposite, which could be termed "wage dispersion," such that, as Halbert and Ingulli point out, "…executives not uncommonly earn 700 times what the ordinary employees do." Pfeffer asserts that wage compression discourages gaming the system: the tendency to waste time trying to outwit the system in order to equalize the rewards. Deemphasizing pay may also have the effect of highlighting other rewards, such as praise, collegiality and meaningful work. We are not underplaying the importance of pay; rather, we contend that greater equity in monetary rewards across organizational levels sends a powerful signal to the organization as a whole about the overall significance and contributions of all the members.

13. Promotion from Within. Such a policy automatically puts a premium on training and development, long-term planning, and seeing the bigger picture. It also avoids all the negativity that can accumulate in good people when outsiders are brought in over them.

Mello himself makes it clear that there is nothing magic in these 13 practices. Research may delineate others in the future, and some of the ones listed here could arguably be condensed into fewer topics. But it's the course set that matters. The above require less lip service and more concrete action. Value the human element, let it be known that this is a keystone of your organization and good things will happen.

If You Want It, Reward It

By now, it should be clear that rewards are reinforcements for the behaviors that precede them. Failure to reward behaviors tends to lessen performance. If this is clear, then why are there so many instances of rewarding unwanted behaviors, and failing to reward those that we wish to encourage? This is the central issue in a classic article by Steven Kerr titled, "On the Folly of Rewarding A, While Hoping for B," which has been widely reprinted in management periodicals for more than 30 years.

Unfortunately, fouled-up reward systems are far from uncommon. Kerr's article lists muddled reward systems that exist in environments as diverse as politics, war, medicine, rehabilitation centers and orphanages, as well as universities and several private companies. Let's take a brief look at orphanages, as an example. Although these institutions are supposedly in the business of finding good homes for children, their "rewards" (i.e., funding) are not based on the number of children placed, but on the number living under their roof. Thus, restrictive adoption policies enhance continued funding, increase the number of people on staff, and lend prestige to the institution's management (who wants to be the head of the smallest orphanage in the state?). While we all hope that orphanages are trying to place children in good homes, we are really rewarding the practice of retaining children in these institutions.

From Chapter 1, you may recall the example of the university president who pleaded for collegial behavior from the faculty by urging them to support the academic activities of other departments across campus. Some faculty did this without organizational reward and others were vocal (out of hearing of the president, mind you) about refusing to do so unless paid. One way to handle this situation would be to require evidence of collegiality on each faculty member's annual review as a prerequisite to admission to the rewards pool. Of course, that would necessitate the founding and funding of a rewards pool instead of giving across-the-board salary increases, which reward organizational membership rather than performance. Across-the-board salary increases tend to *demotivate* high performers. If you want collegiality, reward it or, in this case, refuse to reward the lack thereof.

In one of Kerr's private industry examples, the management of one firm, concerned that much of the organization was dysfunctional, brought in a researcher who identified that:

> ...the same tendencies toward conservatism and apple-polishing at the lower levels, which divisional management had com-

plained about during the interviews, were those claimed by subordinates to be the most rational course of action in light of the existing reward system. Management apparently was not getting the behaviors it was hoping for, but it certainly was getting the behaviors perceived by the subordinates to be rewarding (Kerr, 1975).

Again, reward the behaviors that you want to reoccur, and do so in a timely manner. Never reward behaviors you do not want to see again.

If you want to encourage longevity, then distribute rewards evenly to foster an "entitlement" perspective. If you want to encourage performance, then distribute rewards contingent on the behaviors that are most valued by the institution. Doing so will promote a performance culture that should be dedicated to the customer experience.

Employee Evaluations: A Powder-Keg Issue

We have been blithely speaking about rewards while omitting the processes involved in delivering them. We spoke of distributive and procedural justice, but it is necessary to go a bit further. In the process of distributing rewards, there comes a time when the performances of employees must be assessed and, ultimately, judged. People are funny (meaning peculiar) creatures. For example, they are seldom able to report accurately, even when witnessing the same behavior. There is a Russian saying that is popular among prosecutors and police: "He lies like an eye witness." The phenomenon of conflicting accounts offered by various eyewitnesses to the same event is fairly well-researched, but we won't review it here; rather, we'll take this at face value. The issue with employee evaluations is not just that different people viewing the same behavior will give varying interpretations (which is clearly bad enough), but also that different people are likely to witness varying activities by the people being assessed and so each will judge a different data set. For example, let's say an employee used a forbidden term only once during the entire month, but it was the one time when his supervisor was present. As a result, the employee was "dinged" on his scorecard. The agent in the next cubicle made the same mistake dozens of times, but not one of those instances was witnessed by the supervisor, so no ding occurred, but the neighboring employee heard it clearly and often. Needless to say, this does not promote happy relations between supervisors and employees at evaluation time.

So we have the biases imposed by the inaccurate reporting of witnesses, and variances imposed by sampling. We also have a more insidious source of bias that every school-age child knows about: teacher's pet. This topic was discussed by Gregory Dobbins and Jeanne Russell of Louisiana State University's Department of Psychology, in an article titled "On the Biasing Effects of Subordinate Likeableness on Leaders' Responses to Poor Performers: A Laboratory and a Field Study." In the study, leaders were presented with a vignette describing an incident of poor performance committed by either a liked or disliked subordinate. The researchers found that, while the leaders made similar attributions for the poor performance of liked and disliked subordinates, they were more inclined to punish a disliked subordinate than a liked one.

The Changing Face of Employee Satisfaction

Heretofore, we have written more or less as though all employees are alike. This is largely true, at least, in respect to expectations for distributive and procedural justice, but employees are also varied and this has become all the more so over time. Reflecting back a mere decade ago will convince one that the Hispanic population has swelled dramatically even over this brief period. The number of women in the workforce has surged over the last 25 years so much so that there are now nearly as many women as men working outside the home. The baby boomer generation's approaching retirement has made the advancing age of the workforce a significant factor in staffing plans. All of these reasons have helped to change the face of employee satisfaction over the years. The factors that create employee satisfaction often differ based on the employees' demographics — and employers will need to alter their thinking to create job satisfaction among varying employee groups.

We are indebted to Jennifer Schramm and the Society for Human Resource Professionals (SHRM) for their research and the insights we discuss in this section.

> One of the more interesting aspects that SHRM research highlights is that job satisfaction means different things to different people depending upon their age, gender or other demographic differences. This certainly makes sense and the awareness of these differences can help companies to create policies that maximize job satisfaction for most of its people. This knowledge, coupled with demographic projections can also help us to identify some of the key areas of conflict that may develop over the next decades (Schramm, 2003).

1. Age. As the population ages, benefits such as health care and pensions become ever more important. Unfortunately, both of these popular benefits are becoming ever more expensive to provide. Additionally, elder care benefits are becoming ever more needful, although such are rarely offered in American companies. Work/life balance issues are also likely to increase in popularity in this generation. This is all the more so in that the baby boomers were the first generation to have so many women in the workforce. Although many in this generation want to work past the typical retirement age, they may wish to do so on different terms.

2. Gender. Work/life balance issues loom large for women. In some part, this is because women still perform most of the work in the home, from housecleaning to child nurturing, even while holding down jobs in the workplace. When work/life balance issues prevail, then flex time and shared jobs (with proportionally shared benefits) are viable responses. Shared jobs are not uncommon in Europe, but are nearly unheard of in the United States. In Europe, two people may share a full-time job, split the hours in the office, share a desk and other fixed assets, split the committee assignments and other in-house service issues AND split the full benefits package between them. There is no reason why U.S. companies couldn't offer a similar option. However, here such workers would be considered part-time employees and, as such, not entitled to benefits at all. Elder care and child care issues are also key issues impacting certain demographics. Interestingly, younger men have demonstrated greater interest in flex time and childcare issues than older generations of men. This may signal a change in priorities for the male demographic that will become increasingly important to address over time.

3. Immigration. There has been very little research done on what attracts highly skilled immigrant labor, but if the projected shortfall of skilled labor in the industrialized countries materializes due to aging populations, then research will be required to identify changes in policies that may be necessary to attract that labor.

EQM Strengthens Employee Satisfaction and Performance

Our intent in this chapter has been to review some of the research literature that impacts the most expensive and most important resource for an organization. We believe that distribution of contingent rewards has strongly positive results in both job performance and employee satisfaction. EQM's contribution to employee satisfaction and performance should not be overlooked. Real-time feedback can be a huge assist when performance is substandard. Training can be more efficiently allocated by ensuring that only those who need to improve a given skill get the intervention. When the Rally Cry is not heard by customers and the mistakes have been recorded and transcribed, a basis for retraining is provided. After all, it is not necessary to have long-winded conversations about what was said on a call if the customer's evaluation of the experience has been captured, so transcription from EQM evaluations become less a cost and more a time-saving (and, therefore, cost-saving) initiative. This allows managers to focus on demonstrating to their agents a better way to respond. Remember, people want to receive rewards, and the quickest way to get them is to have errors diagnosed quickly and eliminated via sound training practices. A consistent feedback loop with positive reinforcements for delivering excellent service is key. When people are positively committed to a common set of goals, consistently stellar performance will occur. Customer satisfaction comes from the inside of an organization.

As we've said, rewards lead to satisfaction. We all want happy employees in the contact center, a fact that becomes all the more obvious when we examine the statistics for contact center turnover. Some centers experience 100 percent turnover in the course of a year. It is possible to extrapolate from 100 percent turnover that the people working for these firms are unhappy. While it's likely that there are combinations of circumstances that can be blamed for this, the root causes can be effectively addressed through feedback, reward and equity. EQM can make an important contribution to the welfare of the contact center.

Part II: Science and Research

Chapter 3:
The Necessity of Science

In Part II, we will establish the difference between science and pseudo-science. The present chapter will demonstrate how science in the contact center can be harnessed to hear customer wants and needs so that they can be appropriately addressed.

Chapters 4 and 5 venture into the realm of panaceas by detailing and dissecting two commonly known and utilized research tools that get used inappropriately: benchmarking and Net Promoter. A panacea is, by definition, a "cure all," and such things simply do not exist in the real world. Just as the closest thing we know to a universal solvent is water (which can be easily contained in vessels of glass, plastic and stone, just to name three), there is no one universal curative. In past years, touted universal cures became known by the name "snake oil." They never contained actual "oil of snake" as far as we know, but many were documented to contain large quantities of alcohol, various poisons such as strychnine, mercury and lead, and/or narcotics such as poppy juice, cocaine and opium. While such products may well produce one effect or another, to be certain, such concoctions cannot cure common colds, cancer or arthritis; yet many were touted as curatives for widely disparate illnesses.

Now, small doses of poisons do have some curative powers. Foxglove has long been known as an aid in heart ailments, yet it will kill if given in the wrong dose. Just so, benchmarking has a place in the research portfolio, but only a limited place. As we will later discuss, Net Promoter as promulgated and disseminated, is wrong along multiple dimensions. Nevertheless, the underlying "would recommend" question is based on a long line of solid academic research into word-of-mouth behavior. Again, the essence of Net Promoter has a place in a firm's portfolio of research — just not *every* place.

Chapter 6 will turn our attention to "hard core" science, and we'll discuss at length the detection and correction of bias in research. This is the foundation of good medical practice which has been built up over the years, culminating in longer, healthier lives for those with access to Western medicine. Our goal is to do the same for research undertaken in the customer care industry. The best amelioration for "survey pain" is to evade what can be avoided and build in curatives where evasion is not an option. Apply science rather than snake oil.

While several areas of the organization may be able to contribute to our understanding of customer needs, the customer contact centers are the logical place to collect most customer intelligence. Our first task in this chapter will be to convince you of this necessity. We will do so first by appealing to logic and commonly known information primarily from marketing. Then we will lay out a piece of scientifically conducted experimental research from a financial services environment that concretely demonstrates the efficacy of customer voice.

Secondly, we will discuss why the internal call quality monitoring (IQM) programs that most contact centers currently have in place provide faulty intelligence regarding the satisfaction and wants of their customers. This is not to say that IQM programs are not important or serve no useful ends; to the contrary, such programs can be combined with data from other sources to paint a clear, comprehensive picture of the center's weaknesses that need to be addressed. Simply put, however, it is inarguable that the voice of the customer is not captured via IQM programs.

Thirdly, we will show that scientifically designing the data-capture program, from IQM to metrics to voice of the customer programs, will result in the least-cost, most-gain information for decision making. Specifically, we'll explore the idea that, just as there is malpractice in medicine, there can be, and is, malpractice in measurement programs. It can arise through attempting to design and implement programs in-house that are beyond the firm's understanding and expertise; through purchasing a vendor's software and implementing it in the hopes that it will be right for your application; and/or by hiring one of the many consultants out there whose interest lies in selling a single, cookie-cutter product or approach, without investing the necessary time and effort to tailor it to your needs. In the first case, it's like going into the woods to pick herbs to heal an illness or injury without the appropriate education or guidance. Maybe you'll get lucky and not administer a poison, maybe not. The second case is akin to buying the latest cure-all drug or supplement you see advertised on television. Maybe it's snake oil or maybe it actually works for some ailments, but it's certainly not a panacea for all ailments. And the third is similar to consulting a seemingly competent physician only to find that all of the patients he saw today were given the same prescription: Take two aspirins and call me in the morning. You end up spending additional time, effort and money on visits to other physicians to get the specialized treatment that every patient deserves to receive in the first place. All three instances are malpractice.

Contact Centers Are the Primary Interaction Point

Let us presume that the firm believes that profits derive from meeting the needs of customers. So if the measurement program needs to listen to the voice of the customer (VOC) and provides a mechanism to let them engineer the products and services provided by the company, which area of the firm is best suited to manage this? This is obviously a rhetorical question, and yet, it doesn't mean that we don't need to defend the proposition since, based on the actual practices of many companies, there are many who expect to be able to get VOC data somewhere else.

Marketing is a concept that has been adopted (at least in principle) by nearly every for-profit firm in the world and most not-for-profit organizations, as well. Rooted deep within the marketing concept is the idea of finding out what the customer wants or needs (and here we will use the terms "wants" and "needs" interchangeably although there are important differences between them) and then making that offering available to those customers. The key to profits is through meeting or slightly exceeding customers' needs as effectively (and efficiently) as possible. The implication is that someone knows what the customer wants, informs management, manufacturing, etc., and makes it possible for the product or service offering to materialize.

Traditionally, marketing has thought of itself as the collector and holder of customer intelligence, and that claim is not without some merit. The marketing research department conducts or outsources market research in the form of mining secondary data sources, conducting surveys and panels including focus groups to collect primary customer data, and internal and external audits. Much market research is concerned with listening to *potential* rather than *actual* customers. Product Development is in charge of market research that centers on which product formulation will be favored by which kinds of people as defined by demographics or psychographics. Additionally, research is conducted to test whether a given ad will appeal to the target group for which it was designed. The advertising or promotion departments likely conduct such research. The sales department may also contend that they know customers very well since they interact with them and successfully sell to them on a recurring basis. This argument is particularly appealing when the sales department is in a business-to-business environment, such as selling copiers to business units. However, in companies where the sales department does not interact with the ultimate consumers, such as in channel sales to retailers or wholesalers, there can be little validity to such claims. But even in business-to-business environments, the contact center handles the bulk of customer complaints, questions and comments.

Each and every one of these activities is vitally important, and it is appropriate to have this market intelligence on potential end-users and business-to-business customers gathered within the various marketing department functions. Within this sense, marketing, indeed, listens to the voice of the customer. However, in regards to *actual* rather than *potential* customers, the contact center is a much better outpost for hearing the voice of the customer. No other area within the organization has more continuous, direct contact with customers, yet many companies fail to take advantage of the depth of knowledge available.

The contact center is where the voice of the customer can be heard — and heard often — and reported quickly and accurately to all parts of the organization. The contact center is the measurement focal point that provides the organization with real-time data directly from the customers. Collecting additional pieces of data that become part of the customer intelligence profile is an easy task to accomplish for this department.

In addition to providing numerical and statistical information, the contact center can provide qualitative information. Technology, properly applied and leveraged, allows customers an easy feedback forum to score the products and services provided by the company, to explain their scores and to make suggestions for improvement.

Organizations that put the customer first and leverage the contact center to gather actionable customer intelligence experience the success that the customer satisfaction measurement process can bring to companies. Academics have long known that satisfaction programs increase loyalty, lower transaction costs, reduce failure costs and help to build an organization's reputation in the marketplace (Anderson, Fornell and Mazvancheryl, 2004). This is also general knowledge across contact centers, although it's not always appreciated by their parent companies. However, what doesn't seem to be clear to much of the contact center industry is how to plan and implement a program to achieve these results (hence, the need for this book).

In addition to the previously mentioned advantages, further evidence from academia indicates that there are other benefits that can accrue to firms that institute sound customer satisfaction programs. In one article published in the *Harvard Business Review*, the authors report on the results of a field experiment with more than 200 customers enrolled in a customer relationship program of a large U.S. financial services company. In the research, the randomly selected experimental group participated in a 10-minute survey on the company's products and customer satisfaction. A randomly selected control group was not surveyed. For the next year, neither group received any direct marketing from the company while the various transactions for both groups were recorded: specifically, the purchasing behavior, defection rates and profitability of both groups. The two groups were compared a year later. The researchers found that the surveyed group was more than three times as likely to open new accounts than the control group, was less than half as likely to defect, and was more profitable than the consumers in the control group (Dholakia and Morwitz, 2002).

Remember that the only difference between the two groups was that one was surveyed and one was not; neither group received any direct marketing from the company during the year. The experimental "survey effects" reached their maximum levels months after the survey event and persisted for months longer with new account rates higher, defection rates lower and profitability higher among the surveyed group. This research demonstrates concretely that VOC programs are truly powerful when conducted with due diligence. The impact from this experimental research was sustained and substantial in key measures affecting profitability. The authors attributed the clear impact of the program to the customers' desire to be acknowledged by the company and made to feel important, and to additional mental processing that kept the company top-of-mind when future product choices were made. All of these effects accrued from an elegantly designed, rather simple experimental survey project asking for consumers' opinions (Dholakia and Morwitz, 2002).

The especially nice part of the above endeavor is how elegantly it eliminated numerous biases that could have made interpretation of the results problematic. (Chapter 4 is all about biases and their prevention or amelioration. Here, we will strictly limit the discussion to the cursory level.) There were two randomly selected groups, which eliminated self-selection bias.

Because one group received the treatment and one did not (that is, one was surveyed and one was not) it is possible to see the results of the experimental treatment as opposed to the non-treatment condition. The measures selected for tracking were numerical and behavioral, which makes the results easy to count, compare and not subject to interpretation. That is, either a new account was opened or it was not. Either a customer defected or stayed. Profits from the account were either realized or not. At no point along the way was rater error or observer bias introduced. Lastly, the results were not interfered with by intervening variables, such as solicitations originating from the marketing department of this firm during the period of the study. Therefore, alternative interpretations of the results (such as effective promotions) are impossible.

It's true that neither group was isolated during the time of the study. In fact, numerous other factors definitely transpired, such as advertisements intercepted from a variety of sources, promotional offers from other companies, etc.; however, all things being equal, there is no logical reason to assume that the two groups were differentially affected. It's reasonable to deduce then that those interferences could have had no differential effect on the outcome variables of purchase, defection and profit of one group over the other. The net outcome then is a clearly interpretable result for the intervention; that is, without doubt, *the act of surveying customers leads to increased purchases, decreases in defection rates, and these led, as expected, to increased profits.*

Internal Call Quality Monitoring Is Insufficient

Most managers who maintain high levels of quality service in their centers have implemented an extensive and costly internal call quality monitoring (IQM) program. These programs generally include a sampling of five to 20 live and remote monitoring occurrences per month of an agent's calls with different customers. This sampling of calls is evaluated and scored, the scores are rolled up into composite reports, which are bundled with automatic call distributor (ACD) statistics and are then presented to the contact center manager for regular review. Through this process, the agent is held accountable to a predetermined set of criteria, which often include courtesy, verbal skills, listening skills, product or service knowledge, willingness to help, sales, legal and privacy information requirements, and more depending on the industry, product and service.

The criteria are represented on a monitoring form, which is used by the designated monitor who is responsible for grading the compliance of an agent's calls. There are generally three options for choosing a monitor. Sometimes one person or a team is responsible for evaluating all of the calls. In other instances, the agent's team leader is responsible for this task. There may also be a blending of the two, or even outsourcing the task to a third party.

The monitoring form itself, which acts as a guide for the monitor, is often created by a committee of people in the contact center, by a manager or sometimes by a senior-level executive who has a personal expectation of how a call "should" be conducted. The form is standardized to ensure that all calls are evaluated on the same criteria across agents. In theory, if an agent follows the criteria set forth in the monitoring form, the customer will receive a high level of service, will be satisfied with the service call and the company will retain him or her as a customer.

Since most organizations follow this logic, the majority of IQM programs conclude that most customers are extremely satisfied by the telephonic service experience. Scores naturally migrate to the upper part of the monitoring scoring scale. If there are 100 points available, the majority of the scores are probably 92 or higher, or even 95 and higher. Essentially, the top 10 points on the scale are used, and by all indications the center is doing well.

In reality, this logic is flawed, which can be readily confirmed when direct customer feedback is captured and the internal IQM scores are compared to the customers' directly stated and measured level of service. Theoretically, since both are assessing "call quality," these two scores should be statistically non-significant, meaning they should be essentially the same. So how can one account for a negative double-digit variance? That is, how can one account for internal IQM scores that are in the 90s with directly collected caller satisfaction scores in the 70s or less? How is that possible? What is the problem?

The problem is that all customers want to be taken care of efficiently and effectively, but the elements to accomplish this vary from one person to the next, just as callers' needs vary. Therefore, creating a monitoring form with set criteria that must be adhered to for every call may be inappropriate from the customer's point of view, may contribute to the above mentioned gap between the IQM and VOC programs, and may even create caller dissatisfaction as the agent forces the required criteria into the call.

Consider this example: One of the authors recently needed to schedule a flight with only one day's notice. She called an online travel booking service with which she had a substantial ongoing relationship. After offering the relevant information, she was asked by the agent if she understood the financial penalties for making changes to the ticket after the flight was booked. "Yes, I do," she replied. "Basically, don't make changes or it will cost a boatload of money." After a moment's hesitation, the agent proceeded to recite the entire spiel in detail. The author interrupted to reiterate that she was in a great hurry and would accept the financial and legal ramifications for making a change without having to hear the details. The agent responded that he HAD to go over these details with each caller. "Even though I'm willing to accept the full liability myself without hearing all the details, still I must spend this time?" she countered. "Yes" he said, "I have to read this to you." This was a clear instance where the customer's needs were superseded by the company's rigid call requirements.

Ideally, from the customer's perspective, regulations within the center should place the customer's needs before organizational convenience. Hence, we should conclude that a call monitoring form should be a dynamic instrument that can handle different types of interactions with the ultimate goal being, "The customer was satisfied and a repeat call will not occur." How can you create a dynamic monitoring form and reduce the gap between internal quality scores and customer quality evaluations? By taking a multi-faceted, flexible approach to the call monitoring form or by using different methods to gather perceptions of quality from different audiences.

The criteria covered by your call monitoring form most likely have been revisited and tweaked over time. The form itself may have grown in both length and complexity. Most forms evolve under the assumption that if the agents will follow all of the criteria set forth, then the center is doing well. It's likely that the form you use has already become so long and complex that further flexibility would be hard to build in and difficult to use. Note that adding flexibility to the IQM framework will reduce the ability to obtain solid, comparable, highly reliable evaluations across agents. This reliable comparability across agents is desirable and worth preserving. The logical answer, then, is to pursue the second option: Use different methods to gather perceptions of quality from different audiences.

The optimal solution is to use an internal IQM program combined with a means to hear directly the voice of the customer. This would ensure that the IQM program and its advantages are left in place, while attaining the benefits of hearing what the customers think about their call experience. You can put this proposition to the test within your own contact center environment. Compare your IQM scores against those generated through a direct customer satisfaction response protocol. For the sake of efficiency, validity and reliability, we suggest an automated capture protocol. It is likely that there will be a gap between the high internal IQM scores and your customers' experience of the quality of service they received. If this happens, you're not alone. Evaluation items for the customer should be mapped to the related behaviors that are scored on the IQM form. Does this mean that the questions/items should be identical? No.

If it's not possible for you to compare your own center's scores, we can offer evidence from one of our research projects designed to test the theory that internal IQM scores vary significantly from direct voice of the customer scores. First, let us briefly review the logic behind the research.

Many internal IQM programs attempt to rate aspects of the call that have little correlation with caller satisfaction. Instead, they are based on someone's presumptions about what customers are supposed to think is important. This "someone" is typically a company person operating from the firm's point of view. Without direct customer input, any information regarding call quality is largely speculative. Used in isolation, internal IQM will not produce the return on investment it could if it were combined with an automated customer feedback method. This low ROI (high cost of producing low value) may be the reason why many centers do not monitor more than five calls a month per agent.

Obviously, customers are the best ones to judge how their experience went. From a scientific standpoint, the level of service delivered on a particular call should be immediately assessed. While this rating may seem subjective since it's not a hard metric, such as average speed of answer or a IQM score, the *customers' perceptions* are what really matter. If your customers are not satisfied, all the metrics in the world will be meaningless. But if you know how your customers perceive the service delivered and you have a good set of metrics and IQM scores, the answer to the question "How well is the center performing?" becomes balanced, valid and readily defensible.

Let's look at a research project conducted by Customer Relationship Metrics that proves that IQM scores do not equal the callers' perception of service. A client's monitoring form included 17 items, seven of which could be directly compared to caller evaluations. We examined the call monitoring form and caller evaluations over a five-month period. Our findings are represented in the table below: There was virtually no relationship at all between the callers' evaluation of the experiences and the IQM evaluation. The only statistically significant relationship was related to the variable "tone" and this was not a strong relationship.

The results of this research had a dramatic effect on the IQM program of our customer. The proof that the call monitoring form was not effective from the customers' perspective underscored the need to have a valid answer to how well service was delivered. In addition to a better answer, a significant savings was now possible.

Do Monitoring Scores = Caller Perception of Service?

Caller	Monitoring	Relationship
Knowledge	Knowledge	No
Confidence in solution	Proper solution	No
Courtesy	Courtesy	No
Interest in helping	Empathy	No
Interest in helping	Tone	Yes
Quickly understood request	Listening skills	No
Overall satisfaction	Overall satisfaction	No

2,000 agents, five months of data with four monitoring scores each month and four to eight callers surveyed each month.
Proprietary research from Customer Relationship Metrics

In the original program, each of the center's 2,000 agents were monitored five times per month, with 17 items scored on each call. This equated to 170,000 scores given per month, with four reviews to be completed per hour, requiring 2,500 hours of scoring (not including the feedback time). To complete the 2,500 hours, 63 FTEs were employed at $45,000 per year for a grand total of $2.8 million (again, without feedback and coaching time included). After receiving the results of this research, the center revamped the monitoring form to focus on objective measures. Scoring eight items instead of 17 allowed the center to complete six reviews per hour, requiring 43 FTEs at $45,000 per year for a net personnel cost of $1.89 million. The improvement in the process yielded a savings of $910,000.

Contact center size will vary by firm; however, the direct benefit would apply to all. Savings from the actual time spent on scoring is compounded by the result of having a more effective definition of quality.

The question of how to properly evaluate the quality of the contact center's performance is really three-fold:

1. **Call metrics** to assess the efficiency of the contact center;
2. **IQM program** to ensure compliance with legal, privacy and internal

policies; and

3. **Direct caller evaluation protocol** (VOC program), preferably automated, to evaluate the service from the perspective of the customer.

Guessing at how customers perceive the call experience is not accurate and contributes to inflated monitoring scores. It is entirely possible and profitable to leverage your current investment by making improvements to both the monitoring form and process while adding customer input to your program. Your center's ROI will increase, as well as the quality of information that will be available to manage improvements and to share with upper-level management outside of the center.

Sources and Risks of Survey Malpractice

We rely heavily on an article that we produced previously for the arguments herein (Monger, *Call Center Magazine*, April 2006). We will begin by defining **malpractice**:

> n. an act or continuing conduct of a professional which does not meet the standard of professional competence and results in provable damages to his/her client or patient. Such an error or omission may be through negligence, ignorance (when the professional should have known) or intentional wrongdoing.

Because most of us are accustomed to seeing the term "malpractice" only attached to medical environments, we'll use a medical model to illustrate malpractice here. As the definition indicates, any professional can commit malpractice, whether he or she is an accountant, educator, counselor, manager or consultant. It is worth noting that the malpractice can arise through intentional wrongdoing, but may stem from negligence or ignorance, as well. Negligence implies carelessness or laziness, while ignorance simply indicates lack of training.

As we suggested in the introduction, there are three potential sources of malpractice within the contact center environment: management, software/hardware vendors and consultants. In the case of contact center management, malpractice is most likely due to a lack of education and experience with hard statistics and research methodologies. Most Americans have received little or no training in statistics or research methods, so they aren't able to judge a study's worthiness, much less competently conduct one. As Cynthia Crossen, a long-time reporter and editor for the *Wall Street Journal*, stated in her book *Tainted Truth*:

> ...most people would be ill-equipped to judge a piece of research. American schools, which have largely ignored the explosion of quantitative information in daily life, can and should teach people how to tell whether particular sets of numbers are believable. Learning information skills should be as important to high school and college as a working knowledge of literature, science, economics or communications. High schools should devote some of their mathematics curriculum to everyday statistics. College statistics departments should offer courses for non-majors in the statistics of everyday life. All other university departments should incorporate into their courses training in the field's research methodologies and where and why they can go wrong.

To conduct the quality of research needed to provide VOC intelligence, at a minimum, one would need to attend one research methodology and two statistics courses and least one of which must be in multivariate statistics. Even with this college coursework under one's belt, a competent VOC program would only result if those courses taught what happened to be needed for this application. Even those with an MBA seldom obtain this much training in research or statistics.

If you don't have medical training, you probably wouldn't step forward as an expert in a medical emergency. Nor should you attempt to conduct complex research for which you are unprepared. There is no stigma attached to this lack of expertise as long as one doesn't venture into malpractice by playing "diagnostician," "epidemiologist" or "surgeon" on unsuspecting medical patients, or research designer or statistician for the contact center.

It's not news to anyone in the contact center industry that there are many hardware and software vendors who are willing and able to sell any application. There are some designed for VOC programs and some include the function as an after-thought provision. However, these off-the-shelf applications are unlikely to fit your needs without substantial "tweaking" (at least) or a major overhaul (more likely). Deploying new "solutions" is a headache, as they almost never work as advertised. Further, it takes a lot of time and effort on the part of the computer experts, as well as training for the agents who are meant to employ it. In the end, the initial purchase cost is a "drop in the bucket" compared to the realized cost of implementation. Worse, after all the time, effort and frustration of implementing it, the "solution" may turn out to be a money maker for the seller and a waste for the purchaser. We've heard of instances in which the "solution" was never able to achieve even a small fraction of the promises made presale.

These "solution" providers should be held accountable. Their sales staff may or may not be competent, but, obviously, the commission is their goal. This is entirely understandable human behavior, but it is also malpractice to promise what cannot be delivered, even if it stems from ignorance.

As for the consultants, ignorance should never be an excuse. Theoretically, they are properly educated in statistics, quantitative methodologies and research design to know what is needed. Those who are not qualified to do a job should turn it down. It's the only ethical course of action. However, there are those who are unscrupulous or lazy. Among them are consultants who try to use the same reports repeatedly for multiple customers, who offer the same tired solutions and/or who refuse to do the extra work required to customize the solution for the client who is paying tens of thousands of dollars for the expertise. Cookie-cutter consultants are easy to find, but unless they limit their bids to firms that actually fit within the narrow band of expertise they are willing and able to deploy, then to the extent that they overstep those boundaries, they are guilty of survey malpractice. We know such creatures exist. We have met them and, most likely, so have you.

However they're achieved, measurement programs must meet certain scientific criteria to be statistically valid with an acceptable confidence level and tolerated error. Without these considerations, survey malpractice has occurred. The standard research practices should be observed in industry just as they are in academia. Otherwise, deficient surveys will be created that will most definitely result in invalid conclusions — and the fiduciary responsibility to the company has been compromised when recommendations are made based on erroneous customer data. This is malpractice.

How can you recognize and avoid survey malpractice? The following is a laundry list and short explanation of some tell-tale signs.

Measuring Too Many Things

Trying to capture all the data you need through one survey is a sign of survey malpractice. A five-minute contact should not be measured with a 40-question survey that takes 15 minutes to complete. Limit the goals for each survey and field more of them if you need satisfaction data on multiple areas, such as billing, sales and customer service.

Not Measuring Enough Things

A single overall satisfaction question coupled with an agent courtesy question is not a valid survey. It's necessary to start at the level of constructs and work from there to develop the questions. Without robust construct measurements, there is substantial risk of having inadequate feedback information for agents, you'll be unable to meet incentive and performance goals, and making changes within the contact center will be needlessly hazardous. You can reduce these risks by creating a robust measurement instrument.

Measuring Questions with an Unreliable Scale

Customer satisfaction scales often provide only limited response options for respondents. Sometimes those are excellent, good, fair and poor. But doesn't it make more sense for customers to provide a number similar to the rating scale used in school exams? Everyone can relate to a score of 95 for exceptional work, and 65 as barely acceptable. In cases where respondents are only afforded four- or five-point options, the result is inadequate and limited analysis.

Measuring the Wrong Things or Measuring the Right Things Wrong

Surveys should not be designed to tell you what you *want* to hear, but what you *need* to hear. Don't include questions that were designed simply to make the contact center look good. Ask the tough questions that are likely to pinpoint areas for improvement. Also, ensure that each question serves a purpose in the overall measurement plan, and that you know *a priori* what analysis will be conducted to what purpose. Don't waste valuable resources for the sake of curiosity or inattention.

Asking for an Evaluation after Memory Has Degraded

Although 24 to 48 hours doesn't seem like a long time, it's more time than you should allow to pass if you hope to collect caller's true impressions of the contact center experience. Think about it: Can you remember accurately a five-minute telephone call that took place two days ago? "I have slept since then" is a quip that makes sense, in this case. There is plenty of research on memory that indicates that people's memory of everyday experiences begin to deteriorate almost immediately unless something extraordinary happens to weld it into memory. Two examples of extraordinary happenings include where you were when you heard about 9/11 or where your parents were when they received the news of Pearl Harbor. Thankfully, such tragic occurrences are rare, but, without them, recall degrades rapidly. So if you're taking delayed measurements of customer experiences, you're asking for more than those customers can truly give.

The outcomes from such measurements will result in inaccurate feedback to agents, as well as inaccurate reporting and compromised decision-making for the organization.

Accuracy and Credibility of Service Providers and Product Vendors

As with any technology or service, the user assumes responsibility for applying the correct tool, or applying the tool correctly. You can purchase software to schedule agents, but if you do not apply the functionality correctly, you will be responsible for the error. There are plenty of home-grown tools to field a survey, but you'll assume the liability of survey malpractice if they're used incorrectly. It's easy to locate a service provider that is interested in selling you something, but it usually is something that fits into their approach and not necessarily what you need. So while they sell you the product, you assume the risk.

Wiggle Room via Correction Factors

If you are using correction factors to account for issues in the data or to placate the agents or the management team, some aspect of the survey design is flawed. A common adjustment is to collect 11 survey evaluations per agent and delete everyone's lowest score. With a valid control process, adjustments in the final scores are not necessary. Making excuses for the results or allowing holes to be poked diminishes/undermines the effectiveness of the program and highlights an opening for survey malpractice claims.

No Customer Explanations Collected

In addition to adding important insight for management, customer score explanations (survey comments) enable a more accurate level of individual accountability. In research, this is referred to as qualitative data. The most common error when customers respond to surveys is that they reverse the scale (scale flipping), which means they want to give positive scores, but gave negative ones by mistake. Therefore, comments can be reviewed to ensure correct interpretations of the scale and of the question. Proper assignment of the survey is evident, as well. Survey scoring or assignment errors account for an average of 5 percent to 7 percent of the variation in the scores. Cleaning the data will eliminate this error, lessen the need for correction factors, ensure more reliability in the results and the management decisions that flow from those results, and permit the quality control team to coach with confidence.

As a further value, since the results are all "fairly" achieved, there will be greater acceptance on the part of agents who can be certain that scores intended by the customers are the actual scores received. Then only agents in need of retraining will receive it (saving wasted time in unnecessary training).

Closing Points

There is no substitute for a strong VOC program. While internal IQM programs provide valid intelligence relative to whether policies are being followed by agents, such programs cannot provide any intelligence about how customers perceive their experience. VOC programs must be implemented in the contact center environment, as there is nowhere else in the firm where this data can be collected.

Developing a valid, accurate measurement program requires a background in research methodology and quantitative methodology. Most contact centers lack individuals with this type of expertise and, thus, must rely on external resources to ensure statistically valid results. Unfortunately, this leaves many open to potential survey malpractice, which comes from three key sources within the contact center environment: management, software/hardware vendors and consultants. However, there are several telltale signs that survey malpractice exists within a given VOC program. Knowing how to recognize the signs will help you to take the necessary steps to avoid a wasted, and costly, effort.

Chapter 4:
Benchmarking: The Triumph of Efficiency over Effectiveness

Benchmarking research has been treated as a panacea by its proponents for far too long. As we will make clear, it was not so envisioned by its creators. We hope to return benchmarking to its roots and uses that are legitimate and encourage the substitution of other methodologies for alternative needs. Just as it would be malpractice to prescribe an aspirin as a cure for cancer, likewise, it's malpractice to prescribe benchmarking as a means to hear and understand the wants and needs of customers.

Benchmarking is nearly ubiquitous in the business world. By the mid-1990s, almost four out of five companies in Europe, North America and Southeast Asia used some form of benchmarking (Hastings, 1997). It's also a popular practice in contact centers. It seems that there is always some new study being heralded that everyone MUST read and include in their contact center plans. Like all research methods, benchmarking has certain strengths and weaknesses inherent in its very design. The savvy user of research needs to be knowledgeable about the uses and abuses of various methods so as to select which to use under given conditions.

There are good benchmarking studies that can yield valid, useful information, and others that are cobbled together and essentially without value. However, even the best benchmarking studies provide limited guidance to enhance future performance. This is the nature of benchmarking and no amount of "tweaking" can fix it. Benchmarking is focused on efficiency. Efficiency is good, but effectiveness is better. Remember: We define efficiency as *doing a thing right*. We define effectiveness as *doing the right thing*. Benchmarking studies can help you to do a thing right, but they are uniquely unqualified to help you do the right thing. This is the pain point for those who make extensive and unexamined use of benchmarking studies; the inherent weaknesses are ignored and the results are indiscriminately applied.

In this chapter, we'll provide some definitions of benchmarking that help to make its purpose clear. We'll also offer a brief history of benchmarking, harking back to its origins, purposes, components and types, as envisioned by some of its earliest proponents — which we'll compare with the way benchmarking studies are currently conducted. We'll also touch on the pitfalls of veering so far from the dictated methodology in terms of lost benefits. Finally, we'll discuss the uses and abuses of benchmarking, and the studies that deliver so little they border on malpractice; some are even fraudulent. Together, these points clearly demonstrate why you cannot rely on benchmarking research as the primary or sole guide to running your contact center — or for that matter, any other business — and why caution is necessary when using it as a comparison.

Benchmarking Definitions, Origins and Types

The term "benchmarking" is often casually tossed around, and frequently results in carelessly gathered information meant only to satisfy a benchmarking data request. Hence, it's worthwhile to reflect on the actual meaning of the term. According to *Webster's Third New International Dictionary*, a **benchmark** is:

> 1) a mark in a fixed or enduring object indicating a particular

elevation and used as a reference in topographical surveys and tidal observations; and 2) a point of reference from which measurements of any sort may be made.

In other words, the original meaning of a benchmark was a reference point used to establish other physical features for the purpose of producing maps. The meaning was hence expanded to include reference points on maps of a conceptual rather than merely a physical nature.

The origin of the systematic approach to comparisons that benchmarking represents began in the 1950s in the United States and Japan (Sisson, Arrowsmith and Marginson, 2002). However, benchmarking, as we have come to understand it, harks back to 1979 and the Xerox Corporation's bid to combat competition (Camp, 1989). Originating in its manufacturing operations, the intent was to examine unit manufacturing costs, often by tearing down the machines and comparing them and their efficiency to other competitors.

> Prior to benchmarking, most unit cost and other targets for asset management and customer satisfaction were set internally by using standard budgeting procedures with adjustments for some assumed level of productivity and judgments about what would satisfy customer needs. This process was essentially a projection of past practices into the future. There was little concentration on targets established by the marketplace or by leadership firms with superior functional practices (Camp, 1989).

The effort was subsequently expanded beyond manufacturing into all business areas as a means to lay bare the costs and inefficiencies inherent in the current processes with an eye toward setting goals based on something beyond management "guesstimates." Most non-manufacturing operations had to rely on internal comparisons, for example, with other regional centers undertaking similar non-manufacturing work. It soon became clear that processes were analogous to machinery, and "tearing them down" to better understand the steps and costs involved could improve performance in endeavors outside of manufacturing, as well. "The process was seen as that which needed to be detailed and later compared with the external environment. This later comparison would reveal methods and practice differences which could then be used to determine the benchmark" (Camp, 1989). This meant that competitor's operations had to be examined one operational step at a time.

Interestingly enough, it became clear that studies undertaken in this way *could* uncover superior practices, but were more likely to reveal suboptimal procedures. Further, at best, such studies and copying could lead to *matching* others' competitive position, but was *unlikely* to lead to practices *superior* to those of the competition. Needless to say, simply obtaining competitors' information was difficult at the very least. These factors led to the realization that there are several ways to benchmark, and each had its usefulness.

Eventually the Xerox Corporation settled on this definition for benchmarking.

> Benchmarking is the continuous process of measuring products, services and practices against the toughest competitors or those companies recognized as industry leaders.
> — David T. Kearns, CEO, Xerox Corporation

There are several key issues worthy of note in this definition. First, benchmarking is envisioned as a continuous process rather than as a periodic or one-shot study. The valid argument is that technologies, processes, regulations, etc., change over time and require continual monitoring. It is unrealistic to assume that, once the best practices have been discovered and internalized, nothing will be required again.

The measurement aspect is critical. It is not enough to simply observe. There are two ways to undertake measurement. Word statements that disclose qualitative aspects of best practices are critical, but are often underutilized despite the fact that a metric without the underpinning conceptual material lacks meaning. The most obvious way to reduce observations to numbers is by creating a metric that quantifies the gap between current and best practices. This is the side of benchmarking that is most often the "single-minded measurement that most managers want" (Camp, 1989). But the intention of benchmarking is not to generate operational metrics; rather, it's to better understand the underlying processes leading to superiority. Benchmarking research can be applied broadly in enterprises — products, services and practices are all relevant areas to benchmark.

It is interesting to note that competitors may participate in benchmarking, but they are not by any means the only potential participants or, in some instances, even the best partners. For example, a financial institution that's at the top of its game could be an excellent benchmarking partner for a company in another industry that's interested in error-free document processing.

In summary, benchmarking is not supposed to be a one-off study, but a continuous process aimed at uncovering, analyzing and implementing the best practices available by understanding how those practices are performed.

Robert C. Camp, a world-renowned authority on benchmarking and author of *Benchmarking: The Search for Industry Best Practices that Lead to Superior Performance*, identified at least four types of benchmarking studies — each with certain inherent strengths and weaknesses.

1. **Internal operations** benchmarking studies are among the easiest to complete as full cooperation is to be expected resulting in full disclosure and a total lack of "holes" in the data. Additionally, costs for conducting the study are relatively low and results should be known fairly quickly. Such research, however, requires two entities within the same organization that engage in the same activities. In most cases, such studies would be limited to very large companies that are geographically dispersed.

2. **External direct product competitors** are the "top-of-mind" partners for benchmarking endeavors. However, competitors are often reluctant to share sensitive information, especially if it is relevant to their competitive

advantage, and negotiations to design and implement the study could be lengthy and costly. In addition, the data received would not be subject to independent verification and may not be entirely reliable. It's also important to recognize where a competitor's operations are reasonably comparable and where they are not. Size, for instance, can make some comparisons invalid, since economies of scale can substantially alter the options that can be implemented and, hence, the cost structure. For example, large operations can utilize more sophisticated technology while smaller ones may find the initial investment too high.

3. **External functional best operations or industry leaders** require some thought to ensure that you're selecting the right benchmarking partner. As previously suggested, a banking industry leader may be an excellent partner for a benchmarking study focused on error-free document processing. Catalog giants, such as Lands' End, or even smaller players could teach much about best practices in order fulfillment. When choosing a potential benchmarking partner, it's important to ascertain whether or not the contemplated organization shares the same customer focus and scale as your company. Such studies seldom require sharing of competitively sensitive data, so there is likely to be less reluctance to join the study and more willingness to be forthcoming with information. The beauty of such partnerships is the potential to take the "wheel" invented elsewhere and apply it in a new, compatible environment with reasonable expectations of success. A certain innovative flair is required for this type of study.

4. **Generic processes** may be studied from firms that are widely different. For example, order entry is pretty standard regardless of industry. This type of research lends itself well to uncovering technology and processes that are standard elsewhere, but not utilized within the focal industry. Some additional development may be needed to adapt for the new use, but the idea can arise from a study elsewhere. According to Camp, generic benchmarking holds the greatest potential for revealing best practices, but it also requires the greatest objectivity and receptivity to new applications.

Of particular note is the conscious decision in selecting benchmarking partners inherent in the preceding discussion. Single partners are chosen with known similarities and differences to enhance understandability and applicability given the focal environment. As we will see in the next section, benchmarking, as practiced in the contact center industry, tends to be at variance with benchmarking as envisioned and practiced by its originators and champions.

One last point: Benchmarking is most useful in improving operational efficiency. Operational efficiency means production. All of the early benchmarking literature emphasizes operations and efficiency. Effectiveness is not part of the discussion. This can mean "migraine" levels of pain for the unwary adopter.

Contact Center Benchmarking and Goal Setting: Caution Required

In the contact center industry, benchmarking studies have tended to be broad, industry-spanning research efforts meant to encompass a true cross-section, including sales and technology industry leaders (note these may not be the same firm!), as well as those companies not on the cutting-edge. Large and small, national (and sometimes international) and regional competitors often participate in the same study. Even more difficult to assimilate is the mix of inbound, outbound, high-tech, low-tech, sales versus service-oriented, business-to-business versus business-to-consumer, and who knows how many other contact center types within the same study. The data are aggregated across all these varying contact centers, simple analyses completed, and a final report written that touts the "best-in-class" metrics. This end product ("best-in-class" metrics) was most often the reason for the funded effort.

Those companies that participate in the study receive a copy of the benchmarking report as thanks for their data, and the same report is available to others for a fee. But seldom is much information about the conduct and assumptions underlying the research shared. Caveats to the report are often non-existent, so people make their own assumptions, which may or may not be reasonable. As Cynthia Crossen noted in *Tainted Truth*:

> Behind every piece of published research there is a methodology and a body of data on which the study and its results were based. In survey research [such as benchmarking studies], such information comes in the form of a technical index. Some researchers are generous with this material, some charge for it, and others simply refuse to show it... But without it, there is absolutely no way of knowing whether the research has any value.

Failing to make the technical index available borders on malpractice, as any ethical researcher has an obligation to clearly state the assumptions, methodology and limits of a study's usefulness. There is no such thing as a perfect piece of research. All research has limitations and clearly stating these to the reader is the obligation of every serious, ethical researcher. The less controlled the data collection, the less reliable are the results. The broader the sampling frame, the more variance is introduced and the less applicable the results for any given reader.

The design of the study does make a difference, as illustrated by the following example which investigated the differences between business-to-business and business-to-consumer contact centers. It uncovered substantial differences between the statistics at the two types of centers (Miciak and Desmarais, 2001). This benchmarking study revealed, among other things, that business-to-business contact centers emphasized customer relationship management (CRM) in areas such as acquisition and support, were more likely to use live voice over a voice menu, experienced lower call volumes, received more complex enquiries, and hired staff for technical skills. Consumer contact centers were characterized by more frequently unionized staff, outbound calls that concentrated on customer acquisitions, inbound calls related to transaction processing, use of voice menus rather than live voice, and staff hired for customer relationship traits. Obviously, the operational metrics from these two kinds of centers would vary; combining them in one final report would increase the variance and, hence, make the results less applicable to either type of center. Clearly, perusing the technical index would be a key activity required to relate the results to any given environment.

Business-to-Business versus Business-to-Consumer Contact Centers

	Business to Business	Business to Consumer
Work Environment	Non-union	Union
Call Type	Almost Zero Outbound Calls	Outbound/ Sales Call Common
Traffic Direction	Live Voice	Voice Menus
Call Volumes	Lower Call Volumes	Higher Call Volumes
Complexity of Inquiries	Higher	Lower
Support Activities	Common	Rarer
Inbound Calls	Follow-up/ Delivery	Transaction Processing
Agent Selection Base	Technical Expertise	Customer Relationship Traits

Source: Miciak and Desmarais, 2001

Historically, operational managers have spent a lot of time and effort justifying the existence of contact centers. They have been considered costly (labor, technology, space, attention), non-revenue generating departments (at least on the surface) and, therefore, easy targets for cost-cutting endeavors. Contact center managers needed to justify the existence of these expenses to protect their jobs and budgets, and to continue to pursue the firm's legitimate business interests in service to the customer; however, standards against which to measure the center's performance were necessary. In the past, those standards were generated by higher executives, the contact center managers themselves, or were derived from the center's previous performance with adjustments for some arbitrarily designated level of "improvement." There are obvious problems with each of these approaches, especially when the importance of goals is properly understood.

However they're generated, when based on research, it can be said with confidence that goals have certain effects. Goals direct attention, regulate effort, increase persistence and foster development and application of task strategies and action plans (Locke, 2002). Goals are the targets against which performance is measured. Meeting a goal is meeting the standard and, thus, should garner a reward. Performance below the standard may meet with a variety of negative impacts all the way from denial of pay increases to elimination of the department. Performance above the standard may be met with praise, promotion, additional funding and even a certain amount of organizational clout. Therefore, it is evident that the outcomes are important to the operational manager's career, as well as to the future of the department's employees. A more important, if less personal, point: The organization NEEDS the contact center to gather and assess the voice of the customer, which is the very voice that should drive the organization to future competitive advantage and, hence, profits. In other words, since the outcomes matter, the goals are, and should be, of focal concern.

Ideally, goals should be meaningful, realistically attainable and challenging. "Meaningful" goals advance the welfare of the organization as a whole. "Realistically attainable" goals imply that, given the resources allocated, diligent effort will result in success. "Challenging" goals imply those that are moderately difficult. Easy goals lead to lackadaisical efforts; impossible goals lead to giving up (hence, no effort), while challenging goals lead to higher effort, which prompts higher levels of performance.

It's important to note that firm executives are unlikely to have any experience, much less actual expertise, in contact center work. Whatever goals they articulate may or may not be meaningful, realistic or challenging, and those that are can likely be attributed to serendipity more than anything else. Goals expressed by the contact center manager, on the other hand, generally are realistically attainable, but they may also be (or at least be considered to be) self-serving by being unambitious. If rewards are the valued outcome, and they can only be attained when goals are reached, then it makes sense for the operations manager to set easy goals. If attaining the reward rests on meeting the stated goal, the fact that better performance and higher goals could have been achieved becomes irrelevant. This reasoning, which is readily available to both executives and the operations manager, only leads to a lack of trust regarding goals set by the operations manager.

Goals that are set based solely on historical records that are altered by some arbitrarily set increment are also problematic. They fail to look toward the future. By focusing entirely on the past, new technology and management practices are ignored, and the potential benefits foregone without any consideration. Additionally, if goals are based on historical performance and customer intelligence is absent from the historical data, then any goal set is unlikely to be in service to the customer.

Now the popularity and benefits of benchmarking become apparent. Benchmarking studies substitute external, allegedly unbiased industry aggregated standards in place of arbitrarily or internally generated, potentially biased standards against which to compare contact center performance. The center gauges itself against others in the contact center industry to effect needed changes in service delivery. To create a competitive advantage, benchmarking became part of the way the contact center set its goals and operating targets. Every contact center wants to be as good, or preferably better, than the competition (despite the obvious impossibility inherent in the desire), and it is this fact that needs to be demonstrated when executives ask how the center compares. Note that most direct competitors are not willing to share their performance metrics in a one-to-one relationship, and those that do should be scrutinized to find out why they would willingly make such important competitive intelligence available to those with whom they compete. Therefore, it's often necessary to depend upon benchmarking studies that provide scores collected at arm's length and hope that the participants are from your specific focal industry.

Benchmarking standards of performance have what researchers call face validity: that is, on its face, the standards are a valid, unbiased means of comparison. But, in fact, the face validity may be more apparent than real. This is due in large part to the way benchmarking studies are usually undertaken in the contact center industry. As a research scientist, the use of data points that are suspect causes a high level of discomfort. Rather than looking for any piece of information to produce a response to the comparison question, the source of the data should be critically examined. Is the information part of an official, intelligently designed benchmarking study or simply data collected over time in various studies using variables that share the same names (but may have different definitions), which subsequently were aggregated as an afterthought to produce a "benchmarking" study? Is it known exactly who the participants were, and how they are related to each other and to your firm so that a better comparison can be made? Was the information self-reported by the participants and, therefore, possibly optimistically presented to gain a more favorable comparison? Are the variables being measured explicitly defined so all participants are responding correctly for an apples-to-apples comparison? Understanding the source of the data is imperative as the integrity of the study as a whole or in part can be detrimentally affected by each of the above questions.

We often do not get this sort of critical assessment of the data, though, because disparate companies (via product, market, technology, etc.) are surveyed and undefined variables aggregated. These problems can result in a picture that is fuzzy at best and outright misleading at worst. The benchmarking focus is too much on apparent efficiency and not at all on effectiveness.

Invalid Comparison: Apples to Oranges

But we must consider one critically important question here: Are we comparing ourselves to the right group? If the answer is no, or even that it is unknown, the benchmarking data could be completely irrelevant. As previously suggested, benchmark studies, as typically conducted in the contact center industry, compare everyone against everyone else. There is no thought as to exactly what comparisons are being made. Measurements are different in each organization and those differences are not accounted for in the typical benchmarking study. It is unlikely for the reader to know the specifics of the comparison group. Without those specifics, it is impossible to accurately gauge the applicability of the comparisons being made.

Where's the Customer?

The most important thing to keep in mind is that, while there are several ways to benchmark the performance of the contact center, when all is said and done and the results are in, it is the **customer** who has the final say about whether or not the best practices are being utilized.

So let's say the center ends up going about the benchmarking project the right way. In the end, the metrics and practices are combined so that the numbers have life and can be understood more completely. The center's metrics are compared to a relevant sample of other contact centers that have similar attributes to get as close to an apples-to-apples comparison as possible. Based on these assumptions, the benchmark results should allow operations management to make well-educated business decisions about how to become a best-in-class contact center.

Even though the center is using benchmarking at its best, the most critical piece of the puzzle is still missing... the **customer**. The biggest question that results from a benchmarking report is how the metrics align with caller satisfaction. The efficiency data must be overlapped with the effectiveness data. Unfortunately, this is rarely an output from benchmarking projects, and it is critical to the utility of the study to address the congruence or lack thereof between these two data sets.

Contact center management already knows its center's metrics, and through the benchmarking study, it has identified the best-practice metrics for the focal industry. The next step is to validate the performance metrics with the contact center's *own callers* to determine if there are deficiencies. If there are no gains to be had by achieving the best-of-the-best metric, why announce that as a goal and expend the energy and resources?

Without the customer to validate the metrics, the center's decision-making process cannot help but be flawed. The primary focus should be on effectiveness and, secondarily, on efficiency. Therefore, before undertaking a major improvement program in the contact center motivated by the apparent results from a benchmarking study focused on efficiency, take some time to find out what the *center's customers* think and whether the desired changes would improve their service experience. This is the heart and soul of effectiveness. Why go through the added expense to obtain the nth degree of efficiency when the customer cares more about other things?

While we have used reason to make this case, our belief in the near uselessness of operational metrics to enhance customer satisfaction also rests on research. An empirical assessment of the relationship between caller satisfaction and a number of critical variables was reported in the *International Journal of Service Industry Management.* Of all the critical operational determinants gathered and analyzed in the Purdue University Benchmark Study (almost 500 variables were involved) "only the *percentage of calls closed in the first contact* and *average abandonment* have a significant, albeit weak, influence on caller satisfaction" (Feinberg, Kim, Hokama, de Ruyter and Keen, 2000). The findings from the study defy logic and therefore prove the point that benchmarking operational metrics has little to no bearing on how to engineer the customer experience. To repeat, benchmarking studies are supposed to look at best practices as well as compare metrics, yet they focus almost exclusively on metrics. Those metrics capture operational processes, and operational processes have almost NOTHING to do with customer satisfaction, except for a very weak relationship to *abandonment* and *first-call resolution,* based on this research.

Practices and Metrics:
Two Parts to the Benchmarking Process

The benchmarking process can be divided into two parts: practices and metrics. The tendency, especially in contact centers, is to concentrate on the metrics and neglect the practices. Camp (1989) specifically warns against this. It is easy for managers to work with the metrics and quantitative targets to identify quickly where the contact center stands against the competition. Indeed, it's very important to have comparable information to give operational management the confidence to say some changes need to be made because performance is substandard.

Shortcomings of Typical Benchmarking Studies

Variable definitions are imprecise

Unmatched participants

Self-collected, potentially self-serving data

Randomly assorted participants from multiple industries

Metric focus

Little or no assessment of processes/practices

No customer focus

The problem with this approach is that it's not possible to identify *why* any gap exists just by analyzing the metrics. This is why the practices part is such a useful aspect of the benchmarking process. It allows the methods *behind* the metrics to be identified in order to determine *why* any gaps may exist. Looking at the metrics in isolation can mislead the user and defeat the ultimate purpose for using benchmarking studies.

Another way to defeat the purpose of benchmarking is to chase the performance goals of only one or two perceived leaders in contact center performance. If you do so, you'll always be putting out fires and your new initiatives will constantly fail, because what works for one center is not always (exactly) right for another.

In summary, many benchmarking studies are *ad hoc* collections of variously defined variables collected from unspecified companies from disparate industries aggregated after the fact. Comparisons are often made to inappropriate exemplars; i.e., companies that are not truly comparable. The variables may not be well defined and/or the data self-collected and, therefore, of questionable validity. Benchmarking studies almost exclusively focus on metrics while omitting practices that could help to answer the "why" attached to each gap.

Benchmarking studies can provide valuable operational comparison goals for the savvy user; however, caution is advised to avoid needless pain. Even the best benchmarking research has shortcomings that can only be overcome by using techniques specifically designed to listen to your customers' voices.

Chapter 5:
Net Promoter and EQM

Fads come and go in business, just as they do in the fashion industry — only the period is different. While fashions change seasonally, fads in business may last several years. Witness, for example, employee ownership plans by the score in the 1980s, particularly in transportation firms, but also in some manufacturing companies, as well. Teams were the fad in the 1990s. All would be well in business if only we implemented more teams. Self-directing (managing) teams have been part of the buzz in the 2000s. But the biggest buzz so far in this millennium is Net Promoter. Not only is this concept accepted by some as a panacea for all business woes, but the language has taken on an almost religious fervor.

We intend to rein this language in and specify the real uses of the underlying concept of Net Promoter. All of the above ideas have a place in business, but not every place.

The Net Promoter concept has made a huge splash in the business community over the past few years. Many well-respected, successful companies such as General Electric, Enterprise, eBay and American Express compute, use and tout the Net Promoter Score as the key to the continued success of their firms.

As Net Promoter currently enjoys a privileged place in the press and there are several widely believed misconceptions about it, we have undertaken, in our own small way, to add a dash of clarity to the discourse. Based on empirical evidence published in a well-respected research journal, we believe that Net Promoter, while having value, is clearly not a substitute for a proper EQM program. It cannot provide all that EQM programs backed by CATs® methodology can. It is NOT the "one metric you need," as has been widely publicized. Don't buy snake oil to cure your pain.

Simply stated, our goals for this chapter are to:

1. Define the Net Promoter Score.
2. Explain its logic.
3. Discuss its various adaptations.
4. Examine the empirical evidence: Is it the "SINGLE METRIC" needed?
5. Consider how it compares to key drivers.

When speaking of Net Promoter, we will refer often to two sources: the book *The Ultimate Question,* and the *Harvard Business Review* article, "The One Number You Need to Grow," both written by loyalty expert Frederick F. Reichheld. In his 2003 *HBR* article, Reichheld delineated the Net Promoter Score, based on some 20 years of research. He forcefully contended that customer satisfaction and retention numbers cannot help firms to grow; rather, the only metric linked to growth is positive word-of-mouth (WOM).

The Net Promoter Score

The Net Promoter Score is relatively simple to comprehend: Customers are asked some variation of the question: "How likely is it that you would recommend Company X to a friend or colleague?" The answers are recorded on a 10-point scale. Customers who respond with a 6 or lower are "Detractors," while "Promoters" are the proportion whose scores are 9 or

10. Subtracting the Detractors from Promoters gives the Net Promoter Score.

The equation as envisioned by Reichheld is:

P - D = NPS

Where:
P = (scores of 9 or 10)/n
D = (scores of 6-0)/n
n = number of participants
NPS = Net Promoter Score

It is important to note an anomaly in the Net Promoter Score that seems obvious, but is seldom addressed in the literature either by Reichheld or his proponents: There are multiple ways to get the same Net Promoter Scores, but very different realities would prevail for those identical scores. For example, let us say a company is very polarizing in its policies, which leads to the following results:

P = 50/100
D = 40/100
NPS = 50% - 40% = 10%

In this example, half of the customer base loves us and promotes our business to others. But almost as many (40 percent) are detractors who dislike us. Only 10 percent of our customers are "indifferent" to us.

Now let us assume the following:

P = 20/100
D = 10/100
NPS = 20% - 10% = 10%

Although the calculated Net Promoter Score is the same, there is likely little else that aligns between these two examples. The policies that led to the polarizing of customers are absent in the second example. Nearly everyone (70 percent) is indifferent. Few people "hate" the company, but there are also few who "love" it either. In other words, the company is blasé.

The likely recommendations to help these two imaginary companies would be very different. Company 2 needs a personality. Company 1 has a personality, but needs a "personality-ectomy" to excise it entirely, or a massive makeover at the very least.

Aside from this flaw, it is important to note that you cannot manage a company with a single metric. Even the most casual reading of *The Ultimate Question* makes it clear that, after you ask it, there are other questions to ask and research activities to undertake. It appears to be a single question and is definitely publicized that way; but, in reality, a whole research endeavor must be undertaken to make the Net Promoter Score yield managerially actionable information. Reichheld specifically mentions such activities as call-backs to detractors, focus group research, as well as other activities.

The Logic of Net Promoter

Reichheld begins with the rather appealing and intriguing concept of bad versus good profits, and by defining the Golden Rule. The Golden Rule is exactly what we have been taught in the Judeo/Christian tradition: "Do unto others as you would have them do unto you." In this case, treat your customers as you would like to be treated, which makes immensely good sense.

The Golden Rule is tied to the novel concept of good and bad profits. Clearly, there is no such concept in accounting: all profits are inherently good as far as accounting goes. However, to Reichheld, good profits are those that are derived from expansion of the core business and "with the customers' enthusiastic cooperation... Satisfied customers become, in effect, part of the company's marketing department, not only increasing their own purchases, but also providing enthusiastic referrals."

Reichheld goes on to contend that bad profits are those that come from "captive" consumers. Often, customers do business with you because they are under contract, or because your offering is the least objectionable of those available. These customers are making you money, but only because you are charging them unconscionable fees, outrageous interest or have them held captive. Here is a real-life example: One of the authors has been a customer of a life insurance company for nearly 40 years. She recently received a letter addressed to "only their best customers," with a credit card offer for an "affiliation" card with no annual fee, but with an interest rate as high as 29.99 percent, a $45 late fee, a short payment window that would be hard to hit (hence, increasing the likelihood of late fees), and a cash advance fee with an interest rate that was so high only persons in fear for their lives would exercise such an option. Needless to say, we tossed the offer in our "round file" after much derision and with the comment that "If this is what they offer their 'best' customers, just imagine what type of 'first-born child clause' they would include for the 'average' customer!"

This is the kind of offering that could generate negative profits as the costs of doing business for the customer under these circumstances would engender serious dissatisfaction. One consequence of dissatisfaction is to look for another partner with whom to do business even while the "relationship" continues. That is, profits continue from this customer only so long as the search for viable alternatives continues. Another consequence is negative "word-of-mouth."

Word-of-mouth (WOM) is the concept that underlies Net Promoter. Maybe the simplest definition of WOM is: one individual sharing information with other individuals (Herr, Kardes and Kim, 1991).

That people do, indeed, indulge in WOM is clear. Roughly half of all Americans "often seek the advice of others before making a decision to buy products or services, and about 40 percent feel that people often come to them for purchase advice" (Hawkins, Best and Coney, 2001). Of course, as implied above, WOM can be either negative or positive.

The anecdotal evidence for WOM is substantial, but there appears to be no simple, clear linkage between WOM and sales or other outcome variables. For example, researchers probed the link between volume of WOM and future television ratings and found no consistent relationship (Godes and Mayzlin, 2004).

The Net Promoter Score, on the contrary, is quite straightforward and, at first blush, seems to provide that linkage. (We'll return to this theme when we review the empirical evidence.)

According to Reichheld in *The Ultimate Question*:

> We also realized that two conditions must be satisfied before customers make a personal referral. They must believe that the company offers superior values in terms that an economist would understand: price, features, quality, functionality, ease of use, and all the other practical factors. But they also must feel good about their relationship with the company. They must believe the company knows and understands them, listens to them and shares their principles. On the first dimension, a company is engaging the customer's head. On the second, it is engaging the heart. Only when both sides of the equation are fulfilled will a customer enthusiastically recommend a company to a friend… That's why the 'would recommend' question provides such an effective measure of relationship quality. It tests for both the rational and the emotional dimensions.

It is unfortunate that this rather appealing conceptualization of "two for one" is not supported with specific research to substantiate the assertion. We cannot think of any instance in replicated research where one item is believed to conceptualize two different constructs simultaneously, although there are many instances in which multiple items are used to capture a single construct. Solid research is predicated on items in instruments (that is, questions on surveys) being designed to capture one or a part of one construct. In some cases, constructs are deemed sufficiently complex that multiple items will be written to capture the essence of the single construct. Items that "load" on multiple constructs are always eliminated, as they are not pure. Never before have we seen a single item meant to capture multiple constructs; that is, both the emotive and intellectual dimensions simultaneously via a singular item. We would like to see the empirical evidence that supports this assertion as it is so far out of standard scientific practice.

Some Adaptations of Net Promoter

Although adopted by many companies, Net Promoter also has been **adapted** by others. Some of the adaptations are quite different from what was originally proposed. For example, Reichheld suggests an 11-point scale: 0-10. He argues, reasonably enough, that the zero ending point reduces respondent confusion, as receiving a score of "zero" is never good, while both ones and 10s could be the superior mark depending on the instructions of the researcher.

Several companies use alternative scales. General Electric uses a 1-10 scale, and the Word of Mouth Marketing Association (WOMMA) recommends this as the scale to use with Net Promoter. Enterprise Rent-A-Car uses a 5-point scale and eBay only a 3-point one. (These specific examples were taken from *The Ultimate Question*.) As Reichheld himself asserts, "other scales seem to work."

One company does not even use the "net" in Net Promoter. Specifically, Enterprise Rent-A-Car uses a 1-5 system and "top box" (scores of 5 only) rather than net (Promoters less Detractors). Nevertheless, Enterprise runs a substantial program that it credits to Net Promoter although it has made important changes. Most importantly, they have been very successful in using this metric coupled with other research efforts to "drive" their company to growth and profits.

The Empirical Evidence:
Is Net Promoter the "SINGLE METRIC" Needed?

Some part of the ready acceptance of Net Promoter likely arose from Reichheld's credentials and claims of large studies over many years. The underlying belief is that Net Promoter is rooted in research findings in many firms across many industries for many years.

This perception is bolstered by the language:

…we administered the test to thousands of customers recruited from public lists in six industries: financial services, cable and telecommunications, personal computers, e-commerce, auto insurance and Internet service providers… Eventually we had detailed information from more than 4,000 customers…

All this number-crunching had one goal: to determine which survey questions showed the strongest statistical correlation with repeat purchases or referrals.

In other words, all the above was accomplished in search of the question, "How likely is it that you would recommend Company X to a friend or colleague?" The less research-savvy reader could be forgiven for not realizing that this description pertains to the research used to narrow the list of possible items down to the "ultimate question" rather than to evidence of the efficacy of the Net Promoter metric itself.

It was later research that was accomplished to determine the correlation between NPS and revenue growth rate. Here the language read "over 50 companies… across a dozen targeted industries" (Satmetrix, 2004). However, it turns out, following the logic of Timothy Keiningham and his colleagues in "A Longitudinal Examination of Net Promoter and Firm Revenue Growth," published in the *Journal of Marketing* (July 2007):

In the *Harvard Business Review* article that introduced Net

Promoter, charts for three of the industries examined were presented; the sample sizes in terms of number of firms) were three, five and 10 (Reichheld, 2003). This would mean that the sample sizes for each of the remaining nine industries were approximately 3.6 on average (i.e., [50 − (3 + 5 + 10)]/9 = 3.56. Therefore, industry sample sizes were small.

So although the perception is that Net Promoter is based on large samples and rigorous studies, this is not demonstrably so, at least to date.

Furthermore, Reichheld claims that Net Promoter is the "single most reliable indicator of a company's ability to grow" (Netpromoter.com, 2006). Until recently, there was no independently conducted, clean research to confirm or dispute this claim. (While there were studies conducted by Neil Morgan and Lopo Leotte Rego in 2006, and another by Paul Marsden, Alain Samson and Neville Upton of the London School of Economics and Political Science in 2005, both contained some difficulties that made direct comparisons problematic.) But Keiningham and his colleagues report such an effort in their July 2007 article. While the *JM* is not noted for its readability and user-friendly articles, it is well known for its high-quality research. Fortunately, many who bother to try to understand this article are likely to succeed, as the writers placed the more obtuse arguments in an appendix rather than in the article itself.

To summarize the main points made by Keiningham et al., longitudinal data were used from the Norwegian Customer Satisfaction Barometer (NCSB) from 21 firms and more 15,500 interviewed customers on intention to purchase and recommend. As it turned out, the NCSB's data were an excellent source for testing the Net Promoter hypothesis.

> Unlike most data collection procedures for customer satisfaction, the NCSB identifies customers from the universe of purchasers and then identifies the company from which the customer purchased or consumed rather than starting from an identified company and its lists of customers. If a respondent qualified as a recent purchaser or consumer of a service, he or

she was asked if this service came from the list of companies being measured. If not, the interview was terminated. Each respondent was interviewed for only one service.

As with the Reichheld research, firms were grouped into industries. The Net Promoter score and several other satisfaction indices were computed and compared to revenue growth rates for these industries.

Examination of the correlation tables makes it clear that:

> Net Promoter in no way would be categorized as the "single most reliable indicator of a company's ability to grow" (Netpromoter.com, 2006). Indeed, there is no real indication that average levels of any of the satisfaction/loyalty metrics in Table 1 are significantly correlated with the relative change in revenue within the respective industry.

Keiningham et al. then went a step further. Since they did not have access to Reichheld's raw data, it was impossible to compare their Net Promoter data to other commonly used satisfaction/loyalty indices. But the authors cleverly used the appendix to *The Ultimate Question,* which featured graphs. These were enlarged and the data back-engineered. These graphs summarized data from the American Customer Satisfaction Index (labeled ASCI annual growth) and the other axis "sales annual growth." The R-square reported was .00 indicating that there was no correlation. This finding contradicts not only commonly held beliefs, but also research published in respected journals. That is, the ACSI has a demonstrated, scientifically confirmed relationship with outcomes such as growth, according to the research published in rigorous, reputable journals. Keiningham and his colleagues sought to reconcile these two disparate findings using the data from the back-engineered graphs.

When the Keiningham team compared the results they concluded that:

1. The ASCI looked very similar to the originals, leading to the

conclusion that Net Promoter and ASCI results were very similar when compared to revenue growth rate. Given the .00 correlation reported by Reichheld, this is a very surprising finding.

It is worth taking a moment to think about what is happening.

The first test most scientists run is a simple visual inspection. That is, does this look right? To perform this test, all one needs is to know "in what direction" the results *should* go.

A correlation coefficient of .00 means there is no relationship between the two things being compared. ASCI is a well-known and well-researched measure of customer satisfaction. According to Reichheld, the correlation coefficient between the ASCI and revenue growth is .00, meaning there is no relationship. (This assertion contradicts other research. For example, see, the articles by Anderson, Fornell and Mazvancheryl, 2004; Gruca and Rego, 2005; and Fornell and colleagues, 2006; which are listed in the Reference Library at the back of the book.) Reichheld however contends there is a strong relationship between Net Promoter scores and revenue growth. Logically, therefore, the graphs of ASCI and revenue growth should look very different from Net Promoter and revenue growth.

As we all know, if A = B and B = C, then A = C. Therefore, if the graphs look very similar, then Net Promoter and ASCI must be measuring roughly the same thing.

2. In two of the three industries for which actual comparisons could be made, the ASCI correlations were higher than the Net Promoter correlations.

R2 Values for Growth and Net Promoter and ASCI Scores

	Net Promoter	ASCI
Personal Computers	.68	.76
US Life Insurance	.83	.58
Airlines	.57	.70

Table built from content taken from Keiningham, et al. (2007)

In sum, looking through the empirical evidence at hand, it is not at all clear that Net Promoter is the "one metric you need," as there are others that also do well. This is not altogether surprising as Reichheld himself states: "The 'would-recommend' question wasn't the best predictor of growth in every case… in database software, by monopolies or near monopolies, [and] …in the local telephone and cable businesses." In other words, in the above industries, the Net Promoter Score did not fare well. So in summary, Net Promoter, even by Reichheld's standards, is not "the one metric you need" as it is not the best predictor in certain industries. Indeed, there is clear evidence that other satisfaction measures, namely the ASCI, predict as well or better in some instances.

How Does Net Promoter Compare to Key Drivers?

Recall that external quality monitoring (EQM) is a full, formalized, well-considered research effort. In the contact center environment, it invites callers to participate in an immediate post-call survey (or email, if the contact with the company was via email).

EQM via CATs® then operates at the micro level: one customer at a time. If there is a traumatic service failure, an alarm is sounded allowing immediate recovery efforts to correct the individual problem and save the customer.

The responses across customers are aggregated and submitted to additional analyses to build up managerially actionable recommendations. These analyses inform the business about which activities are drivers of performance. This knowledge allows for the efficient allocation of resources to address those activities likely to result in the largest impact: the biggest "bang for the buck."

In contrast, the Net Promoter metric is a single question and macro in its orientation especially as detailed by Reichheld. Basically, if you don't like the Net Promoter score you get, he urges management to take action to drill down and find out what is driving the score. He suggests managers make follow-up calls and form focus groups. He makes much of having CEOs and district managers putting in the time to take calls from customers: to keep a finger on the pulse of the profit makers. This is actually a great idea. Top people desperately need to understand what is happening at the money level of the company. But all this activity is instigated by the Net Promoter score and from the top down. Why not eliminate the time delay by having real-time data collected? Why not put a program in place that addresses many of Reichheld's concerns automatically, especially as they touch on the contact center?

In no sense are the two approaches mutually exclusive. One could easily have a Net Promoter Score and program as outlined by Reichheld while running an ongoing EQM program with a CATs methodology within the contact center. As we have emphasized before, the Net Promoter concept has value, but it is certainly not the "one metric you need."

Net Promoter and EQM Each Have Uses

In brief then, Net Promoter and EQM programs are not antithetical. They do not work against each other, nor does one necessarily exclude the other. In fact, they can complement, rather than act as a substitute for each other. Using EQM, one can apply first aid on an emergency basis, track issues for systemic changes, and target discipline or retraining based on known facts, just to name a few uses. The Net Promoter program, on the other hand, is a top-down macro approach. Each has its uses.

Chapter 6:
The Science of Research: Detecting and Overcoming Biases

Ever so slowly, human beings have made progress in the treatment of illness. For centuries, humans were bled or had leaches applied indiscriminately to various parts of the body in the mistaken belief that it was necessary to restore the natural balance among the humors of the body: yellow bile, black bile, phlegm and blood. Medical practice would have advanced a lot quicker if this body that every educated physician "knew" to be true had never been invented. Only with the advent of the scientific method could real progress be made in the treating and cure of diseases. Chapter 6 is all about the scientific method in social research.

Academicians have long known that satisfaction programs will increase loyalty, lower transaction costs, reduce failure costs and help to build an organization's reputation in the marketplace (Anderson, Fornell and Lehmann, 1994). This seems also to be known in industry. What doesn't seem to be clear to much of the contact center industry is how to plan and implement such a program to recognize such results. Now the pain comes into focus. How exactly do we avoid survey pain through a scientific research program? Such is the gist of this chapter.

How do we ensure that customer satisfaction results are a profitable business process in the contact center and elsewhere in the organization? To increase the value of the initiative, be certain that the research is done the **right** way, and not only done for the sake of surveying customers. Note that customer feedback results will be used by colleagues regardless of the number of caveats listed in the footnotes, so be diligent in providing valid and credible customer intelligence. The consequences of a poor measurement program and inaccurate reporting can have profound and far-reaching effects in the organization.

Put another way, are you guilty of *survey malpractice* by giving your company faulty information based on inadequate research methods?

Malpractice is a harsh word — it directly implies professional malfeasance through negligence, ignorance or intent. Doctors and other professionals carry insurance for malpractice in the event that a patient or client perceives a lack of professional competence. For contact center professionals and other managers, there is no malpractice insurance to fall back on for acts of professional malfeasance, whether they're intentional or not. Of course, it is much more likely that one would be fired than sued for bad acts, but that offers little comfort. (Chapter 3 introduced this concept.)

Never put yourself in a position where your competence can be called into question. That's why so many call center managers are "skating on thin ice" when it comes to their customer satisfaction measurements: there are demonstrable failings with many of the typical practices used by call center managers. By definition, **an ineffective measurement program generates errors from negligence, ignorance and/or intentional wrongdoing.** You have a fiduciary responsibility to your company — and recommendations made based on erroneous customer data do, indeed, meet the definition of malpractice.

Measurement programs must meet certain scientific criteria to be statistically valid with an acceptable confidence level and level of precision or tolerated error. Without these considerations, you are guilty of survey malpractice. Defending your program with statements like, "it has always been done this way" or "we were told to do a survey" is not sufficient. Research guidelines adhered to in academia apply to the business world, as well. A deficient survey yields inaccurate data and results in invalid conclusions no matter who conducts it. Unnecessary pain and expense are the natural outgrowths of such errors of judgment.

To maximize the return on investment (ROI) for the EQM customer measurement program, and to ensure that the program has credibility, install the science before collecting the data. Make sure that the initial program setup is comprehensive. If there is no research expert on staff, then outsource this to a well-credentialed expert. The alternative is to train someone in the science around creating and interpreting the gap variable from a delayed measurement. Or better still; engage a qualified expert to design a program to measure customer satisfaction immediately after the contact center interaction.

Before assuming that survey malpractice does not or will not apply to your program, consider the following tell-tale signs of errors and biases, which we have reprised from an earlier chapter as they are critical to a good program.

1. Measuring too many things. Your survey of a five-minute contact center service experience takes the customer 15 minutes to complete and includes 40 questions. While everyone in your organization has a need for customer intelligence, you should not be fielding only one survey to get all of the answers.

Should the contact center be measuring satisfaction with the in-home repair service, the accounting and invoicing process, the latest marketing campaign, or the distribution network? Certainly input on these processes is necessary, but don't try to get it all on a single survey.

2. Not measuring enough things. An overall satisfaction question and a question about agent courtesy do not make a valid survey. Without a robust set of measurement constructs, answers to questions will not be found. Three or four questions will not facilitate a change in a management process; nor will they enable effective agent coaching or be considered a valid measure to include in an incentive or performance plan.

3. Measuring questions with an unreliable scale. In school, everyone agreed on what tests scores meant: 95 was an A, 85 was a B, and 75 was a C. Everything in between has its own mark associated with it, as well. Yet, when it comes to service measurement, we tend to give customers limited responses. What do the categories excellent, good, fair and poor really mean? Offering limited response options does not permit robust analysis, and statistical analysis is often applied incorrectly. In addition, using a categorical scale or a scale that is too small (like many typical 5-point survey questions) is not adequate for the evaluation of service delivery.

4. Measuring the wrong things or the right things wrong. Surveys should not be designed to tell you what you *want* to hear, but rather what you *need* to hear. Constructs that are measured should have a purpose in the overall measurement plan. Each item should have a definitive plan for use within the evaluation process. The right things to measure will focus on several overall company measures that affect your center (or your center's value statement to the organization), the agents and issue/problem resolution.

5. Asking for an evaluation after memory has degraded. When we think about time, 24 to 48 hours doesn't seem that long. But when you're measuring customer satisfaction with your service, it's the difference between an accurate evaluation and a flawed one. Do you remember exactly how you felt after you called your telephone company about an issue? Could you accurately rate that particular experience 48 hours later, after other calls to the same company or other companies have been made? That's what you're asking your customers to do when you delay measurement. It opens the door to inaccurate reporting and compromised decision-making, and is also an unfair evaluation of your agents.

Conducting follow-up phone calls to gather feedback about the center's performance is a common pitfall. While the research methodology certainly should have its place in the company's research portfolio, it's less effective than using point-of-service, real-time customer evaluations.

Mail and phone surveys are useful for research projects that are not tactical in nature, but rather focused on the general relationship, product features, additional options, color, etc.

6. **Wiggle room via correction factors.** If you're using correction factors to account for issues in the data or to placate agents or the management team, some aspect of the survey design is flawed. A common adjustment is to collect 11 survey evaluations per agent and delete everyone's lowest score. However, with a valid measurement that includes numeric scores, as well as explanations for scores and a rigorous quality control process, adjustments in the final scores will not be necessary. Making excuses for the results or allowing holes to be poked in the effort diminishes and undermines the effectiveness of the program, and highlights an opening for survey malpractice claims.

7. **Accuracy and credibility of service providers and product vendors.** As with any technology or service, the user assumes responsibility for applying the correct tool, or applying the tool correctly.

There are plenty of home-grown or vendor-supplied tools to field a survey, but, again, *if you do not apply the functionality correctly, you will be responsible for the error.* Keep in mind that some service providers are only interested in selling you something that fits into their cookie-cutter approach, and it will not be customized to your specific requirements.

Questions: The Core of the Survey

Using biased survey results is highly dangerous as operational and personnel decisions will be based on flawed information. The following are some of the pitfalls of relying on mail or delayed phone surveys.

Biases and errors can arise from a variety of sources. Authors of literature on research methods and survey construction vary on the exact terms used and number of biases and errors to avoid, but it's safe to say that there are a great many pitfalls and few safe roads. It is beyond the scope of this text to provide a comprehensive review of these, but some of those that are most likely to occur in the contact center measurement program will be discussed below. These include problems with the questions themselves, instrumentation bias, respondent bias and researcher-created bias.

Historically, in an effort to overcome the myopia stemming from sole reliance on internally generated evaluations of customer satisfaction, companies have turned to mail or phone surveys to augment their understanding of the customers' perception of the service delivery

The research effort is directed toward inquiry, and the questions are the elements that perform that function. The questions, then, are the core; the heart and soul of the endeavor. Although every aspect of the research requires careful planning and execution, the closest possible scrutiny must be reserved for the instrument itself as it is clearly the most essential component. As Pamela Alreck and Robert Settle, authors of *The Survey Research Handbook* claimed, "Their performance [test questions] ordinarily has a more profound effect on the survey results than has any other single element of the survey." Without valid, reliable questions, nothing of any use can be learned.

Questions need to have at least three core attributes: relevance, clarity and conciseness. Relevance means that each question must have purpose within the context of the survey and then focus on that purpose. Clarity implies that each question must be clear as stated to all respondents. Note that some words have different commonly understood meanings based on geography, and even when this is not a problem, nevertheless multiple meanings can be understood without careful regard. Conciseness implies brevity. Essentially say what is needful, all that is needful and nothing more. In general, the longer the question, the more difficult the response task will be. Longer questions increase the likelihood of misunderstanding overall, while increasing the likelihood of forgetting the first part of the question by the time the respondents reach the end.

Beyond relevance, clarity and conciseness, special attention needs to be taken with vocabulary and grammar. In general, it is important to excise all jargon as well as other words not in common usage. Understandability is the key. Toward this end, it is important to use simple sentences. Complex, compound and compound-complex are the other sentence structure types. While occasionally it may be necessary to use a complex sentence construction, compound and complex-compound constructions must strictly be avoided. Not only are they too long and confusing, but they nearly always contain multiple ideas that truly require multiple questions in order to access the desired information.

Instrumentation Bias and Error

Additional instrumentation bias and errors exist, but the number cited varies by author. Upward of 10 such biases and errors can be easily generated. Briefly some of these include use of emotionally loaded terms, questions designed to lead the respondent to answer in a particular way, double-barreled questions in which two questions are contained in a single test item, overemphasis (it's better to understate), over-generalization (which tends to gloss over all detail), over-specificity beyond what participants are likely to be able to give, example containment (which can cue participants to use some exemplars while glossing over others), unstated criteria, double-negative content ("the clerk was never not there"), and over-demanding recall errors.

Respondent-Created Bias and Error

A plethora of response biases exist, and there are controls for some of them. Of the many that could contaminate the measurement programs, we'll give special treatment to self-selection and first-responder biases. In addition, we'll cover recall errors and related topics, such as time delays and the time-gap variable.

    1. The bias of self-selection. Respondents to mail or delayed phone surveys tend to be those customers who have something they really want to say. Such people will tend to generate a bimodal distribution of scores: humps at the ends with a valley in between. Again, we emphasize that time has passed; substantial time, in many cases, lasting as much as days or weeks. Only something that really "stuck in the mind" would occasion someone to respond to an event of only a few minutes duration which happened days earlier. Therefore the bias of self-selection is highly substantial in all mail or delayed phone surveys. This substantial level of bias is an artifact of the methodology. By contrast, the level of self-selection bias is inherently less from a real-time, post-call survey, and this lesser amount of self-selection bias is also inherent in the methodology itself. Those who call into the center may be anywhere along the spectrum of potential responses, depending on why they initiated the call. The sample pool of all callers represents the distribution of customer expectations and perceptions for the customer service channel. Other things being equal, the call event will be fresher and the inconvenience of taking the survey is much less with a "let's do it now" opportunity to respond over the cognitive load of remembering an earlier event that is imposed by all time-delayed surveys. Additionally, instant feedback is likely to be perceived as more likely to be assimilated and used in the center over feedback that is much delayed.

Some of the callers will be "mad as hell" due to the initiating event. Agents who deftly handle such calls (given they have the tools do so) have an opportunity to turn a decidedly negative event in the making into a positive experience. The vast majority are more likely to be calling to fix a problem they see as a relatively small, quick fix, and these folks are neither greatly pleased nor greatly displeased, at least at the outset of the call; that is, the middle-ground people are better-represented in the results from a post service call than from either mail or delayed surveys. All else being equal, the likelihood is that most callers will fall quite naturally into that midrange at the outset of the call and because service provided is basically good, the distribution will (and should) skew a bit to the positive. This expectation is based on the likelihood of neutral to slightly positive expectations pre-call. If the agent performs as expected or better, the scores will naturally tend to rise as the service met or exceeded the pre-call expectation.

Relying only on responses from customers at either or both ends of the satisfaction spectrum, as naturally occurs in mail and delayed calls, paints a distorted view of the centers' activities and its effects on customers. This, in turn, may lead to suboptimal action programs or even the decision to do nothing at all when remedial actions are required. Conversely, expensive retraining, technology upgrades or quality controls could be implemented to fix a problem that is, in fact, a rather isolated incident.

Note that this self-selection bias is not totally eliminated with the use of a post-call survey, but it is minimized compared to delayed methodologies. One must remember that there is no perfect piece of research, and even physicists agree that the act of observing and measuring physical entities tends to alter the phenomena under scrutiny. So to a lesser, non-zero degree, the extremes are more likely to agree to participate than those who are largely indifferent. This is an unavoidable artifact that is highly reduced due to the technology increasing the ease of participation, the relative recency of the event, and the perceived likelihood of feedback being utilized.

2. The first-responder bias (Gendall and Davis, 1993) occurs because the program contacts customers within two or three days (sometimes more) of a service interaction. That is, the survey is conducted well after the original service encounter. The customers who respond to the survey first could be different from the general customer base because they are home at the time and have answered the phone.

Think about the changes in society over the last few years with caller ID, cell phones and both adults working outside the household. All of these social factors, and more, impact who within the customer base actually answers the call to complete the follow-up survey. Even if the measurement team is persistent enough to get a validly sized sample, it may not be representative of the customer base as a whole. Can center management accept this for strategic decision-making? Certainly doing so increases risk.

This factor may be much more important than is obvious because research studies have shown that there are differences between customers who are contacted on the first call and those contacted on subsequent calls (Gendall and Davis, 1993; Robinson and Lifton, 1991; Ward, Russick and Rudelius, 1985). The Gendall and Davis research confirmed that those who are contacted on the first call tend to be more rural, have lower income and less education, are female and older compared to the relevant population as a whole. While this study examined the general public, contact center results may also share specific demographic categories not representative of the entire customer base because the research company calls the telephone numbers on the list until someone answers the phone and completes the survey.

This bias can be fixed by correcting for the sample demographics with analytic techniques, or the problem can be avoided entirely by instituting a real-time measurement program. We'll revisit this topic in some detail later. Either way, the issue is not to be ignored. If the research is to provide valid answers, you must use back-end analytic techniques or real-time measurements.

3. Recall bias is created when participants are asked to think back and remember prior happenings. Measurement programs based on delayed evaluations of a service interaction are predicated on the caller's recall of the interaction. This recall is bound to be faulty. The longer the time frame and the less important or vivid the interaction with the contact center, the larger the recall bias introduced. Anything other than real-time measurement inherently introduces recall bias (error).

Many studies have shown that customers often inaccurately recall information. In some cases customers over-recall, and in others, they under-report past events causing recall bias (Brennan, Chan, Hini and Esslemont, 1996; Sudman, Finn and Lannom, 1984; Sudman and Bradburn, 1974). Over-reporting is the most typical response of consumers when asked to recall events (Brennan, et al., 1996). From a contact center perspective, it may be tempting to characterize this as a good thing since over-reporting drives the interaction scoring higher than deserved. The bias causes the results to be positively skewed and is not an accurate representation of the reality of the service-delivery process. With inflated scores, the management team cannot be expected to make the changes in the contact center that are necessary to maximize the customer experience, increase customer loyalty and boost shareholder wealth.

When asked survey questions, consumer recall of the experience is affected by several factors, including the time allowed to answer each question (differences across interviewers equals interviewer bias), the involvement the customer has with the product/service, the order of the events being recalled, and the presence or absence of comparisons (Sudman and Kalton, 1986; Sudman and Bradburn, 1982). Recall under these circumstances becomes biased and may lead, among other things, to inaccurate assumptions of how consumers will behave when applying the results to business practice (Pearson, Ross and Dawes, 1992).

Researcher-Created Bias

Since researchers are in the business to eliminate biases, it may be counterintuitive to claim researcher-created biases actually exist. Basically, these are divided as designer one-size-fits-all bias, research designs that include delays that could be avoided and the problems that result from those delays, and analyst errors created by using simplistic statistical analysis tools when other tools would provide much better intelligence.

1. One-size-fits-all bias. Be aware that companies that sell research services do not always apply scientific principles to the center's circumstances, but rather seek to squeeze all of their projects into a single mold. Many speak from "their" findings on these project molds, but these findings are often not replicated or validated by research scientists, nor are the findings consistent with the body of research on customer measurement. It is not possible to anticipate the many distortions that can arise from trying to force circumstances to fit into preconceived notions. The output from such a measurement program would need to be subjected to substantial scrutiny in all aspects of the research before any confidence could be placed in it. Since even "canned" research programs are expensive, why not see to it that the contact center gets full value for the money by having the program designed by an expert willing to work within the confines of the center's true parameters? Doing so may or may not be more costly, but it certainly costs less than canned research. You wouldn't buy shoes that were "one size fits all"; why try that kind of research endeavor?

2. Biases inherent in delay designs. Recall bias was discussed above as a respondent bias based on the likelihood of the respondent's faulty memory as the time between the interaction and the measurement increases. Here, we look at it less from the respondent side and more from the designer side.

One of the main objections to substituting a real-time survey methodology for delayed measurement is the desire to evaluate both the service interaction and fulfillment on the same survey. This delay, which is necessary for fulfillment to occur, is unavoidable with this "get it all at once" research plan. However, for an accurate view of the contact center service experience, the evaluation should take place as closely to the time of interaction as possible — it cannot be delayed. Doing so creates a time gap in the contact center's performance results. Mail surveys, in particular, have a long built-in delay. Customers are unlikely to remember the details of a three- or four-minute phone call several days or several weeks after it occurs. The longer the time between a customer's experience and his evaluation, the greater the potential for bias; beyond 24 to 48 hours, recall error rates can be as high as 60 percent.

To overcome the bias, it is necessary to create two separate measurement events: keep the follow-up phone interviews to secure fulfillment, repair or resolution results while capturing the contact center data in realtime. Subsequently, then, it is possible to take the results of the two measurement events and look at them holistically as actionable intelligence to implement positive change for the organization.

Another likely impact of gap variables created by unnecessary delays between performance and measurement is that agents will discount the feedback as non-specific and unreliable. This will certainly create resistance to the feedback and improvement programs, which is justified. Avoid the pain by avoiding the gap variable in the first place.

3. Quantitative analysis of gaps. As previously suggested, collecting customer satisfaction data may seem easy, but deciding on the methodology to gather it has a significant impact on the analysis. As we've stated, it's better to avoid unnecessary time delays that create "gap" variables. However, if a delay methodology will be used anyway, then it must be adjusted to correct the bias (error) that is inherent in this program design. According to scientific research, analyses from delayed evaluations have several biases (errors) and, therefore, are not reliable unless the data is "corrected" through quantitatively accounting for the evaluation gap by creating an additional weighted variable in the analysis. The delayed time or "gap" variable will account for the delay between the service *interaction* and the service *evaluation*, which will allow the researcher to accurately interpret the results. The greater the gap, the greater the bias and the greater the adjustment needed to generate actionable intelligence that the organization can use with confidence. Essentially, the gap is being controlled for statistically within the results, rather than assuming all data to be equal when the evaluations were gathered 24, 48 or 72 hours later (use the exact number of hours).

4. Small sample size. The point of taking a sample instead of surveying the entire population of callers is to save money. However, saving money is foolish if the results of the research cannot be generalized to the population. The sample size must be *large enough* for generalization to be valid. It is important not to cut corners here. If there is insufficient budget to draw a statistically valid sample, then there is no point to doing the research at all. A very complete, but necessarily difficult to understand discussion on sample size can be found in the appendix. We also provide a less difficult to understand, substantially complete discussion of this topic in Chapter 8.

5. Inappropriate or simplistic data analysis. As previously alluded to, a validly worded survey is the foundation of a good survey program. Secondly, an adequate sample size is required. But building a solid foundation goes for naught if the data are not appropriately analyzed. Typically, non-experts consider the analysis complete after computing only frequencies and means. Frequencies are counts of the responses. Means are average responses for the question. For example, let's use a 5-point rating scale for the question: "Overall, how would you rate the service you received on this call?" Assuming this data is collected at TIME 1, the frequencies could look like this:

Rating		Responses
5	excellent service	15
4	good service	25
3	average service	35
2	below average service	20
1	terrible service	05
Total subjects surveyed		100
Mean = 3.25		

(5x15) + (4x25) + (3x35) + (2x20) + (1x5)/100

One possible interpretation of the above would be to say that the typical caller (35 percent) perceived the receipt of average service (a rating of "3"). Alternatively, one could say that, based on the mean, the typical customer perceived an above-average level of service (with "3" as average service, and 3.25 as the mean).

Let us now explore this example set of scores to the same question predicated on the self-selection bias discussed above. This data is taken at TIME 2.

Rating		Responses
5	excellent service	35
4	good service	25
3	average service	05
2	below average service	15
1	terrible service	20
Total subjects surveyed		100
Mean = 3.40		

(5x35) + (4x25) + (3x05) + (2x10) + (1x20)/100

Again, it could be argued that the typical customer perceived the receipt of above-average service, as the mean is 3.40. If the data are examined over time, it could even be concluded that the center's average performance has improved from TIME 1 to TIME 2! But in TIME 1 versus TIME 2, the number of callers who received clearly substandard service was 25 percent and 35 percent, respectively. This should likely be interpreted as an emergency requiring a nearly draconian measure to correct. In actual fact, neither interpretation is likely to be particularly meaningful without other data to confirm it.

Seven Rules for Getting it Right

In addition to adding important insight for management, customer score explanations (survey comments) enable a more accurate level of individual accountability. In research, the collection of comments is referred to as qualitative data. This critical element is often omitted because it may be difficult to collect, process and analyze. Without this feature, a measurement program is immediately susceptible to errors that are not corrected.

When customers respond to surveys, the most common error is reversing the scale (scale flipping). In other words, they want to give positive scores, but, instead, give negative ones by mistake. A review of the comments can ensure correct interpretation of the scale and question. Proper assignment of the survey is evident, as well. Survey scoring or assignment errors account for an average 5 percent to 7 percent variation in scores, pre- and post-quality control. This is the amount of negligent exposure from errors in the data. Controlling for a 5 percent score variation lessens the need for correction factors, ensures more reliability in the results upon which to base management decisions, and allows your QA team to coach with confidence.

The bottom line for quality control is to avoid a need to defend this performance metric as a human resource tool. By instituting stringent quality control, all surveys pass the "Is it fair?" test, and then the right agents are held accountable for the right data. Your center's internal call quality monitoring program requires continuous calibration, rules and guidelines. In other words, a stringent process is needed to be successful. Your survey program is no different.

Research is a science as is the application of the results. "Garbage in equals garbage out." Dirty data is the equivalent of garbage for your measurement program. Considering the implications to staff management, overall call center management, and the center's ultimate value as the relationship manager for the company, it is better to do NO surveys than to do poor surveys. The following criteria will help you to critically evaluate your program or proposed program:

1. Use of the correct measurement methodology. The customer chooses the communication channel to your organization. Your survey of his or her experience should match the channel. Avoid survey "channel slamming" by employing immediate post-call surveys to evaluate telephonic customer service delivery, and email and/or Web surveys to evaluate the electronic channel. Mixed methodologies are likely to create survey malpractice exposure. To avoid survey malpractice, ensure that you are measuring the right things through the right channel.

2. Appropriate length. Protect your response rate and survey validity by fielding a survey that is just right; not too short and not too long. Monitor the point at which respondents drop off to determine if the survey is too long. Consider running more than one survey if the scope of the measurement need grows. Measuring becomes an addiction for those who can benefit from your continuous contact with customers. Don't attempt to measure everything in one survey; simply run additional ones. Don't allow excessive additions to your EQM voice of the customer survey.

3. Actionable results. Information must be more than just "interesting to know" and "what management wants to hear." Customer intelligence drives the organization and should be highly sought after. If your team and company executives are not clamoring for the information, there is room for improvement. Managing the customer experience is continuous, and must be proactive rather than reactive. The contact center is an effective intelligence partner for the company, beyond its own measurement needs. The value that the contact center's measurement program brings to the organization can erase the misconception of being a "cost" center, as long as it is done correctly.

4. Accurate results. Companies waste too much time, effort and resources chasing the wrong improvement efforts, which are derived from questionable survey results. Devote more time, effort and resources to survey design and implementation. Again, NO survey is better than a bad survey. Action on results is expected, so the direction for action must be accurate.

5. Measurement should complement existing programs. Surveying is part of a holistic approach. Call monitoring offers the firm's view of quality, while scientific surveying research offers the callers' view of quality. It should not be one or the other. Use both to complement quality assessment with a holistic view of the caller experience.

6. Retain the customer relationship. Measurement is intended to understand and then to reengineer the experience to be successful for the company and for the customer. When service interactions fail, quantification is not enough. It is irresponsible of the management team not to have immediate triggers to serve as a safety net for the relationship. When building your survey tool, include contact information in case the customer needs additional attention. This way, you will be able to save a customer relationship that might otherwise have been lost. Delayed measurement programs do not include the benefit of an immediate trigger.

7. Request-resolution and problem-resolution must be quantified. The various call-resolution calculations such as first-contact resolution (FCR) are most important from the customers' perspective. Just because your team or the agent views the call as "closed," doesn't mean the customer has the same impression. Reporting and acting on any FCR metric other than the one built up from the perspective of customers is negligence. A series of questions around the resolution topic must be included in your survey.

We all know that "cheap" can sometimes turn out to be very expensive. Cost-only decisions are rarely a comparison of apples-to-apples, although you intend that to be the case. Finding the least expensive survey option will allow you to check off the measurement requirement from your to-do list. However, with a low quality and a low value plan, the survey malpractice implications could easily be more than 100 times your annual measurement budget. Biased and inaccurate results affect the contact center's position within the organization as the momentum of effectiveness breeding efficiency never occurs. The right dials are not tweaked, and improvement is not made and certainly cannot be quantified.

Reflecting back to Chapter 2 on Human Resources, it is obvious that unfair measurement used for performance evaluation causes low agent morale and higher turnover. A lack of quality control enables scores that could be invalid and/or assigned to the wrong agent to be included in the scoring model. With all of these situations in play, unhappy managers equal unhappy agents, which, in turn, equal unhappy customers.

Ignorance about measurement contributes to survey malpractice. Design a customer intelligence plan and secure a greater ROI from the right measurement. View customer-driven quality monitoring to be less of a report card summary and more of a diagnostic tool to achieve best-in-class status. Agents respond to fair and equitable feedback and productive coaching, and this translates to happier customers. Educate and leverage all parts of the company about your measurement program and help them to achieve their goals. If the data are sound and analyzed properly, the results will be sound and, therefore, defendable. This leads to a greater ROI, but more importantly to greater value — to your organization, your employees and, most importantly, your customers.

Survey Malpractice Signs	Ways To Avoid Them
Only numeric responses	Use numeric combined with explanation
Experience-evaluation gap more than one hour	Immediate post-call surveys
Small sample size	Use representative sample at main levels of center
Items measured do not lead to actionable results	Measure the right things in the right way
For resolution percent, only ask: "Was your problem resolved today?"	Significantly inflates the call-resolution metric
No proactive protection of the relationship	An immediate alerting of service failure for effective relationship retention
Scale not connected to actionable results	Give customers, and yourself, a scale that will allow you to get the most information from the data
No quality control	Does it pass the "Is it fair?" test
Measuring five different aspects in one survey	Only ask survey questions related to the experience you want to measure; otherwise, have several surveys in the field

It should take little time and effort to convince executive management that scientifically designed surveying is necessary, but this is often where enormous resources are expended. Instead, the bulk of the effort should be spent on the scientific survey research program design itself.

Many contact center teams analyze what others are doing — either inside or outside the organization — and design and implement a measurement program that is believed to be best-in-class based on those observations. Just because another part of the firm or another center utilizes a particular measurement program does not mean imitation of that program will be right under other circumstances. Don't forget that surveying is a science not to be taken lightly, so follow the guidelines of this science when developing, executing and reporting results of a measurement program, and don't be so concerned with what other entities are doing.

Statistical analysis is not always the most "user-friendly" information.

Sometimes managers and other employees who must utilize the information in decision-making do so without complete understanding of the results (Brandt, 1999). Explaining statistical error corrections is not easy either, so most people tend not to do it at all. However ignoring the error does not mitigate it. When no adjustments are made for the inherent errors, the data will not be representative of the true feelings of the customers.

The consequence of using flawed results is a snowball effect. Decisions for investments in training, technology, marketing and/or research and development will be made with the expectation that they will have impacts which can be quantifiably captured with subsequent measurements. If questionable customer intelligence is the foundation for those decisions, it is quite possible that the wrong decisions will be made on behalf of the customer. Subsequent measurement of the effect(s) gained by the initiative will also be flawed and may or may not substantiate the ROI case. The investment plan is actually a guess made with more certainty than was truly possible. Once a mistake of this magnitude is made, there are certain to be future ramifications relative to credibility. Once credibility is lost, it is hard to regain. So here again, we have more pain that could be avoided with proper planning.

There Is No Standard Mold

Not every research need can fit into a standard mold. If an existing program that is right for another company is borrowed rather than designing an effective program based on the fundamentals of science and the firm's own unique organizational goals, it is important to think through the implications *a priori*. This is a step that is usually omitted to the firm's grief. It is necessary in advance to identify the sources of the supportive research, the quality of the research project, and the potential biases of the findings before being willing to adopt the measurement program. One would proceed with analysis of this data that is believed to provide an understanding of customers' satisfaction with the service experience. The results are then disseminated and used by management to make changes in service delivery in an effort to improve customer satisfaction. But the risk is that, rather than providing actionable intelligence to the organization, the firm is being exposed to a significant risk of loss in regard to customers, revenue and, ultimately, profit. The good news is that all is not lost, even under this highly unfavorable scenario. Most research programs can be repaired, replaced or re-applied to the proper venue within the organization.

This is where the doctors come in. Do it right to start with, or expect to call us later.

Part III takes up the EQM program in great detail. We get down to the details — maybe more than can be absorbed by the typical reader. But, then, we are pain doctors, and we're here to help those who are not able to get it all themselves.

Part III: The Alpha and Omega of the EQM Program

Chapter 7:
The Logic and Benefits
of a Sound EQM Program

We divide the External Quality Monitoring program into three chapters in Part III. First, we tout the benefits and logic behind the program to add some extra motivation to the reader for follow-through. Next, we develop the program itself based on science. Lastly, we provide a host of tips to help with the program.

Physicians use this three-part technique all the time. They tell you that, if you lose weight, your feet and back won't hurt so much, you may not need the diabetes medication any more (which is expensive and has side effects), and it may also ease your depression. These are the benefits and logic behind a weight-control program. Then the program itself, including diet, exercise, rest and whatever else seems needful, including interventions such as a "lap band," stomach stapling or a regime of medications, is detailed. Lastly, the doctor will provide some tips, such as lay out your exercise clothes the night before and put them on as soon as you get up. Then do your exercise first, since you might not to do it at all if you wait.

We social science doctors are keen observers of humans and so have learned from the physicians. We now offer you the same regime, which is tried and true.

Recently, some organizations have responded to the biases described in Chapter 6 and to the need for larger volumes of real-time feedback by adopting interactive voice response (IVR) based surveys. IVR surveys eliminate the delays and high costs associated with declining response rates to mail and phone surveys. In other words, they lessen "survey pain" compared to traditional mail and callback options.

IVR-based surveys are a definite improvement over old ways of soliciting customer feedback, especially in the contact center and service/support/repair environments. However, depending on the available technology, you may encounter problems, such as inflexible scripting and branching options and difficulty obtaining the internal resources needed to manage an ongoing program. Furthermore, capturing qualitative responses and analyzing customer feedback for each agent may not be possible, and effective execution is labor-intensive, as we will discuss later. Most glaringly, if the contact center relies on a low-level IVR tool for data collection, then the true voice of the customer is still missing. Technology is an enabler, but it cannot replace a scientifically designed research program. Simply put, just because you CAN measure, does not mean that you have a GOOD measurement program.

To capture customer intelligence, you need flexible scripting technology. Flexible scripting provides meaningful directions and messages to customers who are willing to participate in the survey (scripting options), and a means to automatically move on to the next logical questions (branching options). Over time, the products, services and policies of the company will change (change being the only constant in the business world) and flexibility is vital to a company's ability to alter its scripting and branching options. Holistically designed, integrated, sponsored programs that facilitate the culture of a Rally Cry for the Customer tend to survive cost-cutting measures, while piecemeal programs make convenient targets. As we will show later, qualitative responses are often key to understanding quantitative data, and it takes dedicated technology to collect and tag this information. Pinpointing the actual agents in need of praise or retraining is critical. Aggregated data alone is an inherently inefficient feedback tool: Agents as a whole will receive feedback, but not the isolated team or individuals most responsible for the specific issue. The boost in morale that an agent receives from a customer's actual words of praise on a job well done is irreplaceable and is the evidence that an agent is engaged and dedicated to the mission. Clearly, the ability to drill down to the level of the team or agent is crucial on multiple fronts. Last, and most critically, we cannot hear the wants and needs of the customer with simple, low-level IVR technology. We need technological sophistication as well as solid design, management planning and flexibility for both the short and long term to accurately gather, evaluate and use customer intelligence.

"Put a Tiger in Your Tank"

"Put a tiger in your tank" is the tag line of an old advertising campaign for Esso Oil Company that featured a smiling tiger. We recommend that you put a performer in your customer intelligence program. To help you do so, we have designed a platform to employ best practices: CATs®.

Advanced IVR survey applications must be a complete process for gathering, analyzing and providing results so management can act upon customer intelligence. Customer Relationship Metrics designed and built such a research platform, known as "CATs®," which stands for completely automated telephone survey. This advanced process utilizes IVR-type technology coupled with sound survey design, extraordinary flexibility in scripting and branching, and the ability to capture the actual recorded voice of your customer. By adopting advanced IVR technology as part of a complete process, it is possible to integrate best practices in customer relationship management into the EQM customer measurement program. Feedback from an advanced IVR program is less expensive per response than either mail or phone surveys (a topic we'll develop later in this chapter).

Here's how the CATs® Advanced IVR program works in a contact center. Callers are greeted with a request to provide feedback at the end of the call to determine the customer's satisfaction with the interaction, i.e., collect the service evaluation from the customer. The agent is unaware of the impending evaluation. When callers finish the transaction with an agent, they are connected to the advanced IVR survey (fully hosted and external or internal). Because the request for feedback is immediate and non-intrusive, completion and response rates are very high with confidence levels of +95 percent.

The customer's own words comprise the qualitative feedback. In addition to being asked to respond to various questions on a numeric scale, respondents are invited to comment on the experience. The CATs® Advanced IVR technology captures the customer's actual words and the transcription complements and elaborates on the scores. The comments are reported in aggregate as well as being attributed to specific calls and specific agents. In other words, the team or individuals can be paired with the feedback to permit targeted, disaggregated feedback to the appropriate level, all the way down to individuals.

Thanks to CATs® Advanced IVR, an alert process automatically initiates at a threshold determined by management. For instance, on a scale of 1 to 9, if a customer rates the overall experience at a 3 or below, the CATs® Advanced IVR technology offers a call-back to the customer and if the offer is affirmed, an immediate email alert is sent containing the customer information and audio file of the comment. The team can then launch a service recovery plan right away, thus avoiding negative word-of-mouth and the potential loss of the future revenue stream from the customer.

The CATs® Advanced IVR program is more robust than a stand-alone IVR system. With it, management gets graphical feedback in the form of an impact and performance chart based on the contact center's key drivers of customer satisfaction. Through their participation in the CATs® survey effort, customers provide feedback, which is interpreted for management's use. That feedback indicates whether the contact center is doing well or poorly and which performance items are important to customers. (These performance and impact terms are explained in greater detail with examples in a later chapter.) What could be more useful to management than the customer's own evaluation of where the center needs to improve?

Combining data collection with research principles led to the need for a formal process of survey calibration between the comments and the data. This is a labor-intensive process for which automation of these steps is not possible. It is no surprise that participants do not always follow directions when completing an evaluation. It is an unavoidable fact of conducting a research program. Therefore, the errors must be corrected using a systematic and consistent approach to obtain the utmost integrity, accuracy and fairness to create report cards from surveys.

Once raw customer feedback is captured, the survey calibration team transcribes and reviews every customer comment. Escalation protocol is applied to each evaluation and the data move through the validation process. Reporting "dirty" data that contain response errors in the performance management system is fundamentally, ethically and legally not an option. For these reasons alone, it is integral that the data reported be accurate. After more than a decade of using the post-call methodology, Customer Relationship Metrics has leveraged the experience from more than 8 million data points to minimize the possibility of measurement error. The option to minimize the importance of this process because it is labor-intensive is malpractice — it is difficult, but you must do it.

Because the Advanced IVR program gathers customer comments, frontline contact center managers can use it as a motivational tool. The spirit of the Rally Cry must be embodied in agent behavior to be heard by your customers. Think of the pride on a young child's face when a parent tacks her spelling test — the one with the big "A" — to the refrigerator door for everyone to see. Like all human beings, agents share a similar sense of pride in their work, and they beam when their successes are publicly praised. Unfortunately, customers who take time to write letters of praise are few and far between. However, many customers will take the time — immediately upon completion of the call — to speak a few words of praise and to validate that the Rally Cry has been heard. The Advanced IVR system records those comments; these are then transcribed and each agent receives a detailed scorecard of his or her contacts after the survey calibration process has been completed.

Benefits of CATs®

Now that we have highlighted some of the advantages of using CATs® as part of an EQM program, let's delve into a more thorough discussion of the topic. After all, a scientifically sound, comprehensive EQM program is a significant investment for the firm. Analyzing the expected outcomes is critical to assessing the project's worth.

Customers, agents, supervisors, trainers and center management can all benefit from this program. Not all companies will benefit in each of the ways listed below, but the potential is there depending on the processes already in use in each company.

Correctly integrating the EQM program into the center's measurement initiative (using CATs® with an Advanced IVR program) results in a host of process improvements that may include any or all of the following:

Agents

• Performance feedback that inspires rather than deters. While no one likes criticism, the words of actual customers often motivate agents by clarifying the issues from a customer's perspective. Simply understanding may not be enough to change behavior (research shows it seldom is), but it can lay the necessary groundwork.

• Receptivity to training initiatives. These initiatives focus on the improvements that customers say a given agent needs.

• Appreciation of praise. While most people claim to be driven by money, research suggests that often motivators of a non-monetary nature are actually more important.

Supervisors

• Clear direction that focuses improvement initiatives in the right areas — those areas that customers say are important to them — is a benefit not to be downplayed. Different teams have different opportunities.

• Avoiding wasted time, money and energy poured into misguided change initiatives.

• Uniting the voice of the customer with operational measurements, resulting in a more balanced scorecard for the center.

Center Management

• Insight into the best ways to stratify the firm's service for different types of customers based on their value or their potential value to the organization.

• Armor to defend the center's purpose, which is the growth and protection of the customer base.

• Increased customer share (and the ability to prove it), leading to a higher ROI for the EQM initiative.

• Statistically valid data collection tools needed to pursue Six Sigma quality in the service delivery processes.

Comparisons of Data Collection Methods

Contact centers measure quality in many ways. The ultimate objective of any EQM program is to answer the question, "How well are our customers served by our contact center and by our company?" The measurement methods utilized are critical to obtaining valid answers to these questions. In today's "commoditized" economy, the only differentiating and competitive advantage a company has is the quality of service it provides. All too often, despite having the best product, companies with poor service fail.

The design of a comprehensive program requires the identification of each interaction channel to be measured and then to complete a comparison of the strengths and weaknesses of several methods. Well-conceived research programs include different methods, such that the weakness of one is ameliorated by the strength of the other. Doing so creates a complete, robust EQM measurement strategy. Once you have attained a holistic strategy, we recommend a balanced scorecard for performance/incentive-based compensation.

The survey methods to be considered should include completely automated telephone surveys, the Internet (including emails), mail and live interviews.

Labor is widely known to be the most expensive production input, so the most cost-effective methods are those that minimize human involvement. The most automated methods include automated surveys, Internet-based and telephone (called CATI, computer-assisted telephone interview) and mail, as a distant last place.

The greatest increase in contacts to an organization comes from Internet-related interaction channels. Thus, Internet surveys are extremely popular because of the perception of low cost, but cannot be used for every measurement situation. When a customer chooses to do business via the Internet, it makes sense to gather their perceptions of quality via the same medium. Internet surveys can be delivered via email, Web site pop-up, or a redirect to a Web page on the organization's Web site (or hosted by a third party). Customer use of Internet and email is not interchangeable. We recommend conducting experiments to determine which method(s) are best for the specific clientele of a given contact center. The Internet methods share some benefits with the CATs® method; however, many people are apt to delete emails unopened and close pop-ups unexamined. There are also software packages designed to block pop-ups and sort out spam. Spam folders are seldom checked, and if your missive lands there, it is unlikely to be read and acted on. Consequently, the participation rates for both Internet and email are lower than for CATs®. When evaluating the use of this method, remember that cheap can be expensive.

IVR technology is another method on the rise. An IVR is less robust than a CATs® survey system due to internal resource limitations, design and analysis issues, such as trunk capacity limitations, report production and the inability to capture customer comments or to provide service recovery alerts, as well as the absence of a survey calibration process. In short, while the use of an IVR alone is better than several other methods, it still does not provide flexibility, the value of customer comments as rewards to agents and training feedback for supervisors, or initiate a service recovery system when an interaction goes bad. And, without a survey calibration process, the effectiveness of the results is marginal.

Mail is the slowest and least economical of the survey solutions. Mail may seem inexpensive, but the actual cost of each survey includes postage out, manual processing upon return, and an entirely different handling system compared to Internet, email, IVR and CATs®. Every human hand involved increases cost and delays feedback. Furthermore, any kind of service recovery activity is ineffective, as the damage has long been done and internalized by the customer by the time mail feedback arrives.

Customers are often completely indifferent when asked to evaluate service 10 days or more after the experience. For most people, a three-and-a-half minute interaction two weeks ago is impossible to recall with much accuracy and, therefore, even with high participation rates (and these are unlikely), the results cannot be considered valid or actionable. Response rates for mail are low and will likely continue to drop as new technologies become commonplace in the average household. The overwhelming volume of junk mail that households receive keeps response rates depressed. After all, from the customer's short-term perspective, this is just another piece of unsolicited mail that more clearly serves the interest of the company sending it than the household that receives it. The survey results matter much more to the firm, center and agent than to the typical customer. Mail surveys are also very impersonal, and any attempt to personalize mail surveys adds expense and time.

The results of mail surveys are difficult to use as an agent feedback tool. As householders, agents also receive volumes of junk mail that they subsequently trash without a second thought. Agents are likely to quickly express their lack of confidence in negative results of a mail survey. In turn, this will increase the volume of "noise" from other agents, who may also feel free to challenge their feedback. (Never underestimate the effects of "groupthink" or "mob rule.") Lastly, as previously noted, the process for mail surveys can be conservatively characterized as lengthy.

Live interviews are the most expensive way to gather customer feedback. Like mail, if the time lapse between the interaction and the call to invite a customer to participate is too long, then the degradation of memory becomes too great for a proper evaluation, resulting in recall bias. Finally, the cost to phone the customer for a live interview adds another layer of expense to the survey effort.

In recent years, outbound calling has fallen into disfavor with customers, and households have taken more creative measures to protect their privacy. These include answering machines, screening calls with number recognition technology, and participation in no-call lists sponsored by both the federal government and some states. While people in Indiana get this service free from the state government, Florida residents pay an annual fee to participate and do so gladly. The result is a smaller population of people participating in telephone surveys leading to small sample sizes and the biases created by that bane. As for the people who are willing to participate, organizations find themselves getting the same feedback from the same people. This non-random drawing of participants exhibits the self-selection bias previously discussed, which, in turn, degrades the results.

Various Data Collection Techniques

	Door-to-door	Mall	Phone	Mail	Fax	Email	Web
Response rates	15%	29%	75%	35-63%	25%	8-37%	26%
Percent bad addresses				0-19%	41%	19-20%	24%
Response time in days (mean)				13-18	9	4-6	7
Number of days to receive 45% response				13		1	
Number of days to receive 80% response				28		9	
Fixed costs				$59	$57	$57	$57
Unit costs				$1.56	$0.56	$0.01	$0.01
Variable costs (200 surveys sent)				$312	$112	$2	$2
Total cost				$371	$169	$59	$59

Table reproduced from *Basic Marketing Research* (2005), Churchill and Iacobucci, Thomson Southwestern, page 226.

Use CATs® to Avoid Survey Pain

A scientifically sound EQM program is the only remedy for survey pain. "While there are many roads to the top of the mountain," some are more efficient and dependable than others. We encourage a combination of data collection techniques to provide dependable, actionable intelligence. Specifically, we urge a sound IQM program harnessed to a scientifically designed EQM program. To eliminate several sources of bias, the CATs® platform surpasses EQM programs that use alternative technologies. It also includes an alert system to undertake recovery initiatives in the event of a service failure. The CATs® platform automates the recording and subsequent transcription of a customer's actual comments, and this feedback aids in training, rewarding and motivating future efforts by the agents. The CATs® platform eliminates a time gap, and therefore the pain, of trying to statistically or otherwise account for the bias imposed by that gap.

"Put a tiger in your tank — Use CATs®" and avoid survey pain.

Chapter 8:
Developing a Scientifically Sound EQM Program

Developing a scientifically sound program to capture customer intelligence through the external quality monitoring (EQM) program is neither simple nor straightforward, but it is the only certain way to avoid survey pain. Each individual element of the program must be scrutinized and weighed for its potential contribution to or elimination of error. Additionally, it is necessary to assess the cost of optimal versus suboptimal options in terms of dollars spent versus benefit or detriment to the validity or reliability of the research. For example, it hardly makes sense to do the "perfect" research (and there truly is no such "critter") if it costs the world to accomplish it.

First, we'll look at the appropriate channel for collecting the customer intelligence data. We argue that the single best channel for collecting this data should be dictated by the means employed by the customer to initiate contact. That is, the best channel is the one selected voluntarily by the customer.

Next, we'll consider the question of sample size. Few people would argue that all customers must be surveyed every time — this is cost-prohibitive. The science of sampling can help determine the appropriate size.

While most contact centers focus solely on quantitative data, qualitative data can be captured at the same time with very little additional cost. Qualitative data is particularly valuable for several reasons, which we'll discuss as well.

Also of concern is the overall quality of the data. Specifically, dirty data has become a hot topic now that data-mining techniques are in vogue.

Finally, we'll turn our attention to data analyses. Often companies settle for averages rather than true scientific analysis techniques. Whether this choice is a "non-choice" where one analyst copied the techniques of his predecessors, a lack of sophistication with statistics or the preference of operational or executive management, the use of superior data analysis routines can definitely enhance decision-making. With the ready availability of analysis routines and plenty of experts willing to sell their advice, there is little reason to settle for mere frequencies and averages.

Rather than simply narrate, we'll provide concrete examples of the analyses and interpretations of data from our own consulting files.

Survey Channel Slamming

When trying to provide the best service to customers, it is not a good idea to create disservice by attempting to force all customers through one communication channel. This is fairly intuitive, and is the reason that most contact centers provide multiple points of access for their customers. Multichannel integration is something almost all contact centers now manage. Providing several channel options for customers reflects that the center is in tune with the customers' desire for high-, medium- and low-touch customer service interfaces. Contact centers can encourage customers to serve themselves on low-touch issues with the cheapest technology and, if done correctly, will not jeopardize customer loyalty. With all the efforts to reduce cost via the use of high-tech/low-touch service channels, it is tempting to force electronic surveys on all customers to lower the cost of measuring customer concern, regardless of the original method of contact. Salespersons offering electronic survey solutions will argue that it makes no difference how customers are contacted, but common sense dictates otherwise. Do not let the science of surveying get lost in the hype. Beware and be aware that cheap can be very expensive, and an "easy, quick fix" may not provide any actionable data.

Customer feedback gathered by a flawed measurement methodology can easily mislead and ultimately misdirect the service strategy. One of the largest and most easily avoided flaws today is "survey channel slamming." The center's measurement strategy must reflect the mission to be customer-focused and an easy-to-reach business partner, and that means congruence with the customer-selected channel of communication. If the customer emails the company, sending a U.S. mail survey to gather an evaluation of the interaction is survey channel slamming. If the customer calls the center for service and receives an email survey, this is survey channel slamming. This flaw in measurement adds a new, yet avoidable, bias to the data-collection effort. Not only that, ignoring customer preferences can generate a service weakness that may create additional dissatisfaction; this undermines the validity of the EQM measurement program. Obviously, survey channel slamming is dangerous to the measurement program and is completely avoidable.

Survey Methods by Contact Channel

Contact Type	Correct Measurement Method
Telephone	Telephone (Automated or Live)
Web/Email	Email
Chat	Email
Mail	Mail

Customer Relationship Metrics

Unless the company conducts a *significant* amount of customer interface electronically, it cannot be confident that a comprehensive and high-quality list of customer email addresses is on hand. Except in the case of online-only companies, businesses cannot assume that all customers have the ability, much less the willingness, to contact the center electronically. Therefore, sole reliance on an electronic method of surveying adds another unnecessary bias to the survey research due to the absence of an important and missing percentage of the customer base.

Customers who call the contact center may not have an email address or may not regularly update their records. This should generally deter the impulse to survey channel slam an email to them to evaluate the service delivered on a telephone call. Centers cannot afford to rely solely on feedback collected electronically because the sample is inherently biased.

Customers also have privacy concerns about how information will be used, especially email addresses. Electronic surveys may be viewed as "spam" and alienate customers or create dissatisfaction with the process itself. This can further weaken the measurement program.

The inability to randomly sample from the customer population due to channel selection bias prevents results from being generalized. So if it is not possible to randomly sample from each channel, then don't measure at all. Invest the available research budget into a statistically viable program that yields results worthy of the management team's attention. The center's return on investment (ROI) will be significantly higher even though the initial cost may be slightly more.

To summarize, to best measure customer service, an immediate evaluation is needed via your customers' preferred channel. If the customer initiates contact telephonically, conduct an immediate post-call survey. If the customer emails, respond with a Web-based survey opportunity.

To measure fulfillment, service or repair issues (or back-office work), a follow-up, delayed survey is appropriate and, here, the use of a complementary survey methodology would not be considered survey channel slamming.

Don't feel pressured to use an "in" but ineffective research program. Remember that just because it is cheap, easy and sold by a personable individual does not mean it is the right data collection methodology. A holistic measurement program for an organization is accomplished by determining the method of measurement for each customer interaction channel and should follow common sense and sound science, and, therefore, use multichannel methodologies.

Getting the Sample Size Right

A crucial issue in survey design is sample size. (Please consult the appendix for the research equations behind sample size.) The sample should be large enough to permit sufficiently precise estimates that serve the research needs, while small enough to fit the available budget (Erdos and Morgan, 1983).

If the entire universe is surveyed (in this case, each caller into a center), there is no need for sampling, and consequently, there is no sampling error. The natural and unavoidable consequence of such a decision is the immense expense. The instant a sample is selected, a sampling error is introduced. The advantage to a random or probability sample is that the error is measurable and, therefore, knowable.

Note well the intention. It is desirable, without incurring the terrific expense of collecting data from the entire universe, to collect data from a subset of the relevant universe, analyze this, and then generalize the results to the universe as a whole. The question becomes, "How many subjects must be surveyed in order to do this?" The answer is fairly complex and depends on the critical effect size, the acceptable *alpha* error or significance level, and the corollary *beta* error.

We can estimate effect size and the measure of variability (or standard deviation around it) by conducting preliminary research or on the basis of similar research conducted in the past. The *alpha* error, or significance level, chosen by the researcher is generally .05 or .01. Sample size is critically affected by the level of uncertainty that the researcher and center are willing to accept. Generally acceptable levels of uncertainty in most research are 5 percent and 1 percent, and relate to the possibility that the conclusion about the null hypothesis (nothing is happening) is wrong. Obviously, a 5 percent or .05 chance of error is less stringent than 1 percent or .01 chance. The more stringent the significance level, the greater the necessary sample size (Kraemer and Thiemann, 1987).

The *beta* error is the likelihood of rejecting the research hypothesis when we should have accepted it. Essentially, this means that we believe the research is *without* value when in fact it *is* valuable. Naturally, we want the probability of making this type of error to be as small as is financially feasible. Computed as 1-*beta*, it is generally known as power and ideally will be .99. Unfortunately, "ideally" is nearly always infeasible as the number of subjects required is usually prohibitive.

An additional layer of complexity results when a stratified or a random sample of several groups is dictated. This is what is required in a contact center, as the desire is to sample a given number of calls each month from each agent. In this way, it is possible to provide feedback to each agent regarding satisfaction scores that can then be useful (but not statistically significant) in coaching. Therefore, it is necessary to draw random samples from each agent's calls totaling a set number of responses for each over the measuring period.

Past experience in the contact center industry tells us that the target rate to evaluate performance at the center level is approximately 400 surveys and is based on the Laws of Random Sampling Theory (explained in the following chart). To have a tolerated error rate of ± 5% (which is commonly acceptable) in the measurement period, it must contain 384 completed surveys. For calculation purposes and to ensure receiving this amount, round the number to 400.

Sample Size Requirements for Levels of Precision (99% to 95%)

Tolerated Error	95 samples in 100	99 samples in 100
1%	9,604	16,587
2%	2,401	4,147
3%	1,067	1,843
4%	600	1,037
5%	384	663
6%	267	461
7%	196	339

The above cells assume that the sample is generated randomly from the population of interest.

Sample size computations only take into account statistical sampling error. Keep in mind that other biases exist and must be accounted for when putting together a measurement program.

A Customer Relationship Metrics measurement program adopts certain practices. The actual number of completed surveys collected each month is multiplied by the cost per to account for the increase/decrease in customer participation. This scenario plans for completing the minimum requirement of 400 surveys per month, per center, to achieve a 95 percent confidence level for center-level reporting. The actual number of completed surveys will vary slightly depending on caller participation. Depending on the number of agents, the target total will be set higher to achieve evaluations for all agents. The rate for the invitation can be increased or decreased to meet a target rate. Sometimes clients ask us to adjust the error rate or confidence level. However, we must first determine the cost/benefit of doing so. Simply put, it may not be economical for the benefits gained. Usually a higher confidence level is more desirable.

Sample size is a critical issue when holding the center accountable for performance scores. To make a generalization with confidence, the metric must be representative of all calls and with an adequate sample size. Skimping on sample size is not worth the savings and it will tend to undermine the confidence with which assertions can be made. Remember that small sample sizes do not generalize and, therefore, are not representative of all service delivered.

Six Sigma initiatives are particularly sensitive to valid measurement data as input into the analysis of initiatives. So if you are considering either Six Sigma or Human Sigma (Fleming, Coffman and Harter, 2005), be aware of the potential need to reexamine the validity and reliability of the measures as well as adequacy of sample size.

Neither Qualitative NOR Quantitative: Both Are Necessary

Most research endeavors use only quantitative measures. This is not particularly surprising. Researchers tend to take a great many statistics classes and, as such, specialize in the manipulation of numbers. Rare indeed is the researcher conversant in non-quantitative methods. Furthermore, qualitative methods are somewhat messier, more time-consuming and often more difficult to coax "proof" from, since most people understand "proof" as a number. Yet the basic fact is unassailable: Qualitative methods have the power to teach what is not already known.

Researchers start out with research hypotheses; that is, they look for what they expect to find. This is the way scientific research is conducted all over the world. But what if the research hypotheses are wrong or, let's just say, not totally right? How do we proceed from here? If qualitative measures were included in the data capture, even a small number, then there is hope of discovering the direction to pursue.

Moreover, subjects make errors in recording their answers or they sometimes feel that there is not a place to list their actual concerns. Providing qualitative data capture provides explanations for pain felt as a customer, suggestions for improving the experience, and can correct for potential biases, as well.

Both kinds of data are needed to give a holistic view of the customer experience; solely one or the other is not enough. Each has its place. Quantitative data collection is imperative for the *score* of the experience and qualitative for the *why* of the score. Quantitative data is usually the scaled item and can easily be analyzed by means, charts and statistical manipulation, and the focus is on the numbers. This type of analysis in isolation can be misleading. Qualitative data provides flexibility — customers can explain their scores and elaborate on their reasoning behind these scores. Qualitative data allows the direct voice of the customer to come through the process.

Clean Versus Dirty Data

The ills of dirty data have been complained of in computer and technology magazines for many years. Dirty data and the need to scrub it is more widely discussed now due to the trend in data-driven decision-making (D3M), sometimes called "data mining" in education (Mercurius, 2005), as well as business and other venues. Dirty data can simply be defined as errors in the data, however they may have accumulated. We most often hear about them in reference to database input errors, and we tend to see solutions to the dirty data problem that rely on quality control at the front end of processes (such as during data input) or the purchase and use of special software designed to detect and repair certain types of errors. However, data errors may not be the result of faulty data input per se, especially when quantitative data capture is automatic, as it is with Customer Relationship Metrics' survey calibration protocol. End-data scrubbing can be a necessary and highly effective means to eliminate some errors.

Recall that one of the aims of a customer survey program is to hold agents accountable for their respective performances within the contact center. Certain outcomes are critically important to both managers and agents, such as incentives, bonuses, praise and recognition, and those outcomes stream from the results of the measurement programs, whether the data are dirty or clean. Agents will scrutinize their performance appraisals for fault if their scores are less than expected. Since the outcomes are important, it behooves all parties to do everything feasibly possible to ensure the cleanliness of the data.

In a customer feedback program designed to hold agents accountable for their performance, one of the most important tasks to perform and one of the most often overlooked processes is the back-end quality control process called survey calibration. Some examples will help to clarify what can be corrected and the impact those corrections can have.

Example 1:

> "The agent who assisted me with my problem was very helpful; however, the generalist, Bonnie Harris, who answered my phone call in the very beginning put me on hold for over five minutes twice and never gave me any kind of an answer. Then she got aggravated whenever I had to be transferred to an agent."

If there is no back-end quality control process, this survey would be assigned to the second agent (as the last one to handle the call). But note that the scores from this survey were based on the performance of the generalist, Bonnie Harris, and were very negative. Based on the customer's explanation, Customer Relationship Metrics removed the survey from the second agent and attached it the rightful owner — Bonnie Harris. Anything less than this due diligence creates "noise" associated with the program. Agents need to focus on the service ratings of THEIR callers and not be presented with any legitimate reasons to spend time discounting the survey results.

Example 2:

> "The comments on this survey were not for this last representative, but for the initial rep I dealt with. I was attempting to get her to cancel some orders and when I asked her to transfer me, she hung up on me."

Once again, if you were not performing a back-end quality control process, this survey would be assigned to the last representative (as the last one to handle the call, maybe the one spoken to when the customer called back). The scores from the survey would be attached to the wrong representative.

Example 3:
> "Please make the first three questions 8s. I made a mistake on grading and didn't catch it until it was too late. I want to make sure Cheryl gets credit for a good job."

In this survey, we see a very common mistake made by customers. Miscoding is a frequent dirty data issue, but our back-end quality control process is designed to catch this and ensure that the customer's true voice is heard.

For believable and defendable results, quality control must be mandated. Customer Relationship Metrics follows a stringent, multiphase survey calibration process. If we did not, agents would be held accountable for poor performance or get the praise that is due some other agent. In either case, letting these errors to go uncorrected would encourage every agent in the contact center to trace down every instance of inappropriately credited feedback, provide ammunition for arguments where results were not as expected and, in general, create more dissatisfaction among agents than necessary. Success or failure of the EQM program is contingent on quality, and should never create dissatisfaction for customers OR employees. The noise and pain described here is totally avoidable. Do not create unnecessary discontent and discomfort.

Because transcription is not "free," there could be a tendency to skip the back-end data cleaning and simply say that the first pass is "close enough." But is it? To what extent does the quality control process affect the scores of the tens of thousands of post-call surveys Customer Relationship Metrics collects each week? On average, between 4 percent and 5 percent of the surveys collected need to be corrected. This may not sound like much, but consider the use made of the results, and what damage dirty-data decisions may do to processes, much less the people, dependent on those results. Clearly, 4 percent to 5 percent is too high.

To show the actual impact of dirty data on the scores, Customer Relationship Metrics tracked the quality control process for one contact center with 110 agents and analyzed its 600 surveys. The results are shown in the following table. Imagine using the dirty data for process decision-making or to reward agents. Better yet, to which numbers would operational management want to be held accountable?

Impacts of Quality Control
110 Reps / 600 Surveys

Raw Data (Before Quality Control)	
Company Satisfaction	54%
Agent Satisfaction	78%
First-Contact Resolution	72%
Pass QC (After Quality Control)	
Company Satisfaction	59%
Agent Satisfaction	84%
First-Contact Resolution	75%

In this instance, customers had much more satisfaction with their experience than initially suspected, both for the company and the agent, and there was higher first-contact resolution than was originally reported. Think about the impact this has on the contact center ROI. Clearly, with dirty data, the ROI was lower in this instance and the credibility of the results could be called into question. Just as importantly, the center's job is to listen to the actual voice of the customer *sans* response errors.

Not Just Averages: Scientific Analysis

Most contact centers that currently collect customer feedback only look at high-level summary results. Most of these customer feedback data reports provide very basic analysis of the information from the caller satisfaction survey, such as frequencies and means. While this information is interesting, it limits insight into the callers' evaluation of service provided by the center. In no sense can these rudimentary reports be said to provide a true scientific analysis of the data. Using these simplistic analyses is akin to having tunnel vision as opposed to a panoramic view.

Managers cannot afford to look at data as a static condition; rather, the relationship between variables is dynamic. In a contact center, changing one input has the potential to drastically affect many outputs. This is known as a "cascading effect" where tweaking one variable is likely to impact several others. Therefore, we must look beyond data as a static summary of numbers into the interrelationships by applying analytics to the data.

From the basic frequencies and means, you cannot determine what elements will *drive change* in overall caller satisfaction. It is possible to know how many customers are satisfied from the individual questions that were asked, but it is impossible to know *why* they feel this way and how the individual variables *impact* overall satisfaction. Without knowing the *why*, one does not have actionable intelligence, which lowers the measurement program's ROI.

The goals of an EQM program are to collect data that provide accurate:

1. PERFORMANCE measures. This is the caller's evaluation of the attributes of service, which is rendered as the mean (i.e., average) level of performance.

2. IMPACT values. These identify the service attributes that are statistically significant to caller satisfaction. These are essentially the drivers of satisfaction. From the customer's point of view, these are what really matter.

The performance means and calculated impact values of each service attribute enable the quantitative identification of areas in which service performance may be below an acceptable level as defined by the data collected from the callers. Management can, with this type of analysis, effectively address specific improvement areas that drive satisfaction and, therefore, contribute substantially to the center's ROI. Without analyzing the relationships, it is not possible to determine which static number truly affects the perception of service delivery.

For the **PERFORMANCE** part of the analysis, the survey results from callers are normalized to a 100-point grading scale. The intent of this step is to aid interpretability. Our mathematical world is founded on base 10, thanks to the fact that humans evolved with 10 digits. So we think and talk in terms of tens and hundreds and fractions thereof, which we call percentages. This lifetime of utilizing the base 10 has fitted us for easy interpretation of base 10 outcomes. We automatically understand what 90 percent means, but would have to do substantial mental processing to relate 8/9ths (which is 88.88 percent) to the real world. For simplicity, outcome scales are often automatically "normalized" to base 10. (Note the term implies anything other than base 10 is not "normal"!)

The alert reader may wonder why the data are not collected in base 10 in the first place. The answer is grounded in sound research considerations. Consider this 5-point scale:

Completely Satisfied	Somewhat Satisfied	Indifferent	Somewhat Dissatisfied	Completely Dissatisfied
1	2	3	4	5

This scale's odd number of options allows callers to express complete indifference as the middle option. Complete indifference is a legitimate choice, and a scale composed of an even number of options (such as a base-10 scale) does not allow for that expression.

Secondarily, contact centers must balance the desire for complete precision in capturing the customer's feelings and the cost and usefulness for doing so. For example, it would be possible to collect caller feedback on a continuous scale rather than the 5-point discrete scale illustrated above. It would look as follows:

Please record your degree of satisfaction with wait time below by placing a mark on the line.

Completely Satisfied   **Completely Dissatisfied**

_____X _____

Theoretically, it would be possible to determine exactly the customer's satisfaction as indicated by the location of the X. But would a respondent to such a scale really feel the difference between the X above and one 1/16th of an inch to the right? This gets to looking more like the appearance of precision rather than actual precision. In reality, few researchers use continuous scales as they are costly to code, require differing data analysis techniques, and do not clearly result in superior understanding of the respondent's intent. Basically, this option costs more and is less clear.

Most research endeavors utilize 5-, 7- or 9-point scales depending on the desired level of precision, and then normalize the output using a transformation table. As long as all output measures are normalized, there are no negative effects of the procedure and interpretability is enhanced.

This data transformation is possible to calculate no matter how fine or gross the graduations of the scale originally used for the surveys. Due to research considerations, many of our clients use a 9-point scale for their immediate post-call surveys, and that scale is normalized (as shown in the chart on the following page).

9-Point Scale Normalized to 100-Point Grading Scale

1	0
2	12.5
3	25
4	37.5
5	50
6	62.5
7	75
8	87.5
9	100

Using this simple data transformation, the results will now appear on a 100-point grading scale. These normalized scores are then analyzed and the mean values for the questions (attributes or variables) involved in the survey become the **PERFORMANCE** bars as seen in the figure on the page 165. These means (or averages) will establish a metric for **PERFORMANCE** on each attribute that can be tracked over time.

Research shows that a normalized **PERFORMANCE** score of 85+ is a level high enough to contribute to customer loyalty, while those below become an area of focus for improvement. However, whether the scores are normalized or not, the mean scores or averages remain a static measure.

The computation of the **IMPACT** scores identifies the caller's assessment of how each question (i.e., attribute or variable) impacts overall satisfaction. This process requires an additional layer of analysis beyond the calculation of mean **PERFORMANCE** scores. The **IMPACT** analysis will quantitatively identify how a change in one attribute can lead to a change in another as well as in overall satisfaction itself.

The **IMPACT** values are computed by regression analysis. This analysis considers the mathematical relationships AMONG the points of measurement so that the results are relational rather than static. As a result, regression analysis of caller satisfaction data concretely demonstrates the amount of impact that each attribute has on overall satisfaction. This allows management to monitor specific areas where changes will raise caller satisfaction with the center and to concentrate on the areas that are most important to the customer. Since this analysis can be provided for each center location, each team, each queue or each type of customer, better defined results and areas targeted for change will become apparent. Therefore, the dollars spent on coaching and training can be maximized by implementing change only for the specific areas that need it most (i.e., provide the "biggest bang for the buck").

An example of a regression model stated in words rather than in symbols follows. Overall satisfaction with the agent is a function of seven variables (or attributes) captured by seven corresponding questions:

1. the agent's ability to quickly understand the reason for the call (Q1);
2. attention to details (Q2);
3. being treated as a valued customer (Q3);
4. the product and service knowledge (Q4);
5. the completeness of the answer provided (Q5),
6. the confidence in the answer/solution instilled by the agent (Q6); and
7. demonstrated ownership of the issue (Q7).

This model is mathematically represented as:

Overall Satisfaction = f (Q1, Q2, Q3, Q4, Q5, Q6, Q7)

This means that overall satisfaction is a function of the answers to questions 1 through 7. By running the regression analysis, we learn what that function actually looks like so that we can say with confidence that certain attributes (questions) impact caller satisfaction more than others. Before we discuss how this is done, let's consider a conceptual example of what we just stated.

My grandmother baked great cakes. She varied the recipe based on what ingredients were at hand and a certain degree of whimsy. We made a game of guessing what ingredients, in what proportion, using what processes had been used to make each creation. A simple cake would be composed of some kind of flour, a sweetener, salt, eggs, a leavening agent, a liquid such as milk, water or fruit juice, and a variety of spices in varying quantities. The frosting was a whole other game. We would taste the cake and judge it based primarily on taste, but also on texture and appearance. Our outcome variables then were taste, texture and appearance.

We always discovered the recipe by making our guesses and then getting the recipe from Grandma. The ingredients (flour, sugar, etc.) are analogous to variables 1 through 7 in the previous example (Q1 understanding, Q2 attention, Q3 treatment, etc.). The exact proportions are analogous to the measurements (for example, 1 cup or 2 teaspoons) used in the recipe and the beta weights that come out the regression equation (which we will discuss in detail below). The performance measure amounts to a judgment on the part of the eaters as to the tastiness, texture and appearance of the cake. In contact center research, the outcome is more likely to be service satisfaction.

With this homey conceptual example in mind, let's see how the regression is accomplished. Once the output from the analysis is available, examine the R-square value. This indicates the amount of variance in caller satisfaction which is explained by the combination of all the attributes that were selected for inclusion in the model. In our example, seven attributes are selected. If the R-square value is above .400, the model is considered a good fit. That is, if the R-square term is above .400, statisticians judge the proposed model to be an acceptable reflection of reality. To further explain this value, if the results show an R-square value of .5126, then 51.26 percent of the variance in caller satisfaction is explained by the attributes that are included in the model. That percentage is generally accepted by the scientific community as strong evidence that the proposed model reflects what is actually happening in the environment under investigation. (There is no direct parallel to our cake example, but conceptually one could say that my Grandmother put a number on my guesstimate recipe, rating how closely my guess would generate the same "tastiness.")

Next, examine the impact that each *individual* attribute (i.e., question) has on caller satisfaction by reviewing the *B* value. This is termed the *Beta* coefficient or the regression weight. The higher the value of *B*, the more impact that attribute has on caller satisfaction. That is, the higher the *Beta* coefficient, the more that attribute contributes to or weighs on the outcome. (Again, let us conceptually see this as the measures, such as cups or tablespoons, and their contribution to the overall resulting cake.)

Then look at the significance values, termed the t-values, from the output. If the values are .05 or less, they are considered to be statistically significant. The attributes that have the highest *B* value AND are statistically significant have the most impact on caller satisfaction. These attributes will generate the largest ROI improvements when undertaking remedial programs (assuming all potential projects have approximately the same costs). When we combine the **IMPACT** drivers of satisfaction identified by the analysis with the measures of **PERFORMANCE**, we see the complete picture of the relationships AMONG the attributes. (So if "tastiness" is the performance variable for a cake, each of the spices will be statistically significant and those with the highest *B* value will contribute the most to "tastiness.")

Customer Relationship Metrics provides the chart below to its clients as an aid to understanding the interrelationships among the variables. The

Regression Analysis Example (Impact and Performance Chart)

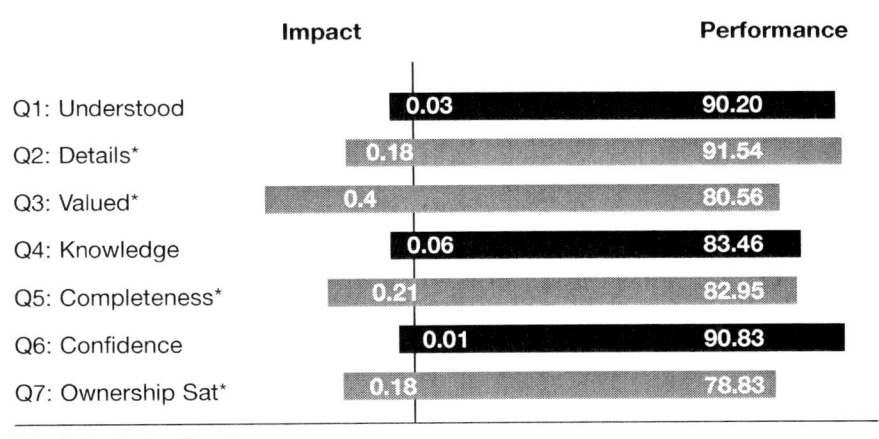

	Impact	Performance
Q1: Understood	0.03	90.20
Q2: Details*	0.18	91.54
Q3: Valued*	0.4	80.56
Q4: Knowledge	0.06	83.46
Q5: Completeness*	0.21	82.95
Q6: Confidence	0.01	90.83
Q7: Ownership Sat*	0.18	78.83

*Statistically significant

drivers of satisfaction are marked with an asterisk because each is statistically significant (t < .05). The IMPACT values on the left are the *B* values (weights) from the aforementioned regression model. The PERFORMANCE scores on the right are the mean scores for each question as rated by the caller and transposed to the 100-point normalization scale. Representing the analysis pictorially assists the users in easily identifying the improvement opportunities with the greatest potential for increasing ROI.

The visual format clearly identifies the areas of focus in which there is the most room for improvement as Q3 Valued (at 80.56) and Q7 Ownership (at 78.83). The **IMPACT** bars indicate that Q3 Valued (at 0.4) is the most important, followed by Q5 Completeness (at 0.21), and Q2 Details and Q7 Ownership (tied at 0.18). So the rule of thumb, as previously stated, is that we should concentrate on those that have the largest impact on caller satisfaction *with* the *lowest* **PERFORMANCE** *scores*. Efforts should go to improving those things that we do not do well which simultaneously matter to the customer. Q2 (Details), Q3 (Valued), Q5 (Completeness) and Q7 (Ownership) are the drivers of satisfaction for this group (center, team or queue). This is true because each is statistically significant (as marked by the asterisk) AND the lowest scores were received on these variables.

The results of this analysis are displayed on the facing page in a decision matrix. This matrix clearly identifies the attributes that offer the best opportunities for action by the center (team or queue). A score of 85 is set as the dividing line between high and low performance. Previous research suggests that a score of 85 or higher is a key level of satisfaction that contributes to customer loyalty. This is represented as a vertical line through the matrix. The horizontal line is set at $t = .05$. Statistically significant attributes are shown above the horizontal line (i.e., $t < .05$) and those that are not are shown below (i.e., $t > .05$). Now, let's tour the four unequally sized quadrants.

Decision Matrix: Results of the Impact and Performance Chart

		Performance	
Impact		0 → 85	85+
Statistical Significance — **Yes**		**Improvement Opportunity** Treating as valued customer Completeness of response Taking ownership of the issue →	**Top Box** Attention to details
Statistical Significance — **No**		**Monitor** Knowledge	**Hold** Quickly understood Confidence in solution

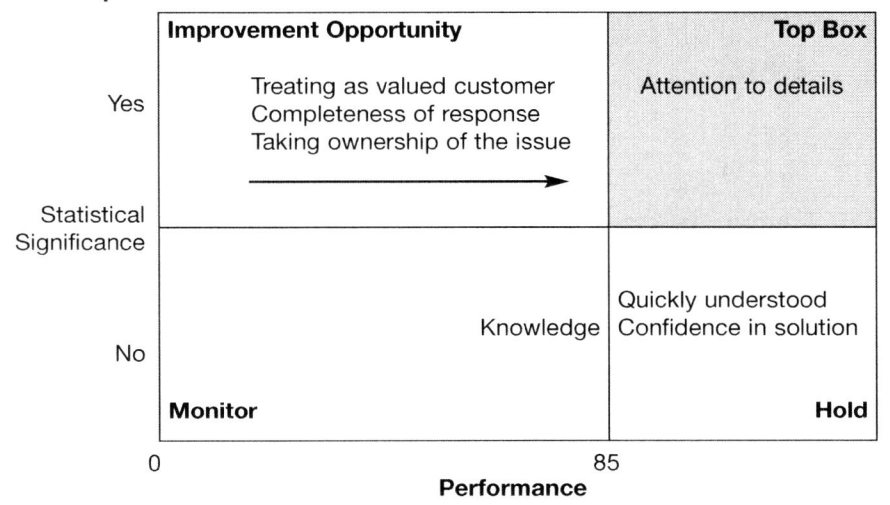

Beginning at the origin, the first quadrant, labeled "Monitor," contains variables with both low **IMPACT** and low **PERFORMANCE**. Such variables that fall into this cell are not performed particularly well (i.e., performance is below the 85 cutoff), but also have little **IMPACT** on ratings of satisfaction. Therefore, no specific managerial attention is required since they matter very little to customer satisfaction. In this particular example, the attribute "knowledge" requires no managerial action.

Moving to the right, the second quadrant, labeled "Hold," contains variables that have attained 85 or better on performance, meaning they are performed well in the center; however, these variables have little **IMPACT** on overall satisfaction as they are not statistically significant. In this case, "quickly understood" and "confidence in the solution" are given superior ratings in **PERFORMANCE**, but neither matter very much to the customer, so there is little reason to invest in either of them. (We already do them well, but the customer does not care.)

Moving up from the second quadrant, one enters the third quadrant: the coveted Top Box. The **PERFORMANCE** rating for variables in the third quadrant are above the 85 threshold for performance, meaning the center delivers these variables very well. Additionally, these variables are important to customers (they have high **IMPACT,** as they are statistically significant). In this example, there is only one variable in the Top Box: "attention to details."

Moving to the left, one enters the critical cell from a managerial standpoint, which is labeled "Improvement Opportunity": only the variables in this fourth cell represent an important improvement opportunity. Variables in this fourth quadrant have high **IMPACT** (as they are statistically significant), but low **PERFORMANCE** (below 85 threshold). In other words, the center is not doing these very well and they are important to customer satisfaction. The variables "treating as a valued customer," "completeness of response" and "taking ownership of the issue" require managerial attention. These then are golden opportunities.

The challenge for management is to move these attributes in the fourth quadrant to the right into the Top Box to be a service differentiator. As the example shows, "attention to details" has a high performance score (over the 85 threshold) and is a driver of satisfaction; therefore, it is in the Top Box. Management would be well-advised to do everything possible within its budget to move "Valued," "Completeness" and "Ownership" into the Top Box, as well. Improving these three will give the center the most return for its investment (assuming roughly equal project costs).

Monitor the variables in the lower row since these do not require an investment at this point in time. In this example, "quickly understood" and "confidence in the solution" have high **PERFORMANCE** scores, but are not drivers of satisfaction and, therefore, are not prioritized for action. But it is worth noting that the results could change over time and move into the top row, in which case the priority changes.

This example demonstrates that customer evaluations cannot be viewed as a static number. The relationship in the matrix is right to left (acceptable or not) and top to bottom (a driver or not). This is a continuous process. As the center improves and invests in important areas, quantification of the results achieved is required to concretely demonstrate the value and the positive ROI for the improvement initiative.

It is also worth noting that the drivers of satisfaction will vary for different sets of data. One team or queue versus another may have different strengths and weaknesses. Don't do the research once and think there is no reason to return again.

The power in this analysis is its ability to accurately pinpoint areas of opportunity. With this intense scrutiny, the center must fish for the right data with the right equipment, which leads to the right analysis for creating change in the center. The results from the EQM program show a high ROI from investment in time and resources for service delivery improvement.

Customer Relationship Metrics recently completed a case study that proves that the differences matter — not only in how the data is collected, but also how it is subsequently analyzed (for the full text go to http://www.metrics.net/Articles.asp). In that case study, the difference is between a negative ROI versus a very large positive ROI. In the negative ROI case, the company dealt with an increase in its annual expenses of over $50,000 and handled more than 800 additional repeat calls per month. In the positive ROI case, the company had an annual savings of almost $190,000 and is handling over 3,000 fewer repeat calls a month. These positive figures translate into increased productivity, lower costs per call, and a lower headcount, in addition to the $190,000 savings. This company realized a one-month payback on their EQM program and increased their ROI not only for the caller feedback program, but for the training and coaching efforts, as well.

Benchmarking with Customer Relationship Metrics: Apples-to-Apples Comparisons

To complement our customers' operational metrics, we at Customer Relationship Metrics not only provide data capturing the Voice of *Their* Customers with our CATs® (Completely Automated Telephone surveys), but also compare it to our Meow benchmarking data. Looking at the best of the best scores (CATs Meow) and the average scores as an apples-to-apples comparison of the CALLER opinions of service delivery are key data points.

For one client last month, their overall call satisfaction received a Top-Box score of 65.0 percent. The center compared its caller evaluations to 63,378 other CATs® scores that had an average of 60.2 percent and a CATs® Meow of 68.9 percent for the same question. This information, when combined with data from the benchmark project they participated in, has more meaning because it includes the callers' perspective.

A second topic of interest to this client was the Top-Box score of 55.8 percent on "treating the customer as valued." For 52,744 comparable CATs® scores, the average was 56.4 percent and the CATs Meow 64.7 percent. This is not a statistically significant difference from the average, meaning that our customer's performance was essentially average. Now it is possible for management to define this as an area worthy of additional focus for improvement in order to reach the CATs Meow level: a change the customer will notice and appreciate.

A Quick Review of Our Main Points

We covered a lot of territory in this chapter and all of it is important to a highly scientific, quality EQM program. The best way to avoid survey pain is to eliminate it in the first place. This has been the primary intent of this chapter.

We first explained survey channel slamming's negative impact on EQM programs. Selection bias, smaller sample sizes and the potential for the survey request itself to create negatives are all fairly simple to avoid. Since nearly all contact centers provide multiple ports of entry for customers, plan to provide survey opportunities congruent with each of these ports. The extra expense is a cheap investment in a quality measurement program.

Next, we explored the requirements of adequate sample size. Make certain the sample size is sufficiently large so as to make the results generalizable to the population of interest. In general, we recommend 400 surveys per center location.

We explained the hidden importance of qualitative data to the EQM program. It is all well and good to hypothesize about what customers find important and then ask questions based on those dimensions. But only customers' actual voices can tell you if something important is missing. Customers' qualitative responses can lead you in new directions. With both qualitative and quantitative data capture, a marvelously holistic picture emerges.

We also emphasized the importance of minimizing dirty data in analytic results. Dirty data only distorts the picture and could lead to faulty business decisions. There are several ways to undertake data-scrubbing and the appropriate method depends on the situation at hand. For our EQM program, we transcribe all qualitative data and correct all survey-flipping (inadvertently reverse scored) instances to ensure that the customers' wishes are embodied in the results. This way, the results are accurate and lead to appropriate management action relative to retraining and rewards.

Last, we urged the use of true scientific analysis over mere means and percentages. The process of normalization aids data interpretation. In addition, a greater understanding of regression uses in the contact center environment leads to improvement opportunities. These opportunities can be clearly understood and attacked using the output from regression such that appropriate investments (i.e., those that matter the most) can be undertaken.

In all likelihood this chapter, dense as it is in content, created some "pain" for readers. It may be necessary to reread this one a couple of times, but it is worth the effort to master this material in the long run. If you never choose to master it yourself, be certain to hire someone who understands and can guide improvement programs through real science.

We turn next to a consideration of some "tips" we have learned over years of research, which will aid those venturing into the customer intelligence realm.

Chapter 9:
Practical Considerations
of the EQM Program

In this chapter, we'll stay away from theory and heavy statistics and limit ourselves to tips and practical issues in the EQM program. Following our survey pain theme, the tips in this chapter tend to be analogous to many common sense health tips.

- Moderate exercise three times a week for 20 minutes
- Eat plenty of fresh fruits and vegetables
- Avoid sugary drinks and saturated fats
- Get six to eight hours of sleep a night

These oft-repeated health tips help us to avoid bodily pain altogether by encouraging a good maintenance program for the body. Many of the tips in this chapter serve much the same purpose: absence of survey pain through reasonable, long-term, sustained research choices. Pain need not be relieved if it is avoided.

Among other things, we'll consider the practicality of the immediate post-call methodology, highlighting the benefits of a blind-to-the-agents system. Additionally, the customers and the company are better served when the callers are not required to decide *a priori* whether they will subsequently participate in a survey. We'll also examine how clever agents can still "game" the system, even with an automatic system in place. Gaming aside, you must attribute the results to the proper agent; otherwise, you waste the power of this system. Increased outbound trunk capacity may be a requirement, and we'll explain why and what happens with insufficient capacity. Furthermore, agents and customers alike will need to break some habits, or the technology cannot produce to its potential. The technology should not drive the research so much as the research should select the technology. We'll glance again at some topics regarding the items and scale points of the instrument. We'll then briefly turn to a reaffirmation of the Net Promoter score in the context of a complete research effort and explain its place in the whole. We encourage aligning the IQM with the EQM programs and suggest ways to do that. Callers are given the opportunity to tell us more than "1" or "5." Through the collection of qualitative data, we can ascertain the "why" behind either number. Last, we'll explain the Alerts feature in greater detail.

Select an Immediate Post-Call Survey Methodology

Methods traditionally used in industry measurement programs are no longer fulfilling their original goals. Some measurement programs are asking the wrong questions or in some cases, such as IQM, they aren't asking ANY questions at all! Many companies are seeking better alternatives to traditional methods of gathering customer intelligence. Customer feedback gathered by a flawed system can easily mislead and ultimately misdirect the service strategy. The measurement system must reflect the mission to be customer-focused and easy to do business with, and that means congruence with the customer-selected channel of communication. Flexibility in the communication channel may, in turn, occasion additional expense.

Center management must balance costs (i.e., keeping talk time low) and customer satisfaction. How does management know, from a customer's perspective, when talk time is too short or too long? What should the supervisors on the floor encourage their agents to improve upon? While on the surface, traditional methods are the most cost efficient, cheap becomes expensive when the customers' needs are not heard accurately and quickly. To best measure the effectiveness of service delivery, an immediate evaluation is needed via the customers' preferred channel.

Determine the Evaluation Process Flow

As the inventors of real-time surveying in contact centers, we get a lot of questions about how to properly conduct measurement programs. There is no simple answer. Every program presents a different set of variables that must be considered to make the program successful. No two measurement programs are exactly alike and no research project is perfect. Regardless of the implementation plan for a post-call measurement program, it is important to employ unique sets of controls to avoid or vastly limit points of failure. One of the most misunderstood aspects of a measurement program is the requirement to have a fully automated or blind-to-the-agent transfer process to the survey for the caller. The program construction must balance technology and human behaviors, even when using a fully automated or blind transfer. A blind-to-the-agent transfer can be used, with great success, when a complete understanding of the strengths and weaknesses are weighed and controls are initiated to limit abuse and failure.

Do NOT Make Customers Pre-Select

When constructing a survey program, two components are critical — the first is the invitation to participate and the second is the survey content. Callers must be informed of the opportunity to evaluate the service before they are served. However, requiring them to decide whether to participate or not before the service experience is ill-advised.

Don't assume that a caller will not change his or her mind from "No, I do not wish to participate" to "Yes, now I do wish to participate." Many survey technology solutions force the customer to pre-select with a "Yes" or "No" response to the invitation prompt. Does your measurement process account for a caller's change of mind? A caller may decide to participate after having a bad experience. This bad experience will be compounded if the agent has no means to transfer the caller (and the caller may not believe this explanation). Or, if a caller is blocked from the survey due to the pre-selection response requirements, the caller may call back in order to take the survey. This is a repeat call — the caller will either not be invited to evaluate the call or will be invited and the call becomes attached to the agent who now receives the call. It is equally plausible that a caller may be "wowed" by the customer service and have a change of heart about participating. They, too, will be blocked from taking the survey. If this delighted customer does not call back, the positive caller feedback is lost and you have added an element of dissatisfaction and possible frustration to the customer when the goal was to measure satisfaction.

Agents Can Still Influence Participation

An initial misperception of post-call surveying is that agents cannot bias survey results in an automated transfer process. While post-call surveying reduces biases associated with time gaps, it is not necessarily a bias-free environment. In order to utilize an automated transfer process, agents must release the call first — in effect, agents must hang up on the callers. The release of the caller by the agent initiates the transfer to the survey system. This is true for both premise-based and hosted survey systems. In the majority of contact center environments, agents allow the caller to end the call. "Never, ever hang up on a customer!" is an established command in the contact center environment.

Some career agents have served customers on the phone for 20 years. A quick calculation tells us that these agents may have taken more than 500,000 calls in their careers, and now we ask them to start hanging up on customers because of this new survey process. Your new measurement program requires a behavior change for the agents that you expect and need on each and every call. How successful will your agents be with a systemic behavior change? In Chapter 2, we spoke at length about employee behaviors and rewards. Remember, you get what you reward, so you will need to arrange contingencies to break this long-standing habit or accept that it will not be broken.

The automated transfer eliminates a lot of bias that would otherwise contaminate the results. Even if the behavior change is working and callers are released by the agents, any agent who suspects a negative rating by the customer may simply not release the caller after the interaction. This prevents the customer from participating in the post-call evaluation. Furthermore, this action by the agent is difficult to identify as noncompliance. This bias and the opportunity for abuse it introduces can tarnish what is, otherwise, a brilliant research strategy.

Assigning the Surveys

As previously discussed, not only can an agent influence who reaches the survey, but inadequate, unsophisticated technology can inaccurately assign survey comments to the wrong agent once a transfer has occurred. To explain, let's say that:

1. A call comes into the contact center.
2. The caller opts to participate in the post-call survey.
3. The caller is routed to agent #1. The agent works with the caller and, at some point, determines that the caller needs to be transferred.
4. The transfer occurs to agent #2 in that contact center or to another physical location.

Your technology must be sophisticated enough to assign the survey response to agent #2's ID number upon transfer to the survey. You cannot ignore this element of the measurement program or you will immediately have problems getting agents to accept the scores as their own. Let's say one customer comment on Bob's report card (agent #1) says that "he was terrific and transferred me to Kelly to finalize the details and she was terrible." Now you have problems. Although Kelly (agent #2) received low scores on the call from the customer, these scores are mistakenly assigned to Bob. Even when all else is technically designed correctly, the issue of assignment needs to be added to the survey calibration protocol.

You May Need More Trunk Capacity

A fully automated or blind-to-the-agent transfer requires outbound trunk capacity to handle the number of calls during the month that will be transferred to the evaluation. Each call occupies two trunk lines (inbound and outbound) instead of just one (inbound). Four hundred or so calls may not cause a need for more capacity, but an incorrect technical design can create thousands of ghost calls. Ghost calls occur when the technology transfers a call to the survey without a caller on the line. If trunk capacity is limited and additional trunk lines are not added, then implementing a blind transfer will cause customers to receive a fast busy signal and block them from the survey. The additional trunk lines ensure that every caller who indicates willingness to participate receives the opportunity to do so. Otherwise, a larger number of callers who want to stay on the line after the agent says, "Is there anything else I can do for you today?" will be unable to provide their feedback when the transfer is lost due to inadequate trunk capacity.

Caller Behavior

Agents are not alone in the need for behavior modifications. The caller must fight the natural reaction to hang up at the end of the call. Callers may hang up and then realize that they did not wait to be transferred to the survey and will call back. Now the issues start — repeat call, incorrect assignment of the call evaluation to the second agent (if selected again) or a need to use the back-up plan for this scenario that satisfies the customer need but loses connection with the agent who initially served the caller, and so on.

Technology Must NOT Drive the Research

A technology-rich contact center is not a guarantee of a successful post-call measurement program. It does mean, however, that you have more functionality to design an effective and fair measurement program.

In all environments, whether technology is rich or poor, consistent across centers in the organization or not, you must consider the callers, the agents, the technical resources (programmers) and the managers of the information when designing a good research program. Technology must support your research efforts, not define them. Contact center agents do not forget injustices (perceived or real) for a very long time, if ever. Subjecting them to an ineffective measurement program, pulling it back at the brink of a mutiny and then reconstructing the process is extremely damaging to the social environment and to the trust between agents and management. The same can be said for a process that even has very small issues. These, in turn, may leak into interactions between agents and customers. In addition, any critical measurement needed for your center will be closely scrutinized when reinstated, argued over, and its implementation possibly delayed. Post-call surveys definitely can and should be fair and balanced and bring considerable value to your quality program rather than pain, debate, accusations and acrimony. Play it safe and have your "ducks in a row" before initiating the project. Secure and pretest all the resources needed to do the job right.

Determine the Service Attributes for the EQM Form

A team consisting of the quality assurance team, the center management team and a key team leader or two from among the agents should outline the survey items. The meeting size should remain small, or the task will easily get off track.

Capture the mission of service delivery — the goal; things that you expect the agents to do for the callers. This is similar to the process used when constructing the internal quality monitoring call form.

Outline the key service attributes and document these as items to be scored by the customer. Adopt the perspective of a customer who is monitoring the call. In addition to evaluation of the agent's overall level of service, identify the specifics to be rated by the customer. The attributes should be general enough that the questions make sense for each kind of customer and each kind of call. Brainstorm the list without trying to write the questions.

A successful EQM program accurately identifies barriers to first-call resolution, provides insight to specific service areas and/or employees in need of improvement, and reduces the loss of any company's most important asset — the customer.

Select the Scale

Most research projects utilize 5-, 7-, 9- or 10-point scales depending on the level of precision or the magnitude of the error that is acceptable. For comparison across research measurement channels, the scale is normalized using a transformation table. The technique of normalization has no impact on the relationship of the data points to one another, i.e., does not affect the results. The procedure is outlined on the facing page to demonstrate the amount of variability in the response choices and how a larger amount of dispersion across the scale is beneficial to the results for both precision and fairness in the results.

Clearly seen in the scale conversions on the facing page is that larger endpoints provide more response choices, which permits more variability in the ratings that directly affects the precision of the results. Research has shown that respondents can differentiate more between their feelings of satisfaction when offered more response categories (Bendig, 1954; Garner 1960). For a 5-point scale, little variation between each scale point is available and on the 100-point scale is a difference of 25 points from one rating to the next. Surveys with fewer response options are "forcing" respondents into a category that causes information loss and renders the results to be

Transformation of the Scales to a 100-Point Scale:

For a 5-Point Conversion:

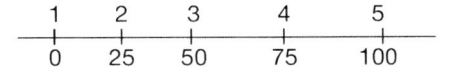

```
  1     2     3     4      5
  +-----+-----+-----+------+
  0    25    50    75     100
```

For a 7-Point Conversion:

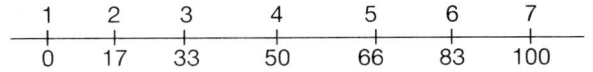

```
  1     2     3     4     5     6     7
  +-----+-----+-----+-----+-----+-----+
  0    17    33    50    66    83    100
```

For a 9-Point Conversion:

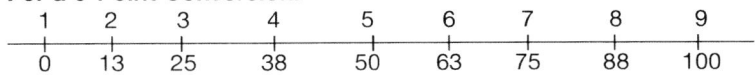

```
  1     2     3     4     5     6     7     8     9
  +-----+-----+-----+-----+-----+-----+-----+-----+
  0    13    25    38    50    63    75    88    100
```

For a 10-point Conversion:

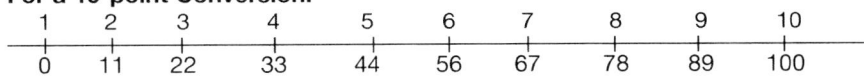

```
  1     2     3     4     5     6     7     8     9    10
  +-----+-----+-----+-----+-----+-----+-----+-----+-----+
  0    11    22    33    44    56    67    78    89    100
```

less reliable than those with more variability (Van Bennekom, 2002). Research also highlights a cognitive difference between a 3 and 4 rating that is smaller than between 4 and 5 rating on the 5-point scale (Van Bennekom, 2002). Applying this logic to the "fairness" test by the agents, one can see the difference in securing a 4 versus a 5 as compared to a 3 versus a 4. Considering that only the 5 ratings will be counted as the desired service level (discussed below), the goal is actually more difficult to achieve with a 5-point scale.

The issue of variability must also be considered along with reliability. Surveys with more response alternatives are more reliable than those with fewer responses (Scherpenzeel, 2002; Alwin and Krosnick, 1991). Surveys that use a 7-, 9- or 10-point scale are most reliable based on several research studies in the academic community (Andrews and Withey, 1980; Andrews, 1984; Alwin and Krosnick, 1991; Bass, Cascio and O'Connor, 1974; and Rodgers, Andrews and Herzog, 1992)

With more scale points, consumers can make better decisions on their experience and give a clearer indication of the experience. Considering the 9-point scale, the difference between each scale point is 12.5 (rounded to 13 in the charts) permitting the respondents to provide a more granular rating of the service experience.

The scale also has implications on the analytics used and on how the results are reported. Referring back to the concept of performance management and the goal of 85 on the 100-point converted scale, successful service is defined by research of satisfaction and its relationship to customer loyalty. The zone of affection is achieved at 4.3 on the 5-point scale (or 85 on the converted scale).

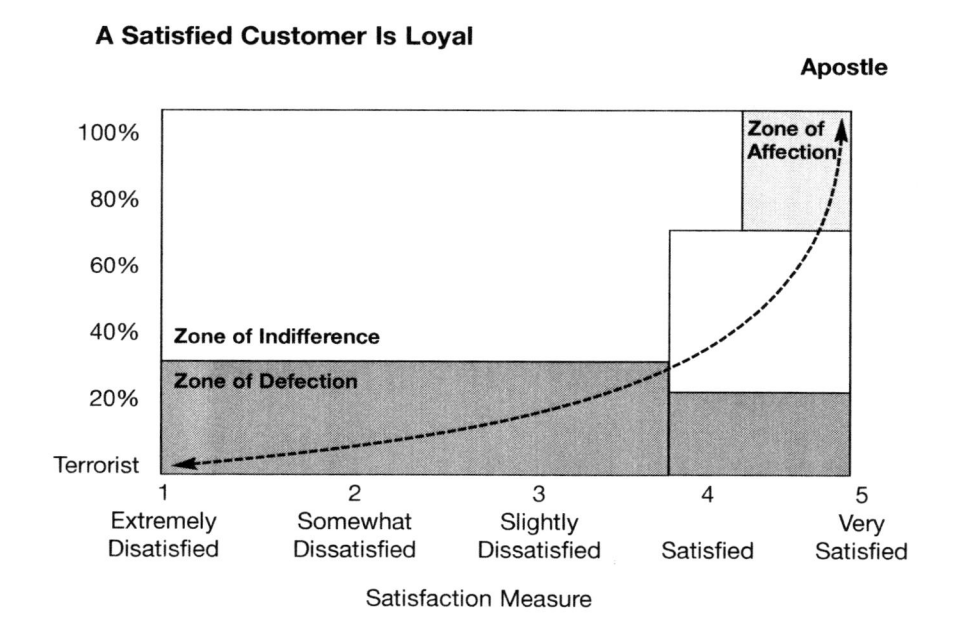

A Satisfied Customer Is Loyal

Apostle

```
100% ┤                                    Zone of
                                          Affection
 80% ┤
 60% ┤
 40% ┤   Zone of Indifference
         Zone of Defection
 20% ┤
Terrorist
         1           2           3           4           5
     Extremely   Somewhat    Slightly                  Very
     Disatisfied Dissatisfied Dissatisfied Satisfied  Satisfied
                        Satisfaction Measure
```

By definition, only a score of 5 on a 5-point scale is considered a successful service experience. On a 7-point scale, only a score of 7 would be delighted, but on the 9- and 10-point scale, both scores of 9 and 10 can be considered in the customer delight category (and therefore successfully meeting the goal). The scale used influences the definition of success for the agent.

Additionally, a scale that allows more dispersion of the ratings also permits the trends in satisfaction (or dissatisfaction) to be more definable. The goal with a post-call survey program is to identify improvement areas using analysis to quantify items that have an impact on the overall satisfaction rating and a scale with endpoints of high versus low is conducive to this analysis (Van Bennekom, 2002). With fewer response choices and less variability/dispersion of the scores, the inherent clustering of the ratings reduces the ability to identify opportunities. This will cause issues when reporting the results as it may cause a question of reliability in your results.

The most commonly used scale for the post-call automated survey methodology is a 1-9 point scale. The reason for its predominance is twofold. Research shows that respondents can differentiate more between their feelings of satisfaction when offered more response categories (Bendig, 1954; Garner 1960). Rating scales with the possibility of a dispersion of the responses are most successful with the automated survey. Additionally, research participants must be able to easily understand and apply the scale to the evaluation process. The 1-9 rating is most easily used with the numbers on the telephone keypad and requires only a one-digit response. In a categorical scale, such as Strongly Disagree, Disagree, Neither, Agree and Strongly Agree, the description of the scale categories must be regularly repeated to ensure the correct application by the respondents. Numerical scales, on the other hand, are far easier for the respondents to retain and to apply.

Key Attributes Versus Net Promoter Score

A primary section of the survey is dedicated to several global questions. One may be the question that Net Promoter scores are derived from:

> How likely are you to recommend this company to a friend?

While we don't discount the inclusion of the Net Promoter question as a critical metric, we do not support the notion that a tactical post-call survey for a contact center can have only that one question. Analyzing the details of the EQM forms is critical to affecting change in service delivery.

For this reason, you should include the Net Promoter question in the global-level set of questions.

Global level concepts – 3 to 5 questions
Likely to recommend
Overall satisfaction with the company/brand/agency
Overall satisfaction with the call
Time to connect to agent

Agent attributes – 6 or 7 questions
Overall service by agent
Knowledge
Professionalism
Confidence in answer provided

Contact Resolution – 3 or 4 questions
Calling about a problem versus question
First time
Number of times
Issue resolution

Contact centers struggle daily to quantify first-contact resolution (FCR), and many estimate the percentage or use an internal procedure to quantify this critical metric. Ultimately, the *caller* should define this metric. The caller's perception of problem resolution is the reality for the contact center management team. Direct and indirect costs are at risk for centers with ineffective problem resolution processes. Repeat calls have a direct cost and unresolved problems significantly degrade customer satisfaction. An EQM program provides the data and the customer explanations that are needed to support action. The survey includes quantification of the occurrence of problems and issues under the names Problem Contact Resolution and Non-Problem (Issues) Contact Resolution.

EQM and ICM Must Complement

The EQM program does not replicate the IQM program, but it certainly complements it as part of the Global Quality Program. After identifying the preliminary list of attributes that the caller will score, conduct an exercise to determine the all-important "What will we do with this information?" test. While many items might be interesting to know, management must be able to act on the answer, or the question cannot be on the survey. Post-call surveys have a goal of completion in two to three minutes (without the optional aspect of explaining the reason for an evaluation).

As an example, imagine that you are running a satisfaction program for a hotel. Critique the following question suggested by the management team:

Rate your satisfaction with the size of the swimming pool.

A swimming pool is an important amenity for a hotel. If the scores from the guest survey indicate that satisfaction is low with the size of the swimming pool, is the hotel management team prepared to act? Will the pool be enlarged? Most likely it is too late to change the size of the swimming pool, so don't ask that question. Consider the customer service attributes about the pool that can be leveraged as a customer benefit, such as the hours with a lifeguard, the dedicated lap swim lanes, or the temperature. If a case cannot be made for making a change based on customer feedback, use the space on the survey to capture something that can be leveraged.

A "complementary item" is usable and has explicit coaching aspects. The list must line up with the internal monitoring items that ultimately define the coaching aspects.

External Quality Monitoring Component	Internal Quality Monitoring Scoring Component
Agent's knowledge of products and/or services	**IQM Component 1:** Agent effectively presented/answered questions regarding fee-related attributes of product and/or service.
	IQM Component 2: Agent effectively presented/answered questions regarding non-fee-related attributes of product and/or service.
	IQM Component 3: Agent effectively presented/answered questions regarding the benefits of product and/or service.
Agent quickly understood the reason for the call	**IQM Component 1:** Agent accurately repeated/rephrased the reason for the call prior to taking any action.
	IQM Component 2: Agent used effective probing questions to uncover the reason for the call.
Agent handled call in a professional manner	**IQM Component 1:** Agent accurately repeated/rephrased the reason for the call prior to taking any action.
	IQM Component 2: Agent branded the call at the opening of the call.
	IQM Component 3: Agent referred to customer by last name [Mr./Ms. _____]
Customer's confidence in the accuracy of the information/ solution provided	**IQM Component 1:** Agent selected strong, action-oriented words to convey information/solution.
	IQM Component 2: Agent conveyed confidence to customer through tone and word choice. Agent avoided use of filler words.
	IQM Component 3: Agent did not generate excessive hold times.

Select the "Why?" Questions

The EQM program combines the quantitative evaluations with the qualitative explanation. Each opportunity for callers to explain their numeric score provides information to make changes based on the customers' perspective — from insights to action. A typical Customer Relationship Metrics survey gives callers three or four opportunities to provide verbal feedback regarding his or her satisfaction with the company, call, representative and/or problem issue. All feedback is transcribed as a separate month-end report. In addition to providing invaluable voice of the customer feedback, these customer comments also allow the Metrics survey calibration team to validate customer survey scores. In order to control the cost of the EQM program, the number of customers who qualify to leave a comment (based on score) is variable, which allows each client some control with respect to the number of comments collected.

Select the Real-Time Alert Triggers

Service recovery is an important component of the measurement program. If a customer experience falls into the failure category (as defined by one or more of your key questions), a call-back offer should be made to the customer. This feature serves as a safety net that delivers significant value by proactively responding to callers who experienced difficulty with the transaction. Research by Customer Relationship Metrics shows that having access to customer comments before initiating the service recovery improves the success rate of the follow-up contact. That is, if the intervention team knows exactly what the customer said BEFORE initiating re-contact with the customer, the probability of a successful recovery is much greater.

The Alert criteria of an EQM program are customizable to meet the needs of the specific business. We have found that these needs may change over time to include or exclude qualifying customers in order to increase or decrease the number of Alerts generated.

It's about Avoiding the Pain

This chapter provided a host of tips and rubrics for use in an EQM program. We hope you will find them practical as you move ever closer to dovetailing the parts of the Global Quality Program into a coherent whole. Doing so permits complementary parts to double-check that the future plans are supported with a variety of current data.

Surveying and its associated pain can and will be reduced or eliminated using the tips in this chapter in conjunction with the previous chapters' guidelines.

We move now to Part IV where we discuss the crucial step of letting others in the company know what has been learned so that appropriate actions can be taken to correct imperfections in the service delivery process and to aid future project planning. Any and all outcomes rest on careful analysis of the programs and justification of the expenses involved. Therefore, we explain the program valuation process, suggest best how to discriminate the lessons of the Global Quality Program, and finally, provide some additional examples of how to turn lessons learned into practical changes.

Part IV: Sharing the Wealth of the EQM Program

Chapter 10:
CLV and ROI in the Center

We all know doctors make use of a variety of physical tools — from rubber hammers to test reflexes to Magnetic Resonance Imaging (MRI) to see beneath the skin in exquisite detail. They also use chemical tools, which we experience as lab tests that draw blood or other bodily materials and convert those substances to numbers that represent health or disease (seemingly like magic to the uninitiated, but as a science to those properly educated).

In this chapter, we'll show you how to build your own tools for much the same purpose in the economic body of the firm as the above-mentioned do for patients' bodies. When the physician prescribes a course of treatment, she often includes one or a series of tests to assess the effectiveness of the treatment. The tools we will build in this chapter include CLV, ROI and even market damage. They serve the same purposes: diagnosis and evaluation of treatment.

To see clearly whether the programs of the contact center are worth the resources expended, we need to place a value on the outcomes just as we needed to value the inputs before initiation. Standard accounting procedures, known and used for centuries, help us to track expenditures and place values on investments. Principles from accounting are the foundation for the now well-known concepts of customer lifetime value (CLV) and return on investment (ROI), which are widely recognized and utilized in contact centers.

We were among the first to talk about these concepts in the contact center environment. Work that was completed by one of us to develop a CLV calculator program was unveiled by a group of Dutch exchange students for demonstration at a Cincinnati conference around 1995. While we did not receive credit for the work, we still have the folder documenting our work, which part of the basis for this chapter. We also incorporate works by other researchers who have written extensively on the topic.

We'll briefly review the concepts and calculations needed to compute CLV and ROI in the contact center environment using successively more complex examples.

Customer Lifetime Value

Customer lifetime value is a concept intended to answer the simple question: "What is the worth of a customer?" At the basic level, it is important to understand this value because when we lose a customer, we do not just lose this sale, but all sales we might have subsequently enjoyed from this customer. Understanding this concretely helps contact center management and executives in the home office to appreciate the "high-stakes game" we undertake when dealing with customers who are experiencing problems.

Basically, we seek to put a value today on a future stream of revenues. This is simply a Present Value problem and any good accounting or finance textbook will provide you with the equation and tables for computing the answer.

The equation is:

$$CLV_t^i = \sum_{t=0}^{n} \frac{CF_t^i}{(1+r)^t}$$

Where:
CLV_t^i = Customer lifetime value of customer i at time t
CF_t^i = Cash flow of customer i at time t
r = Discount rate
n = Number of time periods in the future being considered

While we have made this sound very simple, it is truly a daunting calculation to make by hand and requires some research just to know what numbers to plug in for n, r and t.

The discount rate is the rate at which banks charge your institution for moneys borrowed. Naturally, this rate changes from time to time as financial markets fluctuate and needs for cash in the firm alter with changes in circumstances and plans. Since is it unlikely that anyone in the center actually knows what the rate of interest is for the firm at any given point in time, it is convenient to make all calculations with a predetermined discount rate at least equal to the prime rate at which the Federal Reserve loans to member banks plus 1 percent — unless there is a compelling reason to select something different.

The longevity of customer relationships and the frequency of purchase behavior determine the number of time periods considered. Generally, we convert years of patronage into months, assuming monthly purchases to be the most common likelihood. Of course, the exact details and calculations must match as closely as possible the actual purchase behavior of the average customer in the focal business. But how long do customers stay with a vendor? Certainly businesses can access their records and get some idea of customer churn. People often stay with a financial institution for decades, but may purchase from several manufacturers of small household appliances within a single year. Again, this is a judgment call based on past data, but the best-guess estimate for the focal firm should be the inputs utilized rather than industry wide or wholly assumed inputs.

Computing the cash flow of the customer is not as simple as it might initially seem. You must know, for example, the initial cost to make the first sale (marketing expenses), revenue from that initial purchase, and the expected yearly income from additional sales that flow as a result of the initial purchase.

Take, for example, the purchase of printers for a small business. Suppose it costs $200 in marketing and other expenses to make the initial sale. The printers total $5,000. Supplies (print cartridges) to keep the printers running total $500 per year. The average customer lifetime is 10 years for this product (an overly generous estimate for this type of product). Let's assume a 5 percent interest rate per year (which underestimates the likely rate). More formally we then see:

CF_t^i = $500 per year
+ $5,000 initial purchase - $200 costs to generate = $4,800
r = 5% per year
n = 10 years

Simple math tells us the dollar amounts over the period are:

($500 x 10) + ($5,000 - $200) = $9,800

Although the $4,800 in initial revenue minus costs is in present value, the future stream of $500 per year is not; hence, the present value is overstated by the discount rate of 5 percent per year. To simplify the calculations, assume purchases are made at the rate of one per year for $500. So we need to calculate the present value of a future stream of revenues and add $4,800 to receive the future value of the customer. The present value of the future stream is $3,860.87. To this we add $4,800 for a total customer lifetime value of $8,661 (when rounded). The dollar amounts over the period were overstated by $1,139 ($5,000 - $3,861).

We made these calculations with the help of a Texas Instruments BA-II business calculator purchased back in 1980 or so. Obviously, numerous brands of newer business calculators are available, but this only demonstrates that the calculations do not change over time and even old equipment is very accurate. The keystrokes are simple:

Clear the memory registers
Use financial mode
Hit 5% (for the rate of interest)
Hit 10 n (for the number of periods)
Hit 500 pmt (for payment)
Hit 2nd PV (to calculate the present value)

Doing so yields $3,860.87, to which we add $5,000 for the original purchase, for a total CLV of $8,661.

As an aside, we computed the same problem again using a standard finance textbook that was copyrighted in 1979 (Brigham, 1979). The tables used to generate the answer were originally computed centuries ago and are still useful today. To use this resource, take the same inputs as above and select the correct table to gain the proper multiplier. For most people, selecting the correct table is the tricky part. Invest the time and effort to comprehend which tables to use under which circumstances, or compare the answer with common sense to see whether the result is a realistic possibility. Generally, if the wrong table is selected, the generated answer will not make any sense for the problem under study.

For this problem, we need to access the table that says: "Present Value of an Annuity of $1 per Period for n Period." Next, we scan down the left column to 10 for the number of payments. Then we read across the page to the 5 percent column. The multiplier listed is 7.7217. We multiply that number by the annual payment received (which was $500 in this example) to get $3,860.87, to which we add the present value of the original purchase ($5,000) minus the cost to sell the item ($200). Summing these two gives $8,661, the answer we originally computed with the calculator.

We made this example about as simple as it can be. More realistic estimates require knowing how frequently purchases are made per time period. If purchase frequency is once per month, we would divide the annual discount rate by 12 and adjust n from annual to monthly, as well. Other purchase frequencies would require according adjustments. In fact, to get a realistic result, you must start with realistic input and then make any adjustments to the calculations that realism requires.

Perhaps less obvious is the fact that not all customers are similar, much less the same, with respect to their purchasing behavior with your firm. It adds complexity, but also meaningfulness, to the calculations to place customers in categories that reflect true differences with respect to their purchasing behavior. You've probably heard the old adage that "20 percent of your customers are responsible for 80 percent of the business profits, while 80 percent of customers are responsible for 20 percent of the business profits." Based on this idea (and data from the focal company), we could easily argue that at least two customer groups with differing CLV equations should be created to account for very different purchase behavior. As a result, the values we select in the CLV equation will differ depending on which category of customer is under discussion.

A potentially tricky aspect of all this is that CLV is inherently future-oriented, but requires some past data for judgment calls. Interestingly, customer value does not actually arise from exchanges of the past because they have already been counted in previous periods as revenues and profits; rather, it is the future value of customers that is key. Looked at one way, a good customer of many years who declares herself unwilling to do further business with the company actually has a CLV of zero. Viewed another way, losing the stream of discounted future revenues costs the company very real future profits. In this sense, the present value of rescue and other operations and programs within the contact center have returns on investments that can be calculated, which is the next step.

To review, create classes of customers if there are meaningful differences between customers relative to their behavior with the company. Think of it essentially as creating classes of customers based on their profitability. Subclasses may be necessary in the future as the sources of profitability will vary: some purchase often but in small amounts, while some are less frequent but spend more when they do; some tend to purchase high margin items and others low. The key is to form groups that provide meaningful intelligence.

In their book, *Driving Customer Equity*, authors Roland Rust, Valarie Zeithaml and Katherine Lemon take the CLV calculation further by lessening our fairly restrictive assumptions and substituting more realism. But be aware that more realism means more complications and less ease of construction and use.

For example, in addition to frequency of purchase per period, discount rate and cash flow (which we have already discussed), you could select a planning horizon that limits the analysis to a specific timeframe, which could be longer or (more likely) shorter than the actual customer lifetime value. The authors also incorporate the possibility of customers switching brands, and to use this, you need to specify the most recent brand choice and the estimated probabilities of choosing each brand. Additionally, the average contribution of a purchase to profit could be varied (purchase less cost) since different products have varying profit margins.

CLV Extensions

Once we have a grasp of CLV, we can move on to a variety of extensions that allow us to place values on related concepts. Here we'll examine the values of cross-selling and market damage.

Cross-selling or up-selling is conceptually the simpler idea. Our CLV becomes the sum of the original CLV plus the CLV attached to the additional product. Adding on to our example, let's assume the sale of a second product that is not a substitute for the printers originally sold. Then:

Revenue from the second product	$4,000
Cost to sell	$ 200
Expected yearly additional revenue	$ 300
Additional CLV	$6,117 = (2,317 + 4,000 - 200)
Total CLV (1st + 2nd)	$14,778 = (8,661 + 6,117)

Clearly, cross-selling is advantageous and can make a substantial difference to the CLV of a customer or, by extension, to a customer class by making this activity a goal of the contact center.

Market damage is the harm done first by losing the CLV of the customer plus the loss we sustain due to the customer "bad-mouthing" us to friends and relatives. This damage could be relatively small or huge depending on the assumptions that underpin the calculations.

Before we can take up the market damage example, we must first review the concept of "word-of-mouth." Customers naturally talk to their friends, relatives and coworkers about their purchase experiences. These chats are categorized as positive or negative word-of-mouth depending on whether the customer is relating an experience likely to attract a new customer for the provider or repel them away and into the arms of a competitor. We'll call the number of people who hear about an experience the word-of-mouth factor. This is simply the number of people told about the experience by the person who had it. In the example below, we'll assume that 15 people are told about the experience. To make the calculations manageable by normal humans, we simplify and use a plug-in number; but it should be obvious that not all customers are created equally in this regard. Let's contrast a homemaker who is not employed outside of the home and a university professor with readily available captive audiences of students. It is quite apparent that the professor could do a lot more damage in a short time than the typical homemaker. (We've used this fact with certain recalcitrant retailers in the past to get them to live up to their promises!)

Not every person who hears about an experience will take action based on that intelligence. We call that the influence rate. If 100 people hear about a negative transaction, maybe 99 will do nothing as a result of that intelligence, but one will decide not to give the seller a chance. Note that both the word-of-mouth factor and the influence rate calculations can be empirically derived or based on industry averages. Assumptions based on fantasy are entirely unacceptable.

So here is our example of market damage:

CLV	$1,000
Word-of-mouth factor	15
Influence rate = 1:100	1%
Lost profits per customer =	$1,150 = (15 x .01 x 1,000) + 1,000

As a second example, we can go back to our original CLV example, where we then see the following:

CLV	$8,661
Word-of-mouth factor	15
Influence rate = 1:100	1%
Lost profits per customer	$9,960.15 = (15 x .01 x 8,661) + 8,661
Rounded	$9,960 = 1,299 + 8,661

In both instances, the loss of the original customer is bad enough, but to that loss we must also add the damage done to the company's reputation and revenues due to the dissatisfied customer spreading word of that dissatisfaction.

Taking this up from a single customer to a unit within the contact center, we can look at the market damage from 100 complaints. We will need to assume the fraction of people who actually experience a problem and subsequently complain about it. Note that we base this computation on the idea that only a fraction of those who experience any particular problem will be sufficiently motivated by it to complain to the company. Each of us can attest to this truth from personal experience. If we as consumers complained and got a resolution to each and every thing that went wrong in our economic lives (which are made up of hundreds of transactions a day), we would not have time to make the money to sustain our level of transactions. (Of course, research provides a better estimate, but for purposes of illustration, we'll simply plug-in assumptions.) Here we will peg that fraction at 20 percent or 1/5th. In other words, we assume that if one person complains about a problem, upward of four other people actually experienced that negative event and said nothing to the firm because 20/100 = 5. If 100 customers complain after they experience a problem, then we can readily compute that 500 (100 x 5) people actually experienced the problem in the first place. Let us then assume that we undertake as a contact center to resolve the complaints and we are successful half the time. When we go back to the scenario proposed by our original market damage problem, we get the following:

Number of complaints	100
Percent complaining	20%
Customers experience the problem	500 = 5 x 100
Complaints resolved satisfactorily	50%
Total customers saved through resolution	50 = 100 x resolution rate of .5
Total customers lost	450 = 500 - 50 saved
Market damage	$517,500 = 450 x $1,150

It may help to construct a simulator that provides answers to "if/then" questions. For example, what happens if we increase the word-of-mouth factor by one? Alternatively, we could increase the percent complaining by one or the percent of complaints resolved by one. These examinations of single unit alternations are called "sensitivity" analyses and are very useful for looking at where small changes can exert large impacts. These are more commonly encountered in economics texts rather than in customer satisfaction contexts, but the concept translates well and provides highly useful information when properly approached.

We've shown only a few examples of the usefulness of CLV and market damage calculations. We can help you to create the system that makes the most sense in your business, or you can wade through the scenarios and calculations yourself. Some things should be outsourced to ensure accuracy and realism.

No one wants to engage in self-surgery.

Return on Investment

We move now to the concept that allows us to place dollar values on projects within the contact center context. Return on investment (ROI) is one way to place a value on projects. Two other commonly used methods include cost/benefit ratios and payback period. The first of these entails capturing the costs of a project as well as the benefits achieved by the firm for the outlay and computing the relevant ratio. The second, payback period, computes the amount of time it will take for the project to earn back its costs or, essentially, break even.

Generally, it is more useful to look at the actual return on investment rather than a payback period. Doing so starts with benefits/costs (BCR) ratio such that:

$$BCR = \frac{\text{Project benefits}}{\text{Project costs}}$$

The difference for ROI is looking at net benefits divided by costs converted into a percentage such that:

$$ROI = \frac{\text{Net project benefits}}{\text{Project costs}} \times 100$$

This is the same basic formula used in valuing other projects that are computed as earning/investment, such as in valuing a stock. For example, a stock purchased at $98 and selling a year later for $122 yields a rounded up return of (122 - 98)/98 x 100 = 24.5 percent.

A few words of caution are in order. This process, like most others, works as "garbage in/garbage out." Be careful to fully account for all important aspects and only those that are important. For example, use only the most credible sources of data; where there is a choice of analysis techniques, always select the more conservative of the alternatives so as not to overstate the results. Attempt to isolate the effects of the project so that the true benefits (and problems) are properly quantified and known. Remove outliers from the data because extreme data points are less likely to reflect true events and sometimes exert extreme and superfluous influence on outcomes. Fully load all costs of a program. Note intangible costs and benefits, recognizing that these cannot be (or are not) monetized. Intangibility does not confer irrelevancy; so acknowledge and list these for due consideration. Last, of course, communicate the results to decision-makers.

While the example above concerned a stock, we can also assess the ROI of projects such as a customer satisfaction or retention initiative. The calculations are more complex, but the same principles apply. On the facing page, we have tabled an example for valuing a post-call survey program, starting with a profit and loss statement and moving on to an ROI calculation.

The goal is to move customers up the scale from lower evaluations to higher evaluations [1-4 (not happy) to 8-9 (delighted)]. Research shows that acting on data gathered at the agent level can move delighted or very engaged customers 5 to 10 points a month. Looking at it conservatively, let's say we can only move it by 5 points based on actions taken as a result of the post-call survey program at the agent level plus the benefits realized from our IVR and agent monitoring programs (IQM). A 1 percent improvement in the number of "very engaged" customers will be worth X amount of money in the bank balances of the firm.

In this example, we propose 100,000 customers served multiplied by the monthly value per customer of $50, equaling $5 million as the asset base controlled by the center. Assume that 60 percent of the customers are

VOC Profit and Loss Statement

Asset (Value of Delighted Callers)

Customers Served by Contact Center		100,000	
Monthly Customer Value		$50.00	
Center Asset Base Control		$5,000,000.00	
60.00%	Delighted by experience (Protected) *	$3,000,000.00	
5.00%	% Dissatisfied by experience (Lost) **	$250,000.00	
Revenue Ownership			$2,750,000.00

Cost of Goods Sold

Monthly Contact Center Budget	$2,083,333.00	
Net Protected Revenue		$666,667.00

* percent of 8s and 9s on 9-point scale
** percent of 1s, 2s, 3s, 4s on 9-point scale

©Customer Relationship Metrics

Contact Center EQM ROI

$$\frac{[(\%\text{Delighted Calls} \times \text{Customers Served}) \times \text{Avg. Revenue per Customer}] - [(\%\text{Dissatisfied Calls} \times \text{Customers Served}) \times \text{Avg. Revenue per Customer})]}{\text{Fully Loaded Costs for the Period}}$$

Contact Center ROI 132%

©Customer Relationship Metrics

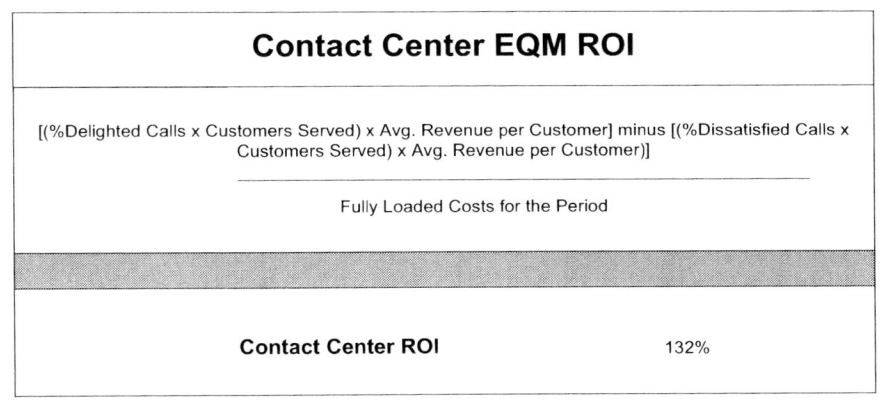

delighted by the experience and 5 percent are disgusted by it. The dollar impact is .6 x 100,000 x 50 = $3 million from those who are delighted. Those unhappy represent a loss to the firm calculated as .05 x 100,000 x 50 = $250,000. Netting these two figures leaves a net revenue result of $2,750,000 for the month, which we call revenue ownership. The revenue ownership must now be reduced by the costs to run the contact center, which we assume to be $2, 083,333, leaving a balance of $666,667. We now transfer these figures into the equation in the second table to get the result of 132 percent return on investment ($2,750,000/2,083,333).

We made numerous assumptions throughout this chapter that would be unnecessary in any real-world application. We would know the center budget, the cost of capital, the number of customers served, and through our IQM program, IVR feedback program and EQM program, we would know how many customers were saved and lost, just to name a few. The necessary data tend to build up over time from the various parts of the business such that the output from one program becomes part of the input for the next analysis.

Remember, in principle, it is relatively simple to complete these calculations; nevertheless, it is quite complex to do so in the real world. The more realistic the model of the firm, the more complex it will be to build today, to modify over time and to interpret with precision.

People do not build their own MRI equipment or run their own blood tests. Rather, the hospital's equipment and personnel, experts all, are deemed to be the superior choice. Again, it is important to emphasize that it is logical and reasonable to hire expertise when it is needed and not readily available within the firm. Proper use of the products of these analyses demands the employment of only top-quality assessment personnel. Second best will not do for mission-critical analyses that will drive the business, so seek out the best rather than the cheapest asset; only utilize those with the education and experience to bring true expertise to the endeavor.

Self-surgery is painful and unnecessary. Don't worry. We are here to stop the pain.

Chapter 11:
Communicating the Results

Maybe the best medical analogy for this chapter is plastic surgery. Plastic surgeons are often believed to practice trivial medicine because so much of their business centers on Botox injections and face lifts for people with more dollars than sense. But a moment of "naked" honesty will reveal that people are personally vain themselves and judgmental of others. This is very nearly a universal truth. A quick look at the hair and skin care aisles of any drug store will provide all the needed evidence for personal vanity. And there are literally hundreds of books and research articles about judgments made by people based on very small evidence, and how those are then generalized to whole populations. (See, for example, the literature on stereotypes from psychology or employee evaluations from Human Resources, just to name two types of literature rich in "snap judgments.") In truth, appearance matters both personally and professionally. We want to look good for ourselves and to avoid the negative judgments of others.

So this chapter revolves around trying to create a good impression for the good work that you've accomplished. Not only is there nothing wrong with this, we argue that it is absolutely necessary to establishing the worth of the contact center.

Taking our analogy one step further, it's worth noting that plastic surgeons also fix cleft palates and other problems that are both unsightly and non-functional. In other words, like other doctors, they fix things. So here we'll demonstrate a few things that can be fixed using data collected from real-time surveys by comparing groups, looking across time or extrapolating to the population at large from the sample data.

Communicating the results of the EQM research effort is a key but sometimes overlooked step in the process. Doing this right can be the difference between renewed funding and cutbacks that cannot be supported; the difference between usable feedback and mass confusion; the difference between having an engaged, motivated group dedicated to the Rally Cry and getting by with handling customer interactions.

Know Your Audience

Who is getting the information? Who is using the information? What specific information are they actually using? It is important to know and understand the answers to these questions before communicating the results. Data must be relevant to the decisions that the audience must make. Actionable data provides answers, direction and purpose.

Here are the audiences that are most likely to require feedback from the EQM program: executive management, operational management of each contact center, teams and individual agents. Each of these audiences will need different data, and graphic or tabular presentations of the data. Additionally, consider when oral presentations will be needed and prepare for those in conjunction with the written reports. Never miss an opportunity to tout the advances made by the program and the benefits achieved.

Reports for Executive Management

As a critical function within the enterprise, any report to executive management must summarize the contribution achieved for the investment made. Beyond a mere presentation of high-level numeric results, an executive-level report should include a summary of the mission, the investment in customer relationship management, the contribution to customer loyalty and sales, a summary of the product, services or process issues identified for enhancement and the results of those initiatives (beyond the contact center).

Looking first and foremost at executive management needs, a first-rate presentation is paramount. Looks matter a good deal at this level, so do not skimp on color graphs and high-quality paper.

Executive Committee Report

In general, such a presentation will require an executive summary, a response questionnaire, a narrative including tables and graphs as appropriate, and a summary/conclusion section.

1. Executive Summary: Give an overview briefly stating the purpose and results of the research. The executive summary must be parsimonious. It should be brief and cogent, wasting no space or words. Make it as objective and clean as possible.

2. Response Questionnaire: Include the survey instruments next. Evaluators of the research need to understand exactly what was asked. It is generally a good idea to include an accounting of the responses to the questions. Those will be readily available from the frequency tables in the analysis printout. You can include both the questionnaire and the responses in this step, hence the name "response questionnaire." It is also possible to include the means for each question if that information will be meaningful to the reader. Some people are sensitive to the order in which the questions are asked, so it is wise to use that order in this section and indicate this clearly. Avoid needless discussion on question order to save time for the important business of selling executives on the value of the research initiative. On the next page is an example of a response questionnaire.

Survey Questions	No. of Responses	Response Scale	Mean Score	Percent Delight
How satisfied are you with our company overall?	538	1-9	77.62	67.00%
How likely are you to purchase additional products from our company in the future?	538	1-9	80.56	74.60%
How likely are you to recommend our products to someone in your family, a friend or a colleague in the future?	538	1-9	79.55	73.30%
Please rate your satisfaction with the ease of using the automated system to reach an agent at the beginning of your call.	538	1-9	74.31	66.40%
Overall, how satisfied are you with our customer service call center?	538	1-9	77.88	72.70%
Please rate how satisfied you are overall with the service provided by this agent?	538	1-9	87.27	85.30%
Please rate your satisfaction with how **quickly** the agent understood the reason for your call.	538	1-9	89.34	86.50%
Please rate the level of ownership the agent took for resolving the reason that you called today.	538	1-9	85.69	83.10%
Please rate the agent's **knowledge** of our products and services.	538	1-9	87.18	82.80%
Please rate the confidence you have in the answer provided.	538	1-9	83.55	84.10%
Please rate the agent's ability to present appropriate options or solutions.	538	1-9	85.69	82.20%
Please rate your satisfaction that the agent treated you as a valued customer.	538	1-9	87.76	87.60%
Were you calling today to resolve a problem?	538	Yes/No	Yes=53.1%	N/A

Including the call you just completed, please enter the number of times you have called about this specific problem or inquiry.	538	Numeric	1.34	N/A
Please press 1 if the problem or inquiry was resolved with the agent today. Press 2 if your problem or inquiry was not resolved on this call.	538	1-2	1=81.4%	N/A

3. Narrative: In the narrative, state the purpose at the beginning and the results at the end, and in between, tell how the research was conducted: who, what, when, where, why, how. Expect to put every piece of important information in the narrative at least twice: once verbally, and at least once more in a table, graph or both. Remember that people do not process information the same way. Some are verbally oriented; others are visual learners, so graphs will be easier to absorb. Still others relate best to numbers — and a table that would put most of us to sleep will sing out loud and clear to them. Include a plan for how the results will be used and outline additional resources needed, including budget, time, space, etc. If the proposed plan can reassign already-available resources without incurring additional expense, then all the better. Put that information in and anything else that supports the argument. Sample components of the narrative section of an executive committee report are shown below.

Example 1

This past quarter, the contact center experienced an unexpected 40 percent increase in call volume, due in large part to the promotional campaign launched in early July. The impact of the large increase in call volume had an adverse effect on operational metrics such as average speed of answer (ASA), average wait time and service level, as well as customer satisfaction levels. As a result, the contact center fell below performance goals on external quality monitoring customer satisfaction metrics for the first time over the last five fiscal quarters.

Voice of the Customer Metrics

	Actual Performance	Goal Performance	Variance from Goal (%)
Call resolution percent	87.43%	90.00%	-2.86%
First-call resolution percent	74.40%	80.00%	-7.00%
Percent repeat calls	13.15%	10.00%	31.50%
Overall satisfaction with company	81.00	85.00	04.71%
Overall satisfaction with call	83.33	87.50	-4.77%
Overall satisfaction with rep	87.63	90.00	-2.63
Percent alerts	5.20%	3.00%	73.33%
Incomplete survey percent	23.40%	18.00%	30.00%
Total number of calls surveyed	1,215	1,300	-6.54%
Percent of total calls surveyed	3.25%	4.50%	-27.78%

Example 2

In an average month, 100,000 customers call into our phone support center. At an average monthly value of $50 per customer, our phone support center has the potential to impact approximately $5 million in revenue. This past year, our phone support center reached performance goals (customer delight of 60 percent, and customer dissatisfaction of 5 percent), representing a 15 percent improvement in performance over the prior year. The result of this improvement is the protection of $750,000 of company revenue. In comparing this figure to the operating costs for this same period, a return on investment figure of 138 percent results.

VOC Profit and Loss Statement

Income (Value of Delighted Callers)		
Customers Served by Contact Center	100,000	
Monthly Customer Value	$50.00	
Center Asset Base Control	$5,000,000.00	
60.00% Delighted by experience (Protected)	$3,000,000.00	
5.00% % Dissatisfied by experience (Lost)	$250,000.00	
Revenue Ownership		**$2,750,000.00**
Cost of Goods Sold		
Monthly Contact Center Budget	$2,000,000.00	
Net Protected Income		**$750,000.00**

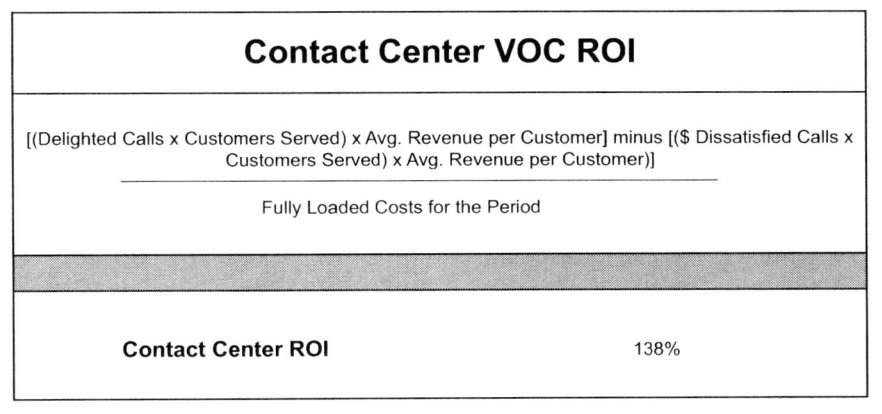

©Customer Relationship Metrics

Contact Center VOC ROI

[(Delighted Calls x Customers Served) x Avg. Revenue per Customer] minus [($ Dissatisfied Calls x Customers Served) x Avg. Revenue per Customer)]

Fully Loaded Costs for the Period

Contact Center ROI	138%

©Customer Relationship Metrics

Example 3

During the first quarter of this year, our contact center once again exceeded the performance of our competitors in the industry. Our domestic location (location 2) contributed to this positive standing, while our offshore location (location 1) continued to struggle to meet performance goals.

4. Summary: The summary/conclusion should again state the purpose of the research, the results of the research, the uses to which the results can be put, and subsequent plans for implementation. This should be much

Question	Location 1 (Offshore) Percent Delight	Location 1 (Offshore) Mean	Location 2 (Domestic) Percent Delight	Location 2 (Domestic) Mean	Client Quarter 1 Percent Delight	Client Quarter 1 Mean	Client Quarter 1 N	Industry Average Quarter 1 Percent Delight	Industry Average Quarter 1 Mean	Industry Average Quarter 1 N
Overall satisfaction with company	53.98%	70.38	76.55%	71.25	62.80%	77.88	6775	54.02%	69.6	34983
Customer contact center adds value	55.88%	72.88	78.32%	74.13	64.70%	79.17	6775	57.00%	73	12673
Likelihood to recommend products	56.95%	69.5	79.08%	70.38	63.80%	75.88	6775	56.66%	68.4	26181
Overall satisfaction with agent	69.15%	78.13	92.01%	77.88	85.60%	89.73	6775	68.07%	76.88	18940
Agent's level of professionalism	74.59%	81.88	91.69%	83.25	84.90%	89.57	6775	74.38%	82	14916
Agent's knowledge of products	69.85%	78.5	91.27%	79.5	81.00%	87.3	6775	69.87%	78.13	33509
Agent provided a clear and complete answer	70.35%	77.25	88.18%	77.25	79.50%	84.93	6775	69.15%	76.13	13917
	Percent		Percent		Percent			Percent		
Problem Resolution: All problem calls	62.09%		92.97%		81.80%			61.80%		
Problem Resolution: First-time problem calls	41.58%		71.94%		58.90%			38.74%		
Call Resolution: All calls	80.47%		92.86%		88.30%			79.54%		
Call Resolution: First-time calls	60.56%		79.12%		68.80%			57.40%		

shorter than the narrative, and should highlight what is successful and useful. It is mission critical to aid executives in understanding the research, so make it clear.

The outlined report is intentionally redundant. It is the writer's job to make it seem less so. Making the same points repeatedly is necessary since this may be the only opportunity to win the case. The idea is to repeat the major points but with more detail from executive summary through narrative, and then summarize again in the conclusion, leaving the reader no choice but to see the absolute rationality of the conclusions. A report should not leave the reader with questions. Make all the necessary information available, place that information into multiple formats, polish the language and present it in an appealing report. Again, it is critical to hold this job to the highest standard. Allocate sufficient time for the best report writer and editor available to do this job.

Reports for Operations Management

The packaging of the external quality monitoring program is an important marketing tool for the contact center and the operational team responsible for its performance. A critical component of the reports is that the research has been executed correctly and the validity of the results is certain. This data informs operational decisions, populates performance management systems and calculates incentives/performance pay. The data is used along with the internal call monitoring data and the operational metrics to provide an accurate assessment of the service function, and to identify directives for each agent and each team.

In addition to providing a snapshot of the service the contact center is providing to customers, operational reports will likely focus on two aspects: location-specific analysis over time and location comparisons. Location-specific data compares the period just past to prior periods and perhaps even to the last year. Such a comparative analysis allows operational management to track changes over time, revealing which interventions yielded the most positive results for a single location.

From a comparison perspective, it is useful for specific locations to be able to rate their performance against their peer locations, as well as the contact center effort as a whole. It can be a source of pride for the successful locations and a spur to more intense efforts for those that lag behind the whole. Continue to make use of multiple formats for the presentation of results. Remember, some readers are more verbal, visual or numerical than others.

The highest tier of the operations-level report is a summary of all feedback collected for all of the contact center locations and departments. This view of the data provides a status report of the past period's performance, which can be compared to prior periods. The table below provides aggregate data regarding customer ratings on each question within the survey. The data found in this table presents % Delight (in this example scores of 8 or 9 on the 1-9 response scale used) and mean score, extrapolated to a 100-point scale.

	Surveys Completed	Mean Score (On 100-Pt. Scale)	Percent Delight
Satisfaction with company	401	80.32	67.9
Likelihood to recommend	401	80.09	70.4
Satisfaction with phone center	401	83.72	74.7
Satisfaction with wait time	401	82.41	74.1
Overall satisfaction with agent	401	92.67	88.3
Q3-Took ownership for resolution	401	92.13	88.9
Q4-Knowledge of products/services	401	91.74	88.3
Q5-Ability to present options	401	91.74	87

On this scale, the lowest service rating (a rating of 1) is equivalent to zero points on the 100-point scale, and the highest rating (a rating of 9) is equivalent to 100 points. The distribution of points is as follows:

Value on 9-point scale	Value on 100-point scale
1	0.00
2	12.50
3	25.00
4	37.50
5	50.00
6	62.50
7	75.00
8	87.50
9	100.00

You can classify customer ratings on key questions into loyalty categories to more closely examine the relationship between customer satisfaction and loyalty. Combine key loyalty questions, including customer satisfaction with the company, the representative and the call itself to create a customer loyalty index (CLI). Customer satisfaction directly relates to long-term customer loyalty that ultimately contributes to shareholder wealth. Trend analysis of CLI is critical to determining if change initiatives are being recognized by customers, reflected in service delivery evaluations, and positively impacting return on investment (ROI).

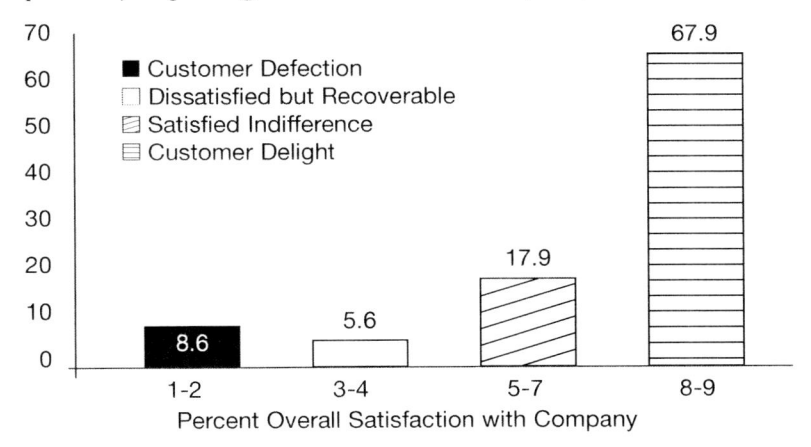

■ Customer Defection
☐ Dissatisfied but Recoverable
▨ Satisfied Indifference
▤ Customer Delight

1-2	3-4	5-7	8-9
8.6	5.6	17.9	67.9

Percent Overall Satisfaction with Company

Four categories are represented in the CLI chart:

- **Customer Delight (horizontal stripes in CLI charts).** The top two categories on the scale (8 and 9) represent customers who are delighted with your company/service/agents. These customers are key company assets that have been preserved through the service experience. Their high scores provide assurance that they will stay with your company, provided you maintain a consistent level of service.
- **Satisfied Indifference (diagonal stripes in CLI charts).** These customers (categories 5-7) represent the primary focus for the next evaluation period. They are generally satisfied, but cannot be counted in the completely loyal category. If presented with an opportunity, these customers may select a different provider. As such, the goal is to move these customers into the delighted category.
- **Dissatisfied but Recoverable (white bar in CLI charts).** Customers in this category (3 and 4) did not have a positive experience and would likely switch, but you may be able to reach out and change their perception by correcting the service experience. As such, timely and informed follow-up is the key to success with this category of customers. These customers should be the secondary focal group.
- **Customer Defection (black bar in CLI charts).** These customers in categories 1 and 2 were very dissatisfied and are most likely to leave your company for an alternative.

The examination of performance means and percentages for key survey questions as described thus far is important, but contributes only part of the information regarding the callers' evaluation of service provided by your centers. The survey data was collected to answer two questions: How are we doing? and What is critical to the quality of the service experience?

- "How" is answered by the caller evaluation of the attributes of service, called a performance measure or the mean level of performance; and,
- "What" is answered by the analytics which identify the service attrib-

utes that statistically impact caller satisfaction, essentially the drivers of caller satisfaction.

The performance means and calculated impact values of each service attribute enable the quantitative identification of areas in which service performance may be below an acceptable level *and* the resulting impact on satisfaction is high. The process of calculating impact values is a little more intricate than the process of calculating mean performance scores. The regression analysis from the caller satisfaction data computes the impact values and identifies the level of impact each attribute has on overall satisfaction. This allows supervisors and managers to concentrate on the areas that are most important to customers.

The combined aspects of service produce an effect that is perceived by the customer. When determining improvement issues, you should consider how the attributes interact, rather than a static attribute-by-attribute evaluation. Therefore, use a regression model to examine the callers' overall perception of the service received during the call. An example model, in words, is:

The rating of overall satisfaction with the agent (Q1) is a function of how quickly the agent understood the reason for the call (Q2), how professional the agent was during the call (Q3), the agent's knowledge of products and services (Q4), the agent providing a complete answer (Q5), the confidence in the information provided by the agent (Q6), and being treated as a valued customer (Q7).

That model, mathematically, is:

$$Q1 = f(Q2, Q3, Q4, Q5, Q6, Q7)$$

By running the regression analysis, you can determine which attributes impact caller satisfaction the most. Combine these drivers of satisfaction with the measures of performance to present a complete picture, as shown on the following page.

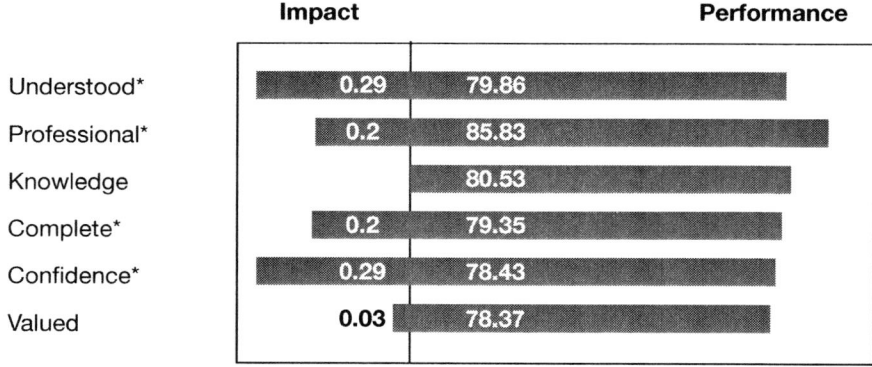

	Impact	Performance
Understood*	0.29	79.86
Professional*	0.2	85.83
Knowledge		80.53
Complete*	0.2	79.35
Confidence*	0.29	78.43
Valued	0.03	78.37

*Statistically significant

Based on the multivariate regression model, "conveying confidence in the response given," "quickly understanding reason for the call," "being professional" and "providing a complete answer" are the most important drivers of satisfaction with the representative for this set of data.

The drivers-of-satisfaction results (presented with the impact/performance chart as above) will vary for different sets of data. One team compared to another may have very different strengths and weaknesses. The power of such analysis is that it narrows the scope of focal areas to a manageable number. The example below shows the chart for Team 1, and on the next page is the chart for Team 2. The drivers-of-satisfaction analysis for the two teams is given pictorially using the bars, but without the actual numbers

Team 1

	Impact	Performance
Treated as Valued*		
Confidence		
Communicating		
Knowledge*		
Ownership		
Understood		

*Statistically significant

Team 2

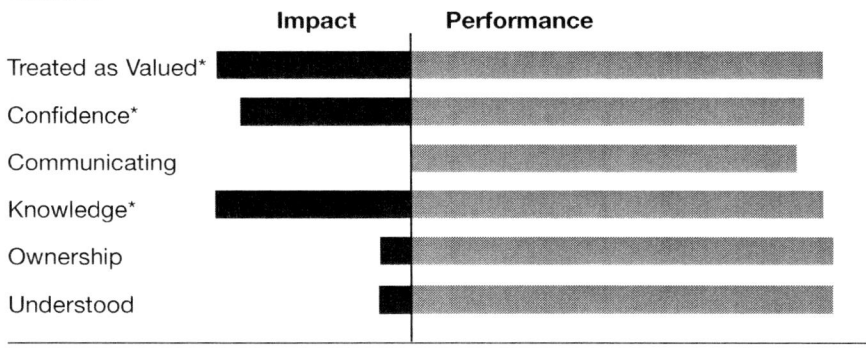

	Impact	Performance
Treated as Valued*		
Confidence*		
Communicating		
Knowledge*		
Ownership		
Understood		

*Statistically significant

for performance and impact. These teams differed only in their leadership and average tenure. Customer types served and location were both similar.

Despite the similarities between these two teams, each team generated different performance means and drastically different impact values. Clearly, Team 2 outperformed Team 1 on every dimension. The results from the surveys define the key drivers for Team 1's customers to be "treated as valued" and "knowledge." Team 2's key drivers also include these two attributes plus "confidence." As Team 2 is receiving higher customer evaluations, Team 1 should emulate the behavior of Team 2 as related to these performance attributes. It is interesting and instructive to ponder "confidence" as a key driver of the superior team while it is absent from the key drivers of the inferior team. Maybe the reason "confidence" is not a key driver for Team 1 can be simply explained by the lesser overall performance of Team 1; in other words, callers simply had less confidence in Team 1 due to lower overall performance along all dimensions as compared to Team 2. Hence, while "confidence" could and did drive overall satisfaction with the agent in Team 2, it could not, and did not, in Team 1. So it all fits together very nicely and provides yet more evidence for the emulation of Team 2 as the "best practices" model for Team 1.

Comparative analysis of different supervisors, teams, locations and departments often reveals service attributes that should be emulated and

Team Comparison with Normalized Data (100 Pt. Mean)

	C1	C2	C3	C4	C5	Q1	Q2	Q3	Q4	Q5	Q6	%
Team A	73.8	80	74.1	79.1	80.6	83.4	83.1	89.4	80.3	80.9	80.6	2.4%
Team B	82.8	81.1	79.9	81.4	81.6	82.4	82.6	88.7	84.8	80.4	80.9	22.3%
Team C	76.1	77.9	77.7	82.2	80.6	81.9	86.2	88	86.4	80.6	81.4	3.7%
Team D	77.4	78.7	78.2	85.4	86.7	89.4	87.2	92.8	91.2	90.2	90.2	5.5%
Team E	69.4	64.2	61.2	66.1	72	70.1	69.9	75	71.2	69.7	68	18.82%
Team F	74.4	75	71.4	81.4	83.3	87.8	89.7	90	87.5	88.9	85.3	2.5%
Team G	73	73.8	74.8	82.8	77.5	81.1	77.7	87.8	78.7	76.5	74.8	2.5%
Team H	95.8	91.7	95.8	100	100	100	100	100	100	100	100	4.67%
Team I	63.4	60.9	62.1	69.8	68.9	68.4	71.1	81.6	72.4	71.4	72.1	16.5%
Team J	64.2	69.4	62.3	69.6	66.9	72.7	71.9	80.6	71.4	70.6	68.1	21.11%

Note: C1–C5 would be general satisfaction criteria; Q1–Q6 would be agent attributes.

others in need of intervention. Based on the table on the facing page, only one of the four teams that represent the largest percentage of completed surveys is a top-performing team (based on mean survey scores). An analysis of the strengths, skills and approaches taken by members of Team B could aid members of the remaining teams in improving their own performance levels. Conversely, analyzing the lower performing teams could identify the unique challenges they face in servicing customers.

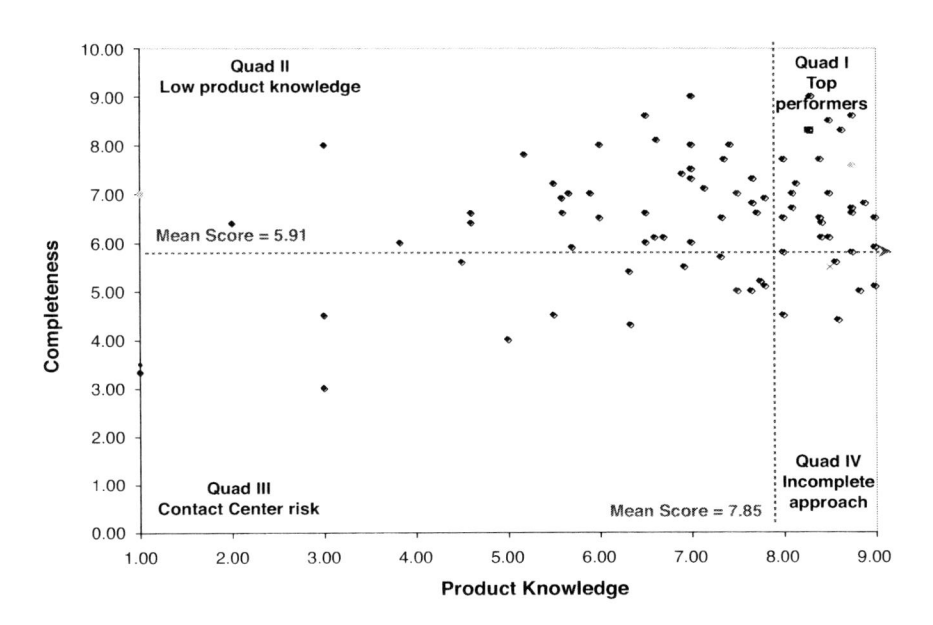

In the example below, we analyzed the characteristics of a low-performing team in order to design corrective training. A drivers-of-satisfaction analysis revealed that "knowledge of the company's products" and "completeness of responses" were the behaviors that had the greatest impact on the customer's perception of the call. We plotted individual performance on these two key behaviors to create a visual profile of the team's makeup. The team's mean scores (on a 1-9 scale) on these two key behaviors divide the scatter plot below into four quartiles. Each quartile represents a unique agent profile, with a known set of strengths and weaknesses. For example, quadrant III, in the lower left side of the scatter plot, represents the call center's risk. These agents are below-average performers on both of the key behaviors that have the greatest impact on customer perception of the service experience. While this quadrant represents a comparatively low percentage of this team's membership, management must conduct an assessment of skill and desire to improve in a timely manner for agents in quadrant III in order to minimize the risk to the contact center and, ultimately, the company's revenue stream.

Let's look at an instance where agent tenure was selected as the differentiating variable among agents. A great deal of time and energy is spent in the contact center industry empowering and developing agents in hopes of ensuring longevity. These actions do not always guarantee that the most tenured agents will be the best performing agents, as was the case in the example below.

Mean Scores — Satisfaction with Representative by Month of Representative Tenure

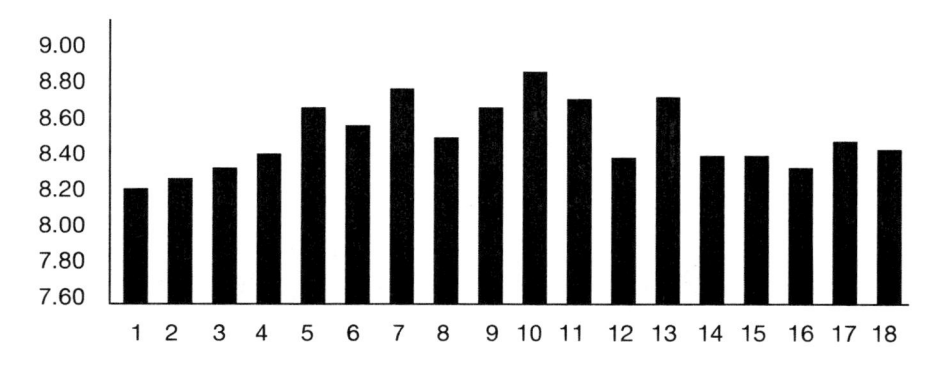

The figure above clearly places peak agent performance at approximately 10 months of tenure. Introducing a performance intervention prior to month 10 of an agent's tenure can extend the peak performance level.

Call resolution plays a key role in driving customer satisfaction. Significant differences in satisfaction scores exist between customers whose calls are brought to resolution and those whose problems/inquiries require follow-up. The following table exemplifies exactly why call resolution is such a key metric.

Was your request resolved during this call today?

	Frequency	Percent	Company Satisfaction	Call Satisfaction	Agent Satisfaction
Yes	1,356	82.1%	79.35	85.33	89.14
No	296	17.9%	35.09	30.70	32.56

Repeat calls also have a dramatic impact on customer satisfaction. Repeated calls by customers are not only costly from the perspective of agent talk time, but also have a fairly severe impact on customer satisfaction with the company, the call and the agent.

Is this the first time you called to resolve this particular Issue?

	Frequency	Percent	Company Satisfaction	Call Satisfaction	Agent Satisfaction
Yes	1,111	67.3%	80.60	84.42	87.07
No	541	32.7%	52.56	57.32	62.43

How many times have you called about this request?

NUM	Frequency	Percent	Cumulative Percent
1	1,111	67.30%	67.30%
2	322	19.50%	86.70%
3	92	5.60%	92.30%
4	38	2.30%	94.60%
5	36	2.20%	96.80%
6	11	0.70%	97.50%
7	4	0.20%	97.70%
8	10	0.60%	98.30%
9	9	0.50%	98.80%
10+	19	1.20%	100.00%
Total	1,652	100.00%	

With a representative sample, we can extrapolate the percentage of repeat calls to all calls taken during the month, in order to calculate the operational cost of repeat calls. The average cost per call is multiplied by the number of repeat calls (as determined by percentages below) for the second, third, etc., calls required. **Keep in mind that the indirect cost is also a factor as it is associated with the significantly decreased satisfaction as shown in the section above.**

The Direct Impact of Repeat Calls
Based on 200,000 calls to resolve a problem in a quarter

Number of Calls by Customers	Percent Total Problem Calls	Number of Additional Calls
2 Calls	27.7%	55,400 x 1 = 55,4000
3 Calls	22.6%	45,200 x 2 = 90,400
4 Calls	16.1%	32,200 x 3 = 96,600
5 Calls	10.3%	20,600 x 4 = 82,400
6 or More Calls	23.2%	46,400 x 5 = 232,000

556,800 x $5 (cost per call) = $2.78 million or $11.2 million annual

The decrease in customer satisfaction can impact revenue 5-10 times this number

From this set of data, it's easy to see how massive the cost of repeat calls can be. To get this, we simply computed the percentage of repeat calls from 2 to 6 or more to get resolution of the problem creating 5 categories. We then multiplied each percent by 200,000 (the number of problem calls) and then multiplied each category by the extra repeat calls needed. Next, we summed across the categories to find the total of additional calls made across all categories. This result was multiplied by the average cost per call of $5.

An analysis of company-level data in this manner provides members of the operational team with a solid understanding of current customer satisfaction levels, the drivers of customer satisfaction and areas in need of improvement. However, examining the data longitudinally reveals performance trends and the impact of interventions.

The figure below is a control chart for call resolution. Control charts are often used in Six Sigma to differentiate between normal and abnormal process variation. Each point in the control chart below represents weekly performance on the key metric call resolution. The thick, black horizontal lines represent the upper (UCL) and lower (LCL) control limits for this metric, based on mean performance and standard deviation of weekly performance around this mean. Any point that resides either below the LCL or above the UCL indicates that the call resolution process is out of control, requiring an intervention.

Performance above the UCL indicates that agents are resolving an abnormally high percentage of calls. On the surface this may seem desirable, but further analysis reveals that resolution was gained at the expense of customer satisfaction. Performance below the LCL could have severe implications on customer satisfaction and contact center costs.

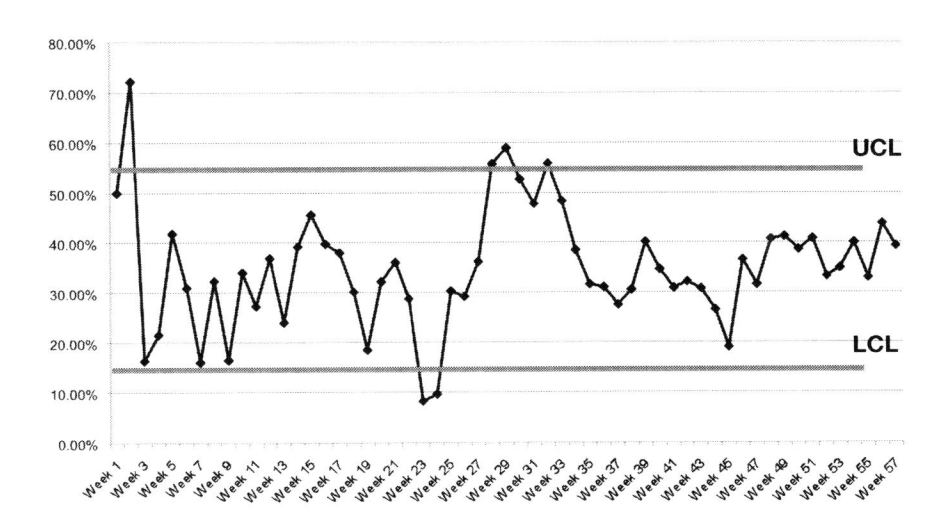

Reports for Supervisors and Agents

Managing a team of contact center agents requires a combination of quantitative and qualitative customer feedback to measure, track, compare and motivate. And the shorter the lag time between a call and the availability of the customer's feedback, the better!

The availability of real-time data expedites a supervisor's ability to identify trends in performance, provide feedback to agents and conduct service recoveries for defective service experiences.

Customer Comment Report

Customers are in a unique position to motivate agents through their positive comments. The knowledge that a customer was impacted by a service experience to the point where he/she would take the time to make it known, is often more effective than any praise given by a peer or supervisor. Conversely, a customer's comment could also shed light on sub-par scores. It is the complement of this qualitative feedback to the quantitative data that allows for a holistic approach to the customer experience.

Since customers are not able to see and have never met the agents they interact with, they create a mental image of what this person must be like using expectations and prior experience as a guide. Consumers categorize others because it makes their lives simpler and provides a feeling of control. Callers, therefore, will know (or think they know) how to approach a situation in which they are dealing with people they don't know because they have already categorized it. They begin with a prototype in mind of what the agent should be like and how the interaction should go. When an agent fits the prototype, and even goes beyond the customer's expectations, then Wow Factor feedback is collected:

- "The young man who helped me was courteous and quite knowledgeable about the company. In fact, if I ever needed anything in the future, I would be tempted to call back repeatedly until I reached him. I would even like to have him over for dinner. Maybe even have some beer and watch some baseball."

- "I found him to be intelligent, quick on the uptake, very pleasant, agreeable and had a sense of humor. That's rare among bankers."

- "Sharon was outstanding. She deserves some additional compensation. This is not one of her relatives. Thank you."

- "I was very impressed with the service that I got today over the phone. There is no way we will ever leave you unless somebody really, really screws something up bad."

This also takes a negative direction when the agent does not fit into the prototype.

- "Your customer service needs to do customer service. When they can't help you or refuse to help you, they follow up with the question: What more can they do to help? Well, they haven't done anything to begin with. A bunch of Cretins."
- "This rep treated me like I was stupid. I didn't appreciate it. You should never treat a customer like they are stupid, even if they are."
- "Your reps are the least informed, ill-equipped and most ignorant people I've ever run into. This bank is the perfect advertisement for any other bank."

We have all suspected that satisfaction and/or dissatisfaction in one's life role may be transferred into other life roles, like an agent taking a bad day out on a customer and vice versa. Frustration or dissatisfaction with a product/service may actually be the result of the consumer feeling frustrated in life roles other than the consumer role. Agents must not only manage the delivery, they must also detect and manage the issue for the caller — all with the company's best interest at the forefront.

- "Thank you for making my depressing life a little bit better with the service that you have given me."
- "The representative was very courteous and kind. I appreciate her. The only problem I've ever had is that our former banker had an affair with my husband. We divorced and now they're married. So, in that area, I'm not satisfied with the services the bank has provided."

Customers also expect to be treated in a manner consistent with their role as the customer in the interaction. Research shows that consumers evaluate service institutions and personnel positively when the personnel treat them as individuals who have specific needs to be met by the service interaction. If agents do not, customers will let you know.

- "The representative was very efficient, and this is true to your company's form. Every time that I have called customer service, I have been given excellent service, and today was no different."
- "It took four phone calls to get a pink slip. I've paid the car off. I deserve the pink slip. The first representative I spoke with said that I would get it in 10 days; it's now been six weeks. On this call, the rep said it was mailed yesterday. Somehow I doubt that, but we'll see. If I don't get it, I'll call you back. I don't mind. I'm retired. I've got nothing to do but call you folks until I get what I want."
- "You can return my calls, which you don't do. I've asked to talk to a supervisor a few times. I haven't gotten a supervisor to give me a call so why should you ask me to waste my time on this survey when you won't have a supervisor call me? I think that's pretty rude. You can call me at XXX-XXX-XXXX. I doubt that I'll hear from you, but it would be really nice if I did. It would make my day and might change my perception of how I've been treated."

Why be concerned with the research behind customer comments? Well, it's a component of increasing customer satisfaction, loyalty and creating a positive word-of-mouth. If you can better understand your customers, you can create a better environment for the service interaction. You can also educate your agents and use this information as a training opportunity for them to garner a better understanding of consumer comments. After all, customers do say the darndest things.

Real-Time Performance Dashboards

By viewing the real-time dashboard below, a supervisor could quickly surmise that today's call resolution and call satisfaction statistics are trending below the month's average. The supervisor now has a goal for the day, as well as a minute-by-minute indicator of his/her success in impacting these key metrics.

Effectiveness Dashboard

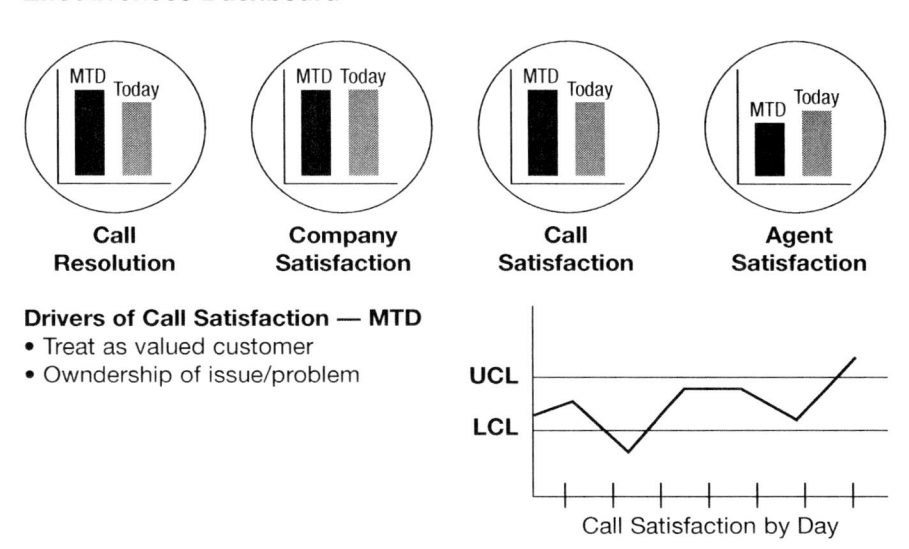

Call Resolution	Company Satisfaction	Call Satisfaction	Agent Satisfaction
MTD / Today	MTD / Today	MTD / Today	MTD / Today

Drivers of Call Satisfaction — MTD
- Treat as valued customer
- Owndership of issue/problem

Call Satisfaction by Day (UCL / LCL)

Real-time dashboard content for executives or other audience members may contain different metrics. A quality assurance manager will drill down into the metrics to review different teams and look within teams for agents who may be struggling.

Real-Time Alerts

The availability of real-time data also allows supervisors the opportunity to recover customers who have had a dissatisfying service experience. Consider these alerts the equivalent of medical emergency room services. Quick diagnosis and treatment of medical conditions can save lives. Quick diagnosis and treatment of dissatisfaction can save customers and profits —

both for today and for the lifetime of the customer. Although the caller may not have been satisfied with the service experience in general, satisfaction with the service recovery experience is significantly related to their intention to repurchase (Boshoff, 1999). If there is no process for service recovery, the relationships of 15 percent of your customers are at risk (if not 15 percent, insert the percentage of your callers who would rate the experience as poor). Customers who have had a service failure that was resolved quickly and properly are more loyal to a company than are customers who have never had a service failure — significantly more loyal (Blodgett, Wakefield and Barnes, 1995; Smith and Bolton, 1998). The key to success is a quick resolution. How quickly do you initiate a recovery plan after the dissatisfying experience? Is there a service recovery plan in operation?

Many contact centers have inadequate processes in place to capture, never mind address, a failure in customer experiences. The process, and its timeliness, leaves too many customer relationships exposed. Service recovery should protect the exposed asset during the call experience (whether that exposure was a direct result of agent behavior or caused by the organization's process). Is recovery of the relationship even possible? It is unlikely if you do not know about it, as only about 5 percent to 10 percent of customers choose to complain to the company (Tax and Brown, 1998). More likely, it results in negative word-of-mouth (market damage) and the discontinued use of your products and services. A lost customer is an easy, low-cost-to-acquire new customer for a competitor AND is customer value lost to your organization.

Components that facilitate timely notification of dissatisfaction enhance service recovery. By instituting a real-time survey, the amount of saved customer relationships will increase not only customer satisfaction, but have a direct link to an increase in customer loyalty. An immediate alert of a failed experience tells an important story. Is there a common issue with a particular agent? Ineffective behavior can be quickly addressed, minimizing the ongoing negative impact for the agent and the organization. Is there a common process issue? Caller dissatisfaction may be rooted in a new policy or procedure. Identify and change the procedure or identify and provide an effective agent response to common aspects of customer dissatisfaction. Extrapolate the findings from the service recovery group and leverage this within your organization.

A real-time alert feature delivers significant value by proactively responding to callers who experienced difficulty with an interaction and are leaving the interaction dissatisfied. The EQM program contains a systematic approach to capture the reason for the customer-defined failure (people, process or technology classifications) to highlight patterns for the organization. Without a framework, proving the effect of a process issue, for example, it is more difficult.

We included the dashboard with this chapter because it communicates to center management the critical elements that must be chronically monitored and managed.

Share the Knowledge

It is so important to share the wealth garnered through EQM programs with all who can use the information to create informed decisions moving forward. Executives select the strategies that propel the organization into the future and need information pertinent to strategic-level analyses. Operations managers need dashboard information to compare performance levels over time and across groups. Agents need concrete feedback in quantitative numbers reflecting their performance, accompanied by the absolute clarity that results from direct verbal feedback from callers. The vividness of qualitative feedback can completely overwhelm the comparatively pallid feedback of numbers.

Properly communicating the results of work well done can bring hearty congratulations, increase political clout and provide absolute proof of the value of the efforts undertaken in the contact center. At lower levels in the organization, proper communication results in better agent performance and lower agent turnover, and lower costs through greater first-time resolution of caller's issues, leading to higher customer satisfaction. Effectively communicating the results of recovery operations from a real-time caller satisfaction protocol can make the economic value of saved customers clear compared to the relatively small costs incurred. Everybody wins when the effort is scientifically planned and executed and the results are shared.

An attractive report is important, but a report making maximal use of the data to illustrate problems and recovery from those problems is crucial. Numerous ways of displaying data and analyses were presented here, and these are just a sample of what can be done by competent "doctors." Personalize the report to the audience such that operational metrics go to the supervisors and units, and more global concerns and victories are central to the story that executives hear. Make a good impression with quality paper, print, binding and use of color.

But most important is to share the health and wealth.

Chapter 12: Actionable Intelligence

We have provided numerous examples throughout the preceding chapters to illustrate our points. Here we will provide a few more to demonstrate how the results from real-time measurement can yield actionable intelligence.

Proficiency of Execution

In the first example (and we have several projects that match this theme), we'll examine the proficiency of execution at the tactical level. In this case, our client identified a number of behaviors that agents could either display or fail to display during a variety of service call types. To make the most of ongoing/developmental training, we used the existing data to create a model identifying which agent behaviors had the greatest impact on customer satisfaction for the two most important communication channels (contact center and electronic).

For the first channel, the agent behaviors measured included:

- The agent's **knowledge** of the company's products and services,

- The agent's ability to convey **confidence** in the information provided,
- The agent's effectiveness in quickly **understanding** the reason for the customer's call,
- The level of **professionalism** displayed by the agent,
- The agent's ability to make the customer feel **valued**, and
- The **completeness** of the responses provided.

Contact Center Channel (Type 1)

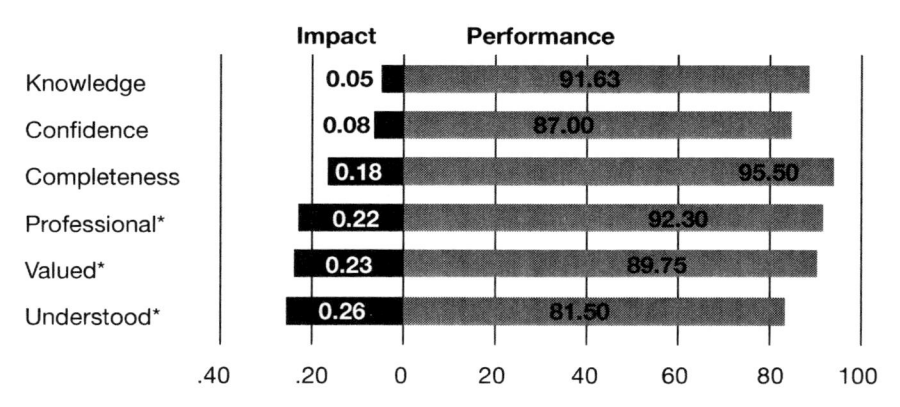

	Impact	Performance
Knowledge	0.05	91.63
Confidence	0.08	87.00
Completeness	0.18	95.50
Professional*	0.22	92.30
Valued*	0.23	89.75
Understood*	0.26	81.50

*Statistically significant

For the second call type, the agent behaviors measured included:
- The agent's **knowledge** of the company's products and services,
- The agent's ability to convey **confidence** in the information provided,
- The agent's effectiveness in quickly **understanding** the reason for the customer's call,
- The level of **professionalism** displayed by the agent,
- The **completeness** of the responses provided,
- The **quality** of the responses provided, and
- The agent's ability to make the customer feel **valued**.

Electronic Channel (Type 2)

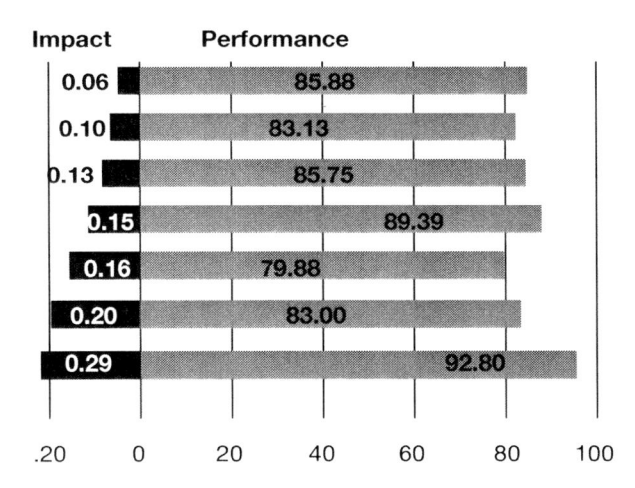

	Impact	Performance
Knowledge	0.06	85.88
Confidence	0.10	83.13
Understood	0.13	85.75
Professional	0.15	89.39
Completeness	0.16	79.88
Quality*	0.20	83.00
Valued*	0.29	92.80

*Statistically significant

Our analysis found that our client is better served by focusing scarce training resources on the behaviors that impact channel-specific customer perceptions of the agent rather than emphasizing everything (which for all practical purposes is the same as emphasizing nothing). The three variables with the greatest impact for the contact center were "quickly understood the reason for the call," "made the customer feel like a valued customer," and "the level of professionalism displayed by the agent." For the electronic channel, the major impact drivers were "made the customer feel valued" and "quality of the response." Armed with this intelligence, our client began to focus ongoing training on perfectly executing these aspects on each interaction (call and email/chat, respectively), while maintaining current levels on the less impactful elements.

Conceptually, it is possible to extrapolate from this example to one in which the focus shifts from training savings to targeted hiring and selection strategies. Let's assume the current selection strategy focused on hiring "people people" and required minimum scores on a valid and reliable empathy paper and pencil instrument for each applicant hired as an agent. Let's say that in this scenario, speed is a key driver of customer satisfaction.

Simple questions that are quick to address make this a high-productivity environment. Under these circumstances, forced hurried production compliance (that is, call time adherence, etc.) drives the agent evaluative system. Now these people-oriented agents are rushed to adhere rather than dealing with customers as people. Their performance may suffer and they will be unlikely to receive as many rewards. High turnover is likely due to a poor fit between the personality characteristics of those hired and the performance requirements of the job. A better selection strategy would center on high-energy, performance-motivated, quick-thinking individuals rather than high-empathy possessors

EQM and IQM Alignment

We take our next example from a study designed to more closely align the internal call monitoring program with the external quality monitoring program. As we suggested in an earlier chapter, the internal program generally consists of supervisors or other designated call monitors who listen to agent-handled calls and rate them along specific dimensions. Those dimensions tend to focus on adherence to legal or managerial considerations. The external quality program focuses on events and results from the customer's point of view. Generally, the customer cares little or none whether the agent tried to cross-sell or whether the caveats of required legalese have been read. The customer is much more likely to care whether the agent "understood" or "had knowledge" and that the cross-selling was a relationship enhancer and not a push.

We also sought to learn whether we could modify the IQM scoring components to more complementarily align the IQM and EQM programs. This study yielded several findings of interest.

We discovered, for example, that the IQM program items only allowed for "yes" and "no" responses. This seriously reduces the variability of responses and results in a "poorer" dataset. Changing the response set to 1-9 results in a "richer" dataset that is more likely to reflect the monitored behaviors. (Note that this would make all the previous data non-comparable to that accumulated going forward. This is an unavoidable result, but the inconvenience is temporary; over time comparable data will be available for period analysis.)

For a comparison between these two scoring methods, see the example below:

IQM Questions	Score (N&Y=0&1)	Score 1-9 (bad to great)
Tone?	1	6
Correct information?	1	9
Relevant information?	1	8
Hold procedures?	0	2
Transfer procedures?	1	9
Total	4	34
Average score	4/5 = 80%	34/45 = 75%

There are five questions on this IQM form. Hold procedures received an N=0 because the agent failed to say, "May I put you on hold while I check that information?" (which would have been the standard response). The agent's score is thus 4 of 5, or 80 percent — not great, but not terrible. Note that the score would also be 80 percent if there had been no hold procedure at all, because there was no such event in the call itself. In other words, there is no real difference between the non-event and the event done at less than standard in a yes/no scoring system.

In the last column, we examine the 1-9 rating options and note that the achieved score was 34 of 45, or 75 percent. In this case, it is readily apparent that the "hold" event took place and that it was poorly handled. The extremely low score for the hold procedure arose because the agent simply said, "hold" before placing the caller on hold, which could only have been worse if the agent had said nothing at all before initiating the hold. The point is that graduations of goodness are possible both to discern and to record which creates the "richness" that we claim for the dataset using the

1-9 system as opposed to simple yes/no.

In the 1-9 scaling, a zero would mean the event did not occur, so instead of 5x9 = 45 potential points, there would only be 4x9 = 36 potential points by which to divide the achieved score. If the hold event simply had been absent from the call, the total score would be 32 and the average would be 32/36 = 89% — a fine score.

So in the Y/N scheme, we don't know whether additional training is needed, while, under the 1-9 scheme, we do know how much of what type of training is required to bring agents up to standard. With little additional input, clients can become more effective, even though some may argue that it is less efficient to have more scoring options.

Additionally, we found that all questions on the client's IQM form were weighted the same. Clearly, some aspects are more important than others and that should be reflected in the endeavor. This can be accomplished by assigning weights based on the center's goals, legal concerns or other managerial priorities. The IQM program, unlike the EQM program, is intended to see from the organization's perspective and protect those legitimate interests; hence, weighting should be designed from this perspective and periodically revised as those concerns fluctuate over time.

In the simplest form, the final score becomes the calculation of the weight of each question multiplied by the score achieved on that question summed across all questions. The table on the previous page is an example of even weighting, which we have expanded into the following table when weights were added.

	1	2	3	4	5
IQM Questions	**Score (N&Y=0&1)**	**Score 1-9 (bad to great)**	**Weight**	**1x3**	**2x3**
Tone?	1	6	2	2	12
Correct information?	1	9	3	3	27
Relevant information?	1	8	3	3	24
Hold procedures?	0	2	1	0	2
Transfer procedures?	1	9	1	1	9
Total achieved	4	34	10	9	74
Potential score	5	45	10	10	90
Average score	4/5=80%	34/45=76%		9/10=90%	74/90=82%

From this table we learn yet more about the agent and what we need to do. It is clear that management judges the possession and dissemination of the correct and relevant information as the most important facets in this center. These make sense, in that wrong information and/or failure to provide the legalese required to protect the company could leave the firm open to legal action. With court awards ranging from petty cash to literally millions of dollars, reducing risk is sound business judgment. The next most important is "tone," and this is also sensible. As discussed in earlier chapters, people make judgments about others based on whatever information is at hand. One of the few cues available to callers is the agent's tone of voice. In this case, the agent's tone was poor quality — maybe due to a cold or to an enduring characteristic that makes the phrase "fingernails on a chalk board" meaningful. Comparisons of IQM ratings over time may assist in determining whether the issue is transient or enduring. If the problem is temporary, it's likely that nothing needs to be done (except recommend medical care to get the agent healthy). If the problem is judged to be enduring, then special assistance may be needed to help the agent overcome what is, in this industry, a disability. Lastly, if it cannot be overcome, this agent may need to be replaced, depending on the degree of importance attached to "tone" and ratings of performance over time. This "disabled" agent could be transferred to the email/Web side of the center where tone of voice is irrelevant. The larger point, however, is that we have some information with which to work. We can now dig down to the basic level to understand the problem and decide whether there are good solutions available.

These suggestions yield an IQM form that is flexible (evaluates the elements present in the call) and goal driven (assigns weights to each question) as well as statistically robust (captures variability via the 1-9 potential levels of response rather than the "present" or "absent" currently in use).

Site Usage

Next, we turn our attention to a study of two sites in different countries. Outsourcing and offshoring are topics of interest to businesses and consumers alike. Substantial evidence suggests that consumers much prefer to deal with agents from their home country, and with good reason.

As we already know, the communication interaction begins with a source that encodes a message, which is sent out over a medium to the receiver, who subsequently decodes that message and reacts to it. Usually, this reaction amounts to encoding a return message and sending it back to the original sender. If the receiver cannot understand properly what the sender is saying, then the receiver cannot formulate an appropriate response. Frustration can occur very quickly for both parties under these trying conditions. We posit that the more important or urgent the transaction, the more quickly frustration will build for the caller; and that frustration goes both ways. Anecdotal evidence suggests that turnover in call centers in foreign countries can be very high, with some agents complaining that Americans are rude when dealing with foreigners. Conversely, many

Americans loathe dealing with foreign agents because often the caller must work harder to complete the transaction, which sometimes takes twice as long as it should have and may still require hanging up only to start over in hopes of getting an American who speaks and understands the common vernacular.

That said, any good economist will declare that offshoring will continue as long as the wage differential between countries for roughly equivalent skills prevails. But what is to be done about the lower caller satisfaction scores? It is not of much use to save agent costs by tapping cheap labor if doing so runs our customers off to do business with our competitors.

In the midst of a project with a human resource benefits firm (where caller interactions could be vital and urgent as they concern medical procedure approvals, among other things), we noticed that the caller satisfaction scores suddenly jumped up for the offshore site and stayed there. On investigation, we found the old "divide and conquer" strategy at work. We often divide our agents into frontline and reserve. Originally, our client placed all agents on the front line, so that as agents finished a call the next would be routed to them. This meant that every call, hard or easy, had an equal chance of being routed abroad. What if the foreign agents take all initial calls? Then if the problem is simple, it can be handled quickly by the cheaper resource. If the problem is complex or communication is clearly poor in the dyad, the call could be routed instantly to the onshore agent for resolution. This is exactly what we found behind the instant jump in offshore caller satisfaction scores. With this strategy, a mix of more and less expensive agents could be used, driving down overall costs, while maintaining acceptable caller satisfaction scores. More importantly, customers would not need to start over (and we know how that displeases callers) because the call could be handed off as needed.

Customer Relationship Metrics continues to conduct research on topics related to offshore service. Please visit www.metrics.net/resources.php for the most current research articles.

NP Sales Versus NP Service

The sales function within every company can easily quantify its contribution to the company by making the cash register ring, so to speak. To quantify the value-added from the support function, a technology company implemented an immediate post-call survey program for the sales and support centers. After two months with the new measurement program, the management team had an obvious customer experience issue with the support center as evidenced in the customer evaluations.

Likelihood to Recommend

	Month 1	Month 2	Month 6
Sales Net Promoter Score =	84.6	85.1	72.5
Support Net Promoter Score =	42.7	43.3	57.5

Overall Agent Experience

Sales (% 8 and 9)	88.6	91.8	85.5
Support (% 8 and 9)	60.6	62.4	75.8

The measurement program implemented for this technology client allowed customers the opportunity to provide verbal feedback, supplementing the quantitative data. Customer comments helped uncover a CRM initiative that had a dramatic impact after only a single fiscal quarter. Analytics uncovered the drivers of dissatisfaction for the support center and the analysis of the survey comments identified the cause of these drivers. The survey data identified sales agents setting unrealistic expectations for order delivery and product specification exceeding needs (excessive upselling) as the largest influencers on the support center Net Promoter scores.

Correcting the actions of the sales force had significant impacts to the Net Promoter scores, the customer experience with agents (both service and sales agents), and to operational costs:

- Reduced the number of problem calls
- Reduced the number of repeat calls for the same issue
- Decreased average handle time (AHT)
- Decreased escalations to a supervisor
- Increased percent adherence
- Increased sales within support environment (warranties, consumables) by providing time to spend more productively — role of support advisor rather than picking up the pieces from broken expectations
- Maintained sales goals

Very few decisions that you make have no effect on the customer experience with your company. Don't be the one who squanders customer intelligence.

Call Resolution

The cost of repeat calls is paid in customer satisfaction and operating dollars. While many inherently understand the frustration that customers feel when resolution requires two, three, four or more contacts, it wasn't until the cost was translated into (operational) dollars and cents that call-resolution percent received as much attention as operational metrics, such as average speed of answer and average handle time.

Data collected from customer surveys revealed that the average customer had to contact the client's call center nearly twice to reach a resolution. Essentially, the contact center was employing twice as many agents as needed to compensate for the sub-par resolution of customer problems and questions. Over a period of seven months, first-call resolution improved, leading to a 22 percent decline in the average calls per customer (from 1.97 to 1.53). When converted into dollars (based on average handle time, average cost per minute and total calls handled per month), the aforementioned improvement translated to a monthly savings in the thousands of dollars.

In just seven months, the improvements cited led to the "elimination" of an estimated 1,000 calls. This client received more than 30,000 calls each month — our monthly survey sample consists of an average of 511 monthly surveys.

In the figure on the next page, the following apply:

- "Fully loaded" call center cost per hour = $20
- Average handle time = 7 minutes
- Sample = 5 percent of population (results extrapolated to entire population of 30,000 monthly callers)
- Results seen in sample reflect results occurring in population
- Survey sample remained "even" across all seven months of study (at an average of 511 surveys)

Savings from Reduction in Repeat Calls

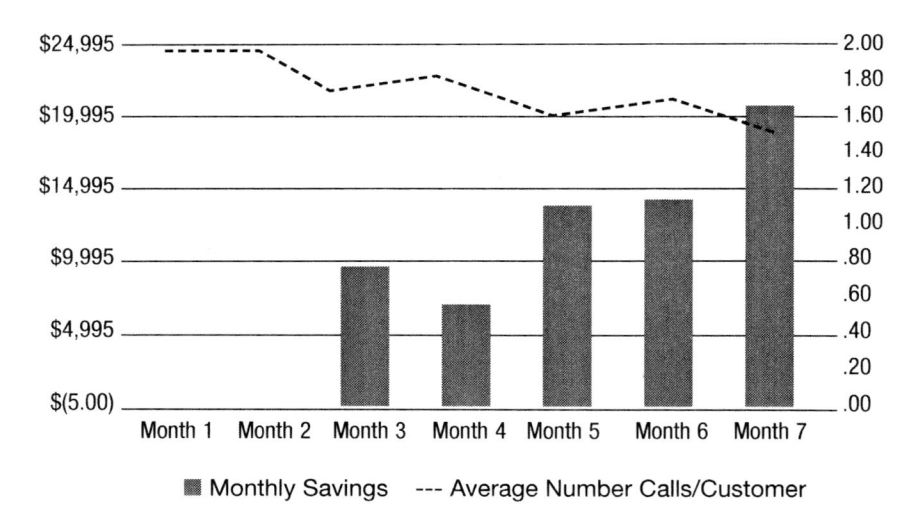

■ Monthly Savings   --- Average Number Calls/Customer

One can readily see that, as the dotted line indicating average calls per customer falls, monthly savings increase. As an added bonus, callers are happier and thus, more likely to remain loyal and bring in additional customers.

Take a Fresh Look at Your Research Efforts

We could continue with numerous other examples, but we hope that we have made the case for scientifically researching the business environment. It is useless to survey endlessly with no goals, no plans and no expertise. Although we often used contact center examples, we have completed numerous projects related to the customer experience with other interaction channels, for organizations that are in the private and public sector, not-for-profit and for-profit. The research principles outlined are for application to any channel.

Transportation companies need to know what riders find appealing and disgusting about the service. Vehicle manufacturers market big-ticket items and depend on servicing those vehicles as well as repeat vehicle purchases to keep them in business. Many state government offices interface heavily with consumers who are also taxpayers deserving of good service. The Bureau of Motor vehicles, State Revenue and other offices need a clear understanding of how to lessen the pain of their customers. Companies that use rebates to encourage sales often make it nearly impossible for consumers to consummate the deal. (We actually had a manager confide to us that their rebate programs were deliberately complex in hopes to gain the sales and have buyers give up before getting the rebate. We bought a $1,000 refrigerator and are still waiting for the $50 rebate. There are thousands more like us who will not buy from that manufacturer again. Properly quantified, it would be clear that gaming the rebate system is bad business, but first someone has to care enough to hire an expert to quantify the situation.)

We hope we have stimulated your interest to the point that you will look to your current research with fresh eyes; that you identify the gaps in the overall measurement system; that you avoid committing malpractice and elevate your organization to be Elite. We are dedicated to providing education and assistance in your quest to remove the pain and to turn customer insights into action.

Appendix

Sample Size Appendix

Many considerations come into play when designing a research study, for example, acceptable error levels and sources of bias. There is no one right way to decide what is acceptable. The following method for determining sample size is a conservative approach, and so would work in many situations. It assumes a simple random sample and a large sample approximation, such as the calls into a contact center.

The Equation

The equation needed for finding the appropriate number of cases to survey for a categorical variable is:

(Py)(Pn) I Std Error2=N

The Standard Error, when multiplied by the coefficient of 1.96, can be thought of as the error term for the entire sample for this item, and Py and Pn represent the proportion of respondents responding "Yes" or "No" to that question. Assign values to Py, Pn and the standard error term, and then solve for N, which is the number of cases.

The Py and Pn Terms

Py and Pn represent the proportion of people responding to each of the categories in a dichotomous variable (a dichotomous variable is one like first-call resolution (FCR), which has only two response choices, "Yes" and "No"). Even multiple-category or continuous variables, like the 10-point scale, can be thought of as dichotomous.

The easiest way to arrive at a number that would work for all the questions on the survey in addition to FCR, is to be as conservative as possible. If we were to use the analogy of an election between two candidates, it is easy to see that the outcome of a close election (where each candidate is expected to receive about 50 percent of the votes) would be harder to predict than a landslide, in which the split in votes might be 80/20. Therefore, a close election might require a larger sample than a landslide would.

It is always safest to maximize the variation by assuming a 50/50 split in responses across questions. Thus, the computation of (Py)(Pn) becomes simple; it is (.5)(.5) or .25. So, the equation now looks like this:

.25/Std Error2=N

Sampling Error

Now that the values of Py and Pn have been set, the next thing to do is to decide the level of accuracy needed for the results. That is, set a sampling error that is acceptable to you. For example, you would like to report that your results are accurate within a range of plus or minus 5 percent (which means you want a confidence interval of 95 percent). This is a typical value to choose, but remember that there is no "right" answer to the degree of accuracy you'd like to attain.

For a confidence interval of 95 percent, divide the sampling error (.05) by 1.96 to determine the standard error:

Standard Error = .05 / 1.96

For a confidence interval of 99 percent, the coefficient to use is 2.576.

So the sample size equation is:

.25 / .006507= N

And finally, solving 384 = N

What This Means

Given this calculation, 384 completed surveys are needed to be 95 percent confident of our overall results, within a range of plus or minus 5 percent. The results will be true 19 out of 20 times.

You can see that these numbers do not change. If you wanted to always have a sampling error of plus or minus 5 percent and always have the most conservative estimate of your response distribution (that is, assume a 50/50 split in responses to your questions), your sample would always be 384.

You could solve for more or less variation of Py and Pn, or you could solve for a different degree of certainty, for example plus or minus 1 percent.

The Finite Population Correction

The sample size derived using the finite population correction produces values for sample size that are extremely similar to the previous uncorrected equation:

$$\frac{2500 * N * (1.96)2}{[25(N-1)] + [2500*(1.96)2]} = \text{sample size}$$

where N is the number in the finite population (like total number of calls) If the number of calls is 162,000 the number of surveys needed to represent the entire group with a 95 percent confidence level is 383.

Note: The Z or t distribution coefficient is determined by the chosen level of confidence, that is, 1.96 for 95 percent, 2.58 for 99 percent, and so on,

For a general rule of thumb for sample sizes, please refer to the table from a generally accepted research methodology book (Backstrom and Hursch, 1963).

Sample Size Requirements for Levels of Precision (99% to 95%)

Tolerated Error	95 samples in 100	99 samples in 100
1%	9,604	16,587
2%	2,401	4,147
3%	1,067	1,843
4%	600	1,037
5%	384	663
6%	267	461
7%	196	339

Reference Library

Adams, John (2006) "Call Center Service: Looking for a Handle to Reduce 'On Hold'; Institutions Like Provident Bank Are Using Call Routing And Data Mining Technology To Reduce Inbound Call Duration And To Improve Overall Service For Customers," *Bank Technology News*, 19(1), p. 22.

Alreck, Pamela L. and Robert B. Settle (1995), *The Survey Research Handbook*, New York: McGraw-Hill.

Alwin, Duane F. and Jon A. Krosnick (1991), "The Reliability of Survey Attitude Measurement: The Influence of Question and Respondent Attributes," *Sociological Methods and Research*, 20(1), 139-181.

Anderson, Eugene W., Claes Fornell and Donald R. Lehmann (1994), "Customer Satisfaction, Market Share, and Profitability: Findings from Sweden," *Journal of Marketing*, 58(3), 53-67.

Anderson, Eugene W., Claes Fornell and Sanal K. Mazvancheryl (2004), "Customer Satisfaction and Shareholder Value," *Journal of Marketing*, 68(October), 172-85.

Andrews, Frank M. (1984), "Construct Validity and Error Components of Survey Measures: A Structural Modeling Approach," *Public Opinion Quarterly*, 48(2), 409-442.

Andrews, Frank M. and Stephen B. Withey (1976), *Social Indicators of Well-Being: Americans' Perceptions of Life Quality*, New York: Plenum Press.

Anonymous (2003), "By the Numbers," *Bank Technology News*, May, 16(5), p.20.

Anonymous (2005), "Call Center Practices Around the World," *Call Center Magazine*, 18(7), 12, 14, 16.

Anton, Jon (2000), "The Past, Present and Future of Customer Access Centers," *International Journal of Service Industry Management*, 11(2), 120-130.

Arussy, Lior (2002), "Don't Take Calls, Make Contact," *Harvard Business Review*, 80(1), 16-17.

Backstrom, C.H. and G.D. Hursch (1963), *Survey Research*, Evanston, IL: Northwestern University Press

Bailor, Coreen (2006), "Keeping Balance in the Center," *Customer Relationship Management*, 10(3), 26-29.

Bailor, Coreen (2006), "Six Common Contact Center Mistakes," *Customer Relationship Management*, 10(2), 26-29.

Bain, Peter, Aileen Watson, Gareth Mulvey, Phil Taylor and Gregor Call (2002), "Taylorism, Targets and the Pursuit of Quantity and Quality by Call Centre Management," *New Technology, Work and Employment*, 17(3), 170-185.

Bass, B.M., W.F. Cascio and E.J. O'Connor (1974), "Magnitude Estimations of Expressions of Frequency and Amount," *Journal of Applied Psychology*, 59, 313-320.

Bearden, William O., Manoj K. Malhotra and Kelly H. Uscategui (1998), "Customer Contact and the Evaluation of Service Experiences: Propositions and Implications for the Design of Services," *Psychology & Marketing*, 15(8), 793-809

Bendig, A.W. (1954), "Reliability of Short Rating Scales and the Heterogeneity of Rated Stimuli," *Journal of Applied Psychology*, 38, 167-170.

Blau, Peter M. (1964), *Exchange and Power in Social Life*, New York: John Wiley.

Blodgett, Jeffrey G., Kirk L. Wakefield and James H. Barnes (1995), "The Effects of Customer Service on Consumer Complaining Behavior," *Journal of Services Marketing*, 9(4), 31-42.

Bolton, Sharon C. and Maeve Houlihan (2005), "The (Mis)Representation of Customer Service," *Work, Employment & Society*, 19(4), 685-703.

Boshoff, Christo (1999), "RECOVSAT: An Instrument to Measure Satisfaction with Transactional-Specific Service Recovery," *Journal of Service Research*, 1(3), 236-249.

Brady, Michael K., J. Joseph Cronin Jr. (2001), "Customer Orientation: Effects on Customer Service Perceptions and Outcome Behaviors," *Journal of Service Research*, 3(3), 231-251.

Brandt, R. (1999), "Satisfaction Studies Must Measure What the Customer Wants and Expects," *Marketing News*, 17.

Brennan, M., J. Chan, D. Hini and D. Esslemont (1996), "Improving the Accuracy of Recall Data: A Test of Two Procedures," *Marketing Bulletin*, 7, 20-9.

Brigham, Eugene F. (1979), *Financial Management Theory and Practice*, 2nd ed., Hinsdale, IL: Dryden Press.

Brown, Lawrence, Noah Gans, Avishai Mandelbaum, Anat Sakov, Haiping Shen, Surgey Zeltyn and Linda Zhaoet (2005), "Statistical Analysis of a Telephone Call Center: A Queuing-Science Perspective," *Journal of the American Statistical Association*, 100(469), 36-50.

Bruno-Britz, Maria (2006), "Opportunity Calling," *Bank Systems & Technology*, 43(1), 20-4.

Burgers, Arjan, Ko de Ruyter, Cherie Keen and Sandra Streukens (2000), "Customer Expectation Dimensions of Voice-to-Voice Service Encounters: A Scale-Development Study," *International Journal of Service Industry Management*, 11(2), 142-161.

Camp, Robert C. (1989), *Benchmarking: The Search for Industry Best Practices that Lead to Superior Performance*, Milwaukee, Wisconsin: ASQC Quality Press.

Cherrington, David L., H. Joseph Reitz and William E. Scott (1971), "Effects of Reward and Contingent Reinforcement on Satisfaction and Task Performance," *Journal of Applied Psychology*, 55, 531-36.

Churchill, Gilbert A., Jr. and Dawn Iacobucci (2005), *Marketing Research: Methods* 9th ed., Mason, OH: Thomson Southwestern.

Crossen, Cynthia (1994), *Tainted Truth: The Manipulation of Fact in America*, New York: Simon and Schuster.

Daniels, Susan E. (2003), "A Model for Customer Service," *Quality Progress*, 36(8), 30.

De Ruyter, Ko and Martin G.M. Wetzels (2000), "The Impact Of Perceived Listening Behavior In Voice-To-Voice Service Encounters," *Journal of Service Research*, 2(3), 276-284.

Dean, Alison M. (2004), "Rethinking Customer Expectations of Service Quality: Are Call Centers Different? *The Journal of Services Marketing*, 18(1), 60-77.

Dholakia, Paul M. and Vicki G. Morwitz (2002), "How Surveys Influence Customers," *Harvard Business Review*, 80(5), 18.

Dobbins, Gregory H. and Jeanne M. Russell (1986), "On the Biasing Effects of Subordinate Likeableness on Leaders' Responses to Poor Performers: A Laboratory and a Field Study," *Personnel Psychology*, 39(4), 759-778.

Erdos, Paul L. and Arthur J. Morgan (1983), *Professional Mail Surveys*, Malabar, Florida: Robert E Krieger Publishing Co.

Feinberg, Richard A., Ik-Suk Kim, Leigh Hokama, Ko de Ruyter and Cherie Keen (2000), "Operational Determinants of Caller Satisfaction in the Call Center," *International Journal of Service Industry Management*, 11(2), 131-141.

Fleisher, Joe (2006), "Costs and Benefits," *Call Center Magazine*, 19(2), 48.

Fleming, John H., Curt Coffman and James K. Harter (2005), "Manage Your Human Sigma," *Harvard Business Review*, 83(7-8), 106.

Fleming, John H., Curt Coffman and James K. Harter (2005), Manage Your Human Sigma, *Harvard Business Review*, July.

Flinders, Karl (2004), "CRM Set for Spending Explosion," *VNUnet.com*, March 8.

Fornell, Claes, Sunil Mithas, Forest V. Morgenson III and M.S. Krishan (2006), "Customer Satisfaction and Stock Prices: High Returns, Low Risk," *Journal of Marketing*, 70(January), 1-14.

Frei, Frances X., Ann Evenson and Patrick T. Harker (2000), "Calling All Managers: How to Build a Better Call Center, *HBS Working Knowledge*, January 11.

Garner, W.R. (1960), "Rating Scales: Discriminability and Information Transmission," *Psychological Review*, 67, 343-352.

Garr, Brian (2005), "Speech Technology: What's the Word of Tomarrow?" *Customer Inter@ction Solutions*, 24(5), 62-64.

Gendall, Phillip and Peter Davis (1993), "Are Callbacks a Waste of Time?" *Marketing Bulletin*, 4(May).

Gilmore, Audrey (2001), "Call Centre Management: Is Service Quality a Priority?" *Managing Service Quality*, 11(3), 153-159.

Gilmore, Audrey and Lesley Moreland (2000), "Call Centers: How Can Service Quality be Managed? *Irish Marketing Review*, 13(1), 3-11.

Godes, David and Dina Mayzlin (2004), "Firm-Created Work-of-Mouth Communication: A Field-Based Quasi-Experiment," *Harvard Business School Marketing Research*, Paper No. 04-03.

Goodman, Paul S. (1974), "An Examination of Referents Used in the Evaluation of Pay," *Organizational Behavior and Human Performance*, 12(2), 170-95.

Grant, Sara, (2005), "Should You Ignore Your Customers?" *HBS Working Knowledge*, April 25.

Gruca, Thomas S. and Lopo L. Rego (2005), "Customer Satisfaction, Cash Flow, and Shareholder Value," *Journal of Marketing*, 69(July), 115-30.

Halbert, Terry and Elaine Ingulli (2006), *Law and Ethics in the Business Environment*, Mason, OH: Thomson West.

Hart, Christopher W.L., James L. Heskett and W. Earl Sasser, Jr. (1990), "The Profitable Art of Service Recovery," *Harvard Business Review*, 68(4), 148-156.

Hastings, M. (1997), Managing the Management Tools, London: *Institute of Management*.

Hawkins, Del I., Roger J. Best and Kenneth A. Coney (2001), *Consumer Behavior: Building Marketing Strategy*, 8th ed., Boston, MA: McGraw-Hill Irwin.

Herr, Paul M., Frank R. Kardes and John Kim (1991), "Effects of Word-of-Mouth and Product-Attribute Information on Persuasion: An Accessibility-Diagnosticity Perspective," *Journal of Consumer Research*, 17 (March), 454-62.

Heskett, Jim (2004), "Are Customer Loyalty Initiatives Worth The Investment?" *HBS Working Knowledge*, March.

Hughes, Alun (2005), "The Evolution of Outbound Call Centre Contact Technology," *Credit Control*, 26(5), 56-60.

Kalyanam, Kirthi and Monte Zweben (2005), "When Customers Want to Hear from You," *HBS Working Knowledge*, November 21.

Kaplan, Robert S. and David P. Norton (2003), "Keeping Your Balance with Customers," *HBS Working Knowledge* July 14.

Kaplan, Robert S. and David P. Norton (2002), "Partnering and the Balanced Scorecard," *HBS Working Knowledge*, December 23.

Kaplan, Robert S. and David P. Norton (1999), "The Balanced Scorecard in Practice," *HBS Working Knowledge*, October 12.

Keiningham, Timothy L., Bruce Cooil, Tor Wallin Andreassen and Lerzan Aksoy (2007), "A Longitudinal Examination of Net Promoter and Firm Revenue Growth," *Journal of Marketing*, 71(July), 39-51.

Kerr, Steven (1975), "On the Folly of Rewarding A, While Hoping for B," *Academy of Management Journal*, 18, 769-83.

Konovsky, Mary A. (2000), "Understanding Procedural Justice and Its Impact on Business Organizations," *Journal of Management*, 26(3), 489-511.

Kotler, Philip and Gary Armstrong (2006), *Principles of Marketing*, 11th ed., Upper Saddle River, NJ: Pearson/Prentice Hall.

Kraemer, Helena Chmura and Sue Thiemann (1987), *How Many Subjects? Statistical Power Analysis in Research*, Newbury Park, CA: Sage Publications, Inc.

Krauss, Michael (2002), "At Many Firms, Technology Obscures CRM," *Marketing News*, 36(6), 5.

Kruger, Justin and David Dunning (1999), "Unskilled and Unaware of It: How Difficulties in Recognizing One's Own Incompetence Lead to Inflated Self-Assessments," *Journal of Personality and Social Psychology*, 77(6), 1121-1134.

Kumar, V., Rajkumar Venkatesan and Werner Reinartz (2006), "Knowing What to Sell, When and to Whom," *Harvard Business Review*, 84(3), 131-137.

Lagace, Martha (2004), "Your Customers: Use Them or Lose Them," *HBS Working Knowledge* July 19.

Li Deng, Xuedon Huang (2004), "Challenges in Adopting Speech Recognition," *Communications of the ACM*, 47(1), 69-75.

Locke, Edwin A. (2002), "Setting Goals for Life and Happiness," in C.R. Snyder and S.J. Lopez (Eds.), *Handbook of Positive Psychology*, Oxford, UK: Oxford University Press.

Mahoney, Manda (2002), "Use the Psychology of Pricing to Keep Customers Returning," *HBS Working Knowledge*, September.

Marsden, Paul, Alain Samson and Neville Upton (2005), "Advocacy Drives Growth: Customer Advocacy Drive UK Business Growth," The Listening Company white paper.

Mello, Jeffrey A. (2007), *Strategic Human Resource Management*, Mason, OH: Thomson South-Western.

Mercurius, Neil (2005), "'Scrubbing' Data for D3M," *The Journal Technical Horizons in Education*, 33(3), 14-18.

Miciak, Alan and Mike Desmarais (2001), "Benchmarking Service Quality Performance at Business-to-Business and Business-to-Consumer Call Centers," *Journal of Business & Industrial Marketing*, 16(5), 340-353.

Morgan, Neil and Lopo Leotte Rego (2006), "The Value of Different Customer Satisfaction and Loyalty Metrics in Predicting Business Performance," *Marketing Science*, 23 (5), 426-39.

Netpromoter.com (2006), "What Is Net Promoter?" [available at http//www.netpromoter.com/netpromoter/index.php].

Nisbett, Richard E. and Timothy DeCamp Wilson (1977), "Telling More Than We Can Know: Verbal Reports on Mental Processes," *Psychological Review*, 84(3).

Pearson, Robert W., Michael Ross and Robyn M. Dawes (1992), "Personal Recall and The Limits Of Retrospective Questions In Surveys," in J. M. Tanur (ed.) *Questions about Questions: Inquiries into the Cognitive Bases of Surveys*, New York: Russell Sage Publications.

Pfeffer, Jeffrey, Toru Hatano and Timo Santalainen (1995), "Producing Sustainable Competitive Advantage through the Effective Management of People," *Academy of Management Executive*, 9(1), 55-73.

Pontes, Manuel C.F. and Colleen O'Brien Kelly (2000), "The Identification of Inbound Call Center Agents' Competencies that are Related to Callers' Repurchase Intentions," *Journal of Interactive Marketing*, 14(3), 41-49.

Prabhaker, Paul R., Michael J. Sheehan and John I. Coppett, (1997), "The Power of Technology in Business Selling: Call Centers," *The Journal of Business & Industrial Marketing*, 12(3/4), 222-235.

Reichheld, Frederick F. (2006), "A Satisfied Customer Isn't Enough." *HBS Working Knowledge*, March 6.

Reichheld, Frederick F. (2006), *The Ultimate Question: Diving Good Profits and True Growth. Boston:* Harvard Business School Press.

Reichheld, Frederick F. and Phil Schefter, The Economics of E-Loyalty, *HBS Working Knowledge*, July 10, 2000.

Reichheld, Frederick F. (2003), "The One Number You Need to Grow," *Harvard Business Review*, 81(December), 46-54.

Rigby, Darrell K, Frederick F. Reichheld and Phil Schefter (2002), "Avoid the Four Perils of CRM," *Harvard Business Review*, 80(2), 101-109.

Robbins, Stephen P. (2005), *Organizational Behavior*, Prentice Hall Inc.

Robinson, Linda and Donald Lifton (1991), "Reducing Market-Research Costs — Deciding When to Eliminate Expensive Survey Follow-Up," *Journal of the Market Research Society*, 33(4), 301-8.

Rodgers W.L., Andrews, F.M. and Herzog, A.R. (1992), "Quality of Survey Measures: A Structural Modeling Approach," *Journal of Official Statistics*, 8 (3): 251-275.

Roethlisberger, F.J. and William J. Dickson (1939), *Management and the Worker*, Cambridge, MA: Harvard University Press.

Rotfeld, Herbert Jack (2000), "Misplaced Marketing Meanwhile at the Service Desk: "Hello! Is Anyone Here?" *The Journal of Consumer Marketing*, 17(7), 573-4.

Rust, Roland T., Valarie A. Zeithaml and Katherine N. Lemon (2000), *Driving Customer Equity*. New York: The Free Press.

Satmetrix (2004), "The Power Behind a single Number: Growing Your Business with Net Promoter," Satmetrix Systems white paper, [available at http://www.satmetrix.com/pdfs/netpromoterWPfinal.pdf].

Scherpenzeel, A. (2002), Why use 11-point Scales? http://www.swisspanel.ch/file/doc/faq/11pointscales.pdf

Schmidt, Frank I. and Jon E. Hunter (1983), "Individual Differences in Productivity: An Empirical Test of Estimates Derived from Studies of Selection Procedure Utility," *Journal of Applied Psychology*, 68, 407-414.

Schramm, Jennifer (2003), *Job Satisfaction Survey Report*, Society for Human Resource Professionals.

Schwab, D.P. and L.L. Cummings, (1970), "Employee Performance and Satisfaction with Work Roles: A Review and Interpretation of Theory," *Industrial Relations*.

Sheth, Jagdish and Atul Parvatiyar, "The Evolution of Relationship Marketing," *International Business Review*.

Simpson, Mike and Dimitra Kondouli (2000), "A Practical Approach to Benchmarking In Three Service Industries," *Total Quality Management*, 11(4-6), S623-S630.

Sisson, Keith, James Arrowsmith and Paul Marginson (2002), "All Benchmarkets Now? Benchmarking and the 'Europeanisation' of Industrial Relations," presented to the ESRC "One Europe or Several" *Programme*, 2002.

Smith, A.K. and R. N. Bolton (1998), "An Experimental Investigation of Customer Reactions to Service Failure and Recovery Encounters: Paradox or Peril?" *Journal of Service Research*, 1 (1), 65-81.

Sudman, Seymore and Norman Bradburn (1974), *Response Effects in Surveys: A Review and Synthesis*, Chicago: Aldeme Publishing Company.

Sudman, Seymore and Norman Bradburn (1982), *Asking Questions: A Practical Guide to Questionnaire Design*, San Francisco, CA: Jossey-Bass Publishers.

Sudman, Seymore, A. Finn and L. Lannom (1984), "The Use of Bounded Recall Procedures in Single Interviews," *Public Opinion Quarterly*, 48(2), 520-524.

Sudman, Seymore and G. Kalton (1986), "New Developments in the Sampling of Specil Populations," *Annual Review of Sociology* (12)1, 401-30.

Tax, Stephen S. and Stephen W. Brown (1998), "Recovering and Learning From Service Failure," *Sloan Management Review*, 40(1), 75-88.

Teinowitz, Ira, "'Do Not Call' Does Not Hurt Direct Marketers," *Advertising Age*, 76(15), 3, 95.

Van Bennekom, Fred C. (2002), Customer Surveying: A Guidebook for Service Managers, Boston, MA: *Customer Service Press*.

Wallace, Catriona M., Geoff Eagleson and Robert Waldersee (2000), "The Sacrificial HR Strategy in Call Centers," *International Journal of Service Industry Management*, 11(2), 174-184.

Ward, James C., Bertrum Russick and William Rudelius (1985), "A Test of Reducing Callbacks and Not-at-Home Bias in Personal Interviews by Weighting At-Home Respondents," *Journal of Marketing Research*, 22(1), 66-73.

DMA VIEW ON... Call centers feel TPS pinch. (1 October). *Marketing Direct*, 59.

Index

Academy of Management Executive 257

Academy of Management Journal 255

Adams, John 251

Advertising Age 259

Agent behaviors 233-234

Aksoy, Lerzan 255

Alerts, criteria 187
- real-time 229
- triggers xiii, 187

Alpha error 151

Alreck, Pamela 116, 251

Alwin, Duane F. 181, 251

American Customer Satisfaction Index (ACSI) 106

American Express 97

Anderson, Eugene W. 65, 107, 111, 251

Andreassen, Tor Wallin 255

Andrews, Frank M. 181, 251, 257

Annual Review of Sociology 258

Anton, Jon 251

Armstrong, Gary 19, 255

Arrowsmith, James 83, 258

Arussy, Lior 251

Assignment errors 79, 125

Au Bon Pain 49

Automated transfer process 176

Automatic call distributor (ACD) 67

Autotrader.com 25

B value 165

Backstrom, C.H. 249, 251

Bailor, Coreen 251

Bain, Peter 252

Bank Systems & Technology 252

Bank Technology News 251

Barnes, James H. 230, 252

Base 10 160

Basic Marketing Research 145

Bass, B.M. 181, 252, 258

Bearden, William O. 252

Bell Telephone 20

Benchmarking xii, xiii, 15-16, 29, 61-62, 81-88, 91-96, 169, 253, 256, 258
- standards 91
- studies 15-16, 81-82, 85, 87-88, 91-92, 94-96

Benchmarking: The Search for Industry Best Practices that Lead to Superior Performance 85, 253

Bendig, A.W. 180, 183, 252

Benefits/costs ratio (BCR) 201

Best, Roger J. 101, 255

Beta coefficient 165-166

Beta error 151-152

Bias
- agent influenced 176-177
- first-responder 117
- instrumentation xii, 115, 117
- one-size-fits-all 121
- recall 120-121, 144
- researcher-created xii, 115, 121-125
- respondent-created xii, 117-121
- self-selection 66, 118-119, 124, 144

Blau, Peter M. 48, 252

Blind-to-the-agent transfer 175, 178

Blodgett, Jeffrey G. 230, 252

Bolton, R. N. 258

Bolton, Sharon C. 252

Boshoff, Christo 230, 252

Bradburn, Norman 120-121, 258

Brady, Michael K. 252

Branching options 136

Brandt, R. 130, 252

Brennan, M. 120, 252

Brigham, Eugene F. 195, 252

Brown, Lawrence 252

Brown, Stephen W. 230, 258

Bruno-Britz, Maria 252

Burgers, Arjan 253

Call Center Magazine 73, 251, 253

Call metrics 72

Call resolution 243-244

Call, Gregor 252

Camp, Robert C. 83-86, 94, 253

Cascading effect 159

Cascio, W.F. 181, 252

CATs® (Completely Automated Telephone survey) 27, 98, 108, 137-138, 140-143, 145-146, 169-170
 - advanced IVR technology 138
 - CATs® Meow benchmarking data 169-170

Chan, J. 120, 252

Cherrington, David L. 36, 39, 253

Churchill, Gilbert A. 145, 253

CitiBank 29

CNN 48

Coffman, Curt 154, 253

Completely Automated Telephone survey (CATs). See CATs®.

Computer telephony integration (CTI) 30

Computer-assisted telephone interview (CATI) 142

Coney, Kenneth A. 101, 255

Confidence level 76, 112, 153, 249

Consumer Behavior: Building Marketing Strategy 255

Cooil, Bruce 255

Coppett, John I. 257

Correction factors 78-79, 115, 125

Credit Control 255

Cronin, J. Joseph Jr. 252

Crossen, Cynthia 74, 88, 253

Cross-selling 197-198, 236

Cross-training 51

Cross-utilization, of employees 51

Cummings, L.L. 37, 258

Customer comment report 226

Customer equity 197, 257

Customer Inter@ction Solutions 254

Customer lifetime value (CLV) xiii, 17, 22, 191-200
 - calculation 197
 - equation 193, 196
 - extensions xiii, 197

Customer loyalty index (CLI) 215-216

Customer relationship management (CRM) 19, 21, 88, 137, 207, 242, 251, 254-255, 257

Customer Relationship Metrics xiii, 11, 71-72, 137, 139, 149, 153, 155-158, 165, 169, 187, 241

Customer Satisfaction Measurement (ICMI's Member Research Report on) 50

Customer satisfaction
 - drivers-of-satisfaction, analysis 218, 221
 - drivers-of-satisfaction, results 218
 - equation 26
 - impact analysis 162
 - impact drivers of 165
 - impact scores 162
 - impact values 159, 162, 166, 217, 219

Customer Surveying: A Guidebook for Service Managers 259

Daniels, Susan E. 253

Data collection, methods xii, 141-145

Davis, Peter 119, 254

Dawes, Robyn M. 121, 256

de Ruyter, Ko 94, 253

Dean, Alison M. 253

Decision matrix 166-167

Delayed survey methodologies 119, 122

Deng, Li 256

Department of Motor Vehicles 20

Desmarais, Mike 88-89, 256

Dholakia, Paul M. 66, 253

Dickson, William J. 36, 257

Dirty data xiii, 126, 148, 155, 157-158, 171

Dobbins, Gregory H. 55, 253

Dunning, David 11, 256

Eagleson, Geoff 259

eBay 97, 103

Employee ownership 49-50, 97

Employee(s)
 - evaluations xi, 54, 205
 - hypotheses on performance drivers 36-41
 - satisfaction xi, 36-41, 55, 57

Employment, security 47-48

Empowerment 50

Enterprise 6, 97, 103, 206

Enterprise Rent-A-Car 103

Equity theory xi, 41-43

Erdos, Paul L. 151, 253

Esslemont, D. 120, 252

Esso Oil Company 137

Eureka 49

Evenson, Ann 254

Exchange and Power in Social Life 48, 252

Executive committee report 207, 209

External quality monitoring (EQM) xi-xiv, 13-14, 16-18, 23, 25, 32, 35, 57-58, 97-98, 108-109, 113, 126, 131, 133, 135, 137, 140-141, 145, 147, 149, 157, 159, 169, 170-171, 173, 174, 179-180, 183-189, 204, 206, 209, 213, 231, 236, 238
 - alignment with IQM 236-240

Feinberg, Richard A. 94, 253

Financial Management Theory and Practice 252

Finite population correction 249

Finn, A. 120, 258

First-call/contact resolution (FCR) 127, 158, 184, 247

Fleisher, Joe 253

Fleming, John H. 154, 253

Flexible scripting technology 136

Flinders, Karl 20, 254

Florida Medicaid 21

Florida Memorial University 44, 51

Fornell, Claes 65, 107, 111, 251, 254

Frei, Frances X. 254

Gans, Noah 252

Garner, W.R. 90, 180, 183, 228, 254

Garr, Brian 254
Gendall, Phillip 119, 254
General Electric 97, 103
Ghost calls 178
Gilmore, Audrey 254
Godes, David 254
Golden Rule, The 100
Goodman, Paul S. 42, 254
Google 30-31
Grant, Sara 254
Gruca, Thomas S. 107, 254
Halbert, Terry 44-45, 51-52, 254
Handbook of Positive Psychology 256
Harker, Patrick T. 254
Hart, Christopher W.L. 254
Harter, James K. 154, 253
Harvard Business Review 66, 98, 104, 251, 253-254, 256-257
Hastings 81, 255
Hatano, Toru 257
Hawkins, Del I. 101, 255
Hawthorne experiments 36
HBS Working Knowledge 254-257
Herr, Paul M. 101, 255
Herzog, A.R. 181, 257
Heskett, James L. 254-255
Hini, D. 120, 252
Hokama, Leigh 94, 253
Houlihan, Maeve 252
How Many Subjects? Statistical Power Analysis in Research 255
Huang, Xuedon 256
Hughes, Alun 255
Human Sigma 154, 253

Hunter, Jon E. 49, 258
Hursch, G.D. 249, 251
Hypotheses, over-rewarded 43
Iacobucci, Dawn 145, 253
IBM 44-45
IBM Principles 45
Incentive pay 49
Industrial Relations 258
Influence rate calculations 199
Information sharing 50
Ingulli, Elaine 44-45, 51-52, 254
Institute of Management 255
Interactive voice response (IVR) 28-30, 136-140, 142-143, 202, 204
 - surveys 136
 - technology 137-138, 142
Internal call quality monitoring (IQM) xi, 13-14, 16, 62, 67-72, 79, 125, 145, 174, 179, 185-186, 202, 204, 236-240
 - alignment with EQM 236-240
 - form 70, 237-238, 240
 - program 14, 62, 70-72, 79. 145, 185, 204, 236, 238
 - scores 68-71
Internal Revenue Service (IRS) 20
International Business Review 258
International Journal of Service Industry Management 94, 251, 253, 259
Irish Marketing Review 254
Jennifer Convertibles 31
Job performance 57
Journal of Applied Psychology 36, 39, 252-253, 258
Journal of Business & Industrial Marketing (The) 256-257
Journal of Consumer Marketing (The) 257

Journal of Consumer Research 255

Journal of Interactive Marketing 257

Journal of Management 255

Journal of Marketing 104, 251, 254-255, 259

Journal of Official Statistics 257

Journal of Personality and Social Psychology 256

Journal of Service Research 252-253, 258

Journal of Services Marketing 252-253

Journal of Technical Horizons in Education (The) 256

Journal of the American Statistical Association 252

Journal of the Market Research Society 257

Kalton, G. 121, 258

Kalyanam, Kirthi 255

Kaplan, Robert S. 255

Kardes, Frank R. 101, 255

Kearns, David T. 84

Keen, Cherie 94, 135, 253

Keiningham, Timothy 104-106, 108, 255

Kelly, Colleen O'Brien 257

Kerr, Steven 52-54, 255

Kim, Ik-Suk 94, 253

Kim, John 101, 255

Kondouli, Dimitra 258

Konovsky, Mary A. 44, 255

Kotler, Philip 19, 255

Kraemer, Helena Chmura 152, 255

Krauss, Michael 20, 255

Krishan, M.S. 254

Krosnick, Jon A. 181, 251

Kruger, Justin 11, 256

Kumar, V. 256

Lagace, Martha 256

Lands' End 86

Lannom, L. 120, 258

Law and Ethics in the Business Environment 44, 51, 254

Laws of Random Sampling Theory 152

Lehmann, Donald R. 111, 251

Lemon, Katherine N. 257

Lifton, Donald 119, 257

Lincoln Electric 49

Live interviews 142-143

Locke, Edwin A. 90, 256

London School of Economics and Political Science 105

Louisiana State University's Department of Psychology 55

Mahoney, Manda 256

Malhotra, Manoj K. 252

Management and the Worker 36, 257

Managing Service Quality 254

Mandelbaum, Avishai 252

Marginson, Paul 83, 258

Market damage 191, 197-200, 230

Marketing Bulletin 254

Marketing Direct 259

Marketing News 252, 255

Marketing Research: Methods 253

Marketing Science 256

Marsden, Paul 105, 256

Mayo, Elton 36

Mayzlin, Dina 102, 254

Mazvancheryl, Sanal K. 65, 107, 251

Mello, Jeffrey A. 44, 46, 52, 256

Mercurius, Neil 155, 256

Miciak, Alan 88-89, 256

Mithas, Sunil 254

Monger, Jodie v, vii-viii, 73

Monitoring form(s) 68-73

Moreland, Lesley 254

Morgan, Arthur J. 151, 253

Morgan, Neil 105, 256

Morgenson, Forest V. III 254

Morwitz, Vicki G. 66, 253

Mulvey, Gareth 252

Narrative 207, 209, 213

NASCAR 46

Net Promoter xii-xiii, 15-16, 61-62, 97, 98, 99, 100-109, 174, 183-184, 242-256, 258
- detractors 98-100, 103
- promoters 98-99, 103
- Net Promoter Score (NPS) xii-xiii, 97-100, 102, 104, 106, 108-109, 174, 183, 242
- Netpromoter.com 105-106, 256
- sales 241
- service xiv, 241

New Technology, Work and Employment 252

Nisbett, Richard E. 256

Nordstrom 49-50
- Nordstrom Rules 50

Normalization 16, 166, 171, 180

Norton, David P. 255

Norwegian Customer Satisfaction Barometer (NCSB) 105

O'Connor, E.J. 181, 252

Offshoring 27, 45, 47, 49, 240-241

Operations-level reports 213-214

Organizational Behavior 47, 254, 257

Organizational Behavior and Human Performance 254

Outbound trunk capacity 174, 178

Outsourcing 6, 19, 22, 68, 240

Parvatiyar, Atul 258

Peapod 25

Pearson, Robert W. 121, 255-256

Performance
- rating 167
- scores 153, 162, 166, 168, 217

Personnel Psychology 253

Pfeffer, Jeffrey 47, 49, 52, 257

Plato 51

Pn Terms 247

Pontes, Manuel C.F. 257

Prabhaker, Paul R. 257

Principles of Marketing 255

Professional Mail Surveys 253

Proficiency of execution xiv, 233

Profit and loss statement 202

Programme 258

Psychological Review 254, 256

Psychology & Marketing 252

Public Opinion Quarterly 251, 258

Purdue University Benchmark Study 94

Py 247-249

Qualitative data 16, 78, 125, 148, 154-155, 170-171, 174
- responses 136, 171

Quality Progress 253

Quantitative data 16, 136, 148, 154-155, 171, 226, 242
- analysis 122

Questions about Questions: Inquiries into the Cognitive Bases of Surveys 256

Rally Cry for the Customer xi, 9-11, 14, 17, 25-26, 35, 57, 136, 139, 206

Real-Time Performance Dashboards 229

Recruiting, selectivity 49

Rego, Lopo Leotte 105, 107, 254, 256

Regression analysis 16, 162-163, 165, 217
- model 163, 166, 217-218

Reichheld, Frederick F. 98-100, 102-109, 257

Reinartz, Werner 256

Reitz, H. Joseph 36, 39, 253

Reports 206-232
- customer comment 226
- executive committee 207
- for executives 206-213
- for operations management 213-225
- for supervisors and agents 225-232
- real-time alerts 229-231
- real-time performance dashboards 229

Response Effects in Surveys: A Review and Synthesis 258

Response questionnaire 207

Return on investment (ROI) xiii, 7, 17, 71, 73, 113, 128, 130, 141, 150, 158-160, 165-166, 168-169, 191-204, 210, 215
- calculation 202

Rewards 27-28, 35, 37-43, 52-54, 57-58, 90, 142, 171, 177, 236
- distributive justice 43
- procedural justice concept 43-44, 54-55, 255

Rigby, Darrell K. 20, 257

Robbins, Stephen P. 41, 44, 257

Robinson, Linda 119, 257

Rodgers W.L. 181, 257

Roethlisberger, F.J. 36, 257

Ross, Michael 121, 256

Rotfeld, Herbert Jack 257

Rowan & Martin's Laugh-In 20

R-square value 164

Rudelius, William 119, 259

Russell, Jeanne M. 55, 253

Russick, Bertrum 119, 259

Rust, Roland T. 257

Sakov, Anat 252

Sample size xii, 16, 123, 129, 147, 151-154, 170, 247-250

Sampling error 151, 153, 248-249

Samson, Alain 105, 256

Santalainen, Timo 257

Sasser Jr., W. Earl 254

Satmetrix 104, 258

Scale flipping 78, 125

Schefter, Phil 257

Scherpenzeel, A. 181, 258

Schmidt, Frank I. 49, 258

Schramm, Jennifer 56, 258

Schwab, D.P. 37, 258

Scott, William E. 36, 39, 253

Scripting options 136

Self-directed teams 50

Self-selection 66, 117-119, 124, 144

Sensitivity analyses 200

Service recovery 138, 142-143, 187, 230-231, 252, 254

Settle, Robert B. 116, 251

Sheehan, Michael J. 257

Shen, Haiping 252

Sheth, Jagdish 258

Simpson, Mike 258
Sisson, Keith 83, 258
Six Sigma 141, 154, 225
Sloan Management Review 258
Smith, A.K. 230, 258
Society for Human Resource Professionals (SHRM) 56
Sociological Methods and Research 251
Southwest Airlines 49
Speech recognition technology 29
Standard error 247-248
Stanford University 47
Statistical error corrections 130
Strategic Human Resource Management 44, 256
Streukens, Sandra 253
Sudman, Seymore 120-121, 258
Survey Malpractice xi, 15, 63, 73-79, 81-82, 88, 112-113, 115, 126, 128-129, 139, 245
Survey Research 249, 251
Survey Research Handbook (The) 116, 251
Survey
    - calibration 139, 142, 155-157, 178, 187
    - calibration protocol 155, 178
    - channel slamming xii, 126, 148-150, 170
    - comments 78, 125, 177, 242
    - communication channel methods 149
    - errors 111-131
    - post-call xiii, 108, 118-119, 150, 174, 177, 183, 202, 241
    - questions 115-117
    - response scales 180-183
    - scoring 79, 125
    - Internet 142
    - mail 122, 143, 253
    - phone 114-118, 136, 137
    - time-delayed 118

Symbolic Egalitarianism 51
Tainted Truth (The) 74, 88, 253-254
Tax, Stephen S. 20, 230, 258
Taylor, Phil 252
Teinowitz, Ira 259
Texas Instruments 195
Thiemann, Sue 152, 255
Thomson Southwestern 145, 253
Tomlin, Lily 20
Total Quality Management 258
Toyota 46
Ultimate Question (The) 98, 100, 102-103, 106, 257
Upton, Neville 105, 256
Uscategui, Kelly H. 252
Van Bennekom, Fred C. 181, 183, 259
Venkatesan, Rajkumar 256
VNUnet.com 254
Voice of the Customer (VOC) 13-14, 16-17, 19, 21-23, 25, 62-63, 65-70, 73, 74, 75, 79, 90, 126, 136, 141, 155, 158, 187, 210
    - VOC program 73-74, 79
Wage compression 51-52
Wakefield, Kirk L. 230, 252
Waldersee, Robert 259
Wall Street Journal 45, 74
Wallace, Catriona M. 259
Wal-Mart 48, 51
Waltrip, Michael 46
Ward, James C. 119, 259
Watson, Aileen 252
Webster's Third New International Dictionary 82
Wetzels, Martin G.M. 253
Wilson, Timothy DeCamp 256

Withey, Stephen B. 251

Word of Mouth Marketing Association (WOMMA) 103

Word-of-Mouth (WOM) 22, 30, 62, 98, 101-102, 138, 198-200, 230, 255

Work, Employment & Society 252

Working Knowledge 74, 254-257

Wow Factor feedback 226

Wright, Dr. Karl 51

Xerox Corporation 83-84

Zeithaml, Valarie A. 257

Zeltyn, Surgey 252

Zhaoet, Linda 252

Zweben, Monte 255

How to Reach ICMI Press

We would love to hear from you! How could this book be improved? Has it been helpful? No comments are off limits! You can reach us at:

Mailing Address: ICMI Press
102 South Tejon, Suite 1200
Colorado Springs, CO 80903
Telephone: 719-268-0305, 800-672-6177
Fax: 719-268-0184
Email: icmi@icmi.com
Web site: www.icmi.com

About ICMI

The International Customer Management Institute (ICMI) is one of the call center industry's most established and respected organizations. Founded in 1985, ICMI delivered the industry's first management-level conferences, educational programs and publications.

While ICMI's path-breaking work continues, the mission remains much the same: to provide resources and expertise that help individuals and organizations improve operational performance, attain superior business results and increase the strategic value of their customer contact services. Today's ICMI melds the traditional focus on consulting, training, and high-level engagement with UBM's strength in media and events to create a powerful one-stop-shop resource. Through the dedication and experience of its team, uncompromised objectivity and results-oriented vision, ICMI has earned a reputation as the industry's most trusted source for:

- Consulting
- Training
- Publications
- Events
- Professional Membership

Through constant innovation and research, ICMI's consulting and training services have become the industry's gold standard. ICMI publications, such as *Call Center Magazine* and *Call Center Management Review,* and events, including the Annual Call Center Exhibition (ACCE) and Call Center Demo and Exhibition conferences, continue to lead the industry. And ICMI's growing membership community now includes professionals representing organizations in over 50 countries.

Order Form

QTY.	Item	Member Price	Price	Total
	Call Center Management On Fast Forward: Succeeding In Today's Dynamic Customer Contact Environment**	$33.96	$39.95	
	Survey Pain Relief: Transforming Customer Insights into Action	$29.71	$34.95	
	It's Better to be a Good Machine than a Bad Person: Speech Recognition and Other Exotic User Interfaces in the Twilight of the Jetsonian Age**	$33.96	$39.95	
	How to Build a Speech Recognition Application: A Style Guide for Telephony Dialogues	$80.75	$95.00	
	Customer Centricity through Workforce Optimization	$29.71	$34.95	
	Call Center Handbook Series A Career for the 21st Century** The Voice of Your Company: Conversational Skills for Customer Service Reps** Your Pivotal Role: Frontline Leadership in the Call Center**	$11.01 ea.	$12.95 ea.	
	Driving Peak Sales Performance in Call Centers**	$33.96	$39.95	
	Call Center Technology Demystified: The No-Nonsense Guide to Bridging Customer Contact Technology, Operations and Strategy**	$33.96	$39.95	
	ICMI's Call Center Management Dictionary: The Essential Reference for Contact Center, Help Desk and Customer Care Professionals**	$21.21	$24.95	
	ICMI's Pocket Guide to Call Center Management Terms**	$5.12	$5.95	
	ICMI Handbook and Study Guide Series Module 1: People Management** Module 2: Operations Management** Module 3: Customer Relationship Management** Module 4: Leadership and Business Management**	$169.15 ea.	$199.00 ea.	
	Topical Books: **The Best of *Call Center Management Review*** Call Center Recruiting and New Hire Training** Call Center Forecasting and Scheduling** Call Center Agent Motivation and Compensation** Call Center Agent Retention and Turnover**	$14.41 ea.	$16.95 ea.	
	Forms Books Call Center Sample Monitoring Forms** Call Center Sample Customer Satisfaction Forms Book**	$42.46 ea.	$49.95 ea.	
	Software QueueView: A Staffing Calculator CD ROM* Easy Start™ Call Center Scheduler Software CD-ROM*	$41.65 $254.15	$49.95 $299.00	
	Call Center Humor: The Best of Greg Levin's "In Your Ear" Satire Columns, Volume 4**	$8.45	$9.95	
	The Call Centertainment Book**	$7.61	$8.95	
	Shipping & Handling @ $5.00 per US shipment, plus .50¢ per* item, $1.00 per** item and $2.00 per*** item. Additional charges apply to shipments outside the US.			
	Applicable State Sales Tax will be Applied			
	TOTAL (US dollars)			

❏ Please send me information on ICMI's publications, services and membership.

Please ship my order and/or information to:

Name _____

Title_____

Industry _____

Company_____

Address _____

City_____State/Province _____

Country_____Postal Code _____

Telephone (   )_____

Fax (   )_____

Email_____

Method of Payment (if applicable)

❏ Check enclosed (Make payable to ICMI Inc.; U.S. Dollars only)

❏ Charge to: ❏ American Express   ❏ MasterCard   ❏ Visa

Account No._____

Expiration Date _____

Name on Card _____

Fax order to:	719-268-0184
call us at:	800-672-6177 or 719-268-0305
order online at:	www.icmi.com
or mail order to:	102 South Tejon, Suite 1200
	Colorado Springs, CO 80903

Please contact us for quantity discounts. For more info on our products, please visit **www.icmi.com**